EDUCATION, INEQUALITY AND SOCIAL CLASS

Education, Inequality and Social Class provides a comprehensive discussion of the empirical evidence for persistent inequality in educational attainment. It explores the most important theoretical perspectives that have been developed to understand class-based inequality and frame further research. With clear explanations of essential concepts, this book draws on empirical data from the UK and other countries to illustrate the nature and scale of inequalities according to social background, discussing the interactions of class-based inequalities with those according to race and gender.

The book relates aspects of inequality to the features of educational systems, showing how policy choices impact on the life chances of children from different class backgrounds. The relationship between education and social mobility is also explored, using the concepts of social closure, positionality and social congestion. The book also provides detailed discussions of the work of Pierre Bourdieu and Basil Bernstein, two important theorists whose contributions have generated thriving research traditions much used in contemporary educational research.

Education, Inequality and Social Class will be essential reading for postgraduate and advanced undergraduate students engaged in the study of education, childhood studies and sociology. It will also be of great interest to academics, researchers and teachers in training.

Ron Thompson is a Principal Research Fellow at the University of Huddersfield. His main research interests are in social class and educational inequality, and he has written extensively on young people and educational marginality. He is co-author of *Education, Work and Social Change* and *NEET Young People and Training for Work*.

EDUCATION, INEQUALITY AND SOCIAL CLASS

Expansion and Stratification in Educational Opportunity

Ron Thompson

Routledge
Taylor & Francis Group

LONDON AND NEW YORK

First published 2019
by Routledge
2 Park Square, Milton Park, Abingdon, Oxon OX14 4RN

and by Routledge
52 Vanderbilt Avenue, New York, NY 10017

Routledge is an imprint of the Taylor & Francis Group, an informa business

British Library Cataloguing-in-Publication Data
A catalogue record for this book is available from the British Library

Library of Congress Cataloging-in-Publication Data
A catalog record has been requested for this book

ISBN: 978-1-138-30635-6 (hbk)
ISBN: 978-1-138-30637-0 (pbk)
ISBN: 978-1-315-14174-9 (ebk)

Typeset in Bembo
by codeMantra

CONTENTS

FIGURES AND TABLES

Figures

Tables

ACKNOWLEDGEMENTS

Producing any book is a lengthy and demanding project, and I would like to thank the staff at Routledge for their support and patience throughout this process, particularly Will Bateman, Emilie Coin, Chloe Barnes and Heidi Lowther. The process of copyediting and proofreading was ably supported by Emeline Jarvie of codeMantra. I am also grateful to the University of Huddersfield for providing the research fellowship that made it possible to undertake such an extended project and to those colleagues who have been a particular inspiration – especially Roy Fisher, Lisa Russell and Robin Simmons. To Margaret, I am immensely grateful for her patience and understanding during eighteen months of writing.

1

INTRODUCTION

Inequality is a central theme in the sociology of education, and the relationship between educational attainment and social origins is the subject of an extensive academic literature. However, inequality of educational opportunity also raises important questions of justice and value; it is a political issue as well as an intellectual challenge. Radicals such as Thomas Paine proclaimed education as a human right over 200 years ago, and in his essay *Education* [1815], the philosopher James Mill argued that 'all the difference which exists between classes or bodies of [people] is the effect of education' (Burston 1969, p. 52). Nevertheless, progress towards universal education left many forms of inequality largely unchanged. Even in Western liberal democracies, where writers such as John Dewey (1930) expressed the view of mass education as a precondition for legitimate government, educational opportunities beyond the elementary stage were often bitterly contested. As Andy Green points out in his book *Education and State Formation*:

> Whilst radical reformers preached human freedom and intellectual development, dominant education ideologies ... were often more concerned with social control, moral conformity and political acquiescence than human emancipation.
>
> (Green 2013, p. 39)

Such attitudes have not been entirely left behind, and in twenty-first century England, debates on grammar school education and curriculum change reflect the struggles over educational opportunity of earlier generations. By contrast, liberal theories of education emphasize rationality, progress and universal values, positioning educational practices based on social closure and control as a relic of the past. In the form of these theories that has dominated political thinking on education for many years, liberal principles are related to the increasing complexity of modern society. Education is held to be an essential factor in the social division of labour, allocating people to occupations according to their aptitude and skills. From this point of view, economic efficiency depends on utilizing the abilities of the whole population, making educational opportunity an economic as well as a moral imperative. Consequently, we should expect to see inequalities in education decline significantly over time. However, there is substantial evidence that this is not the case, and a more accurate picture is that the focus of inequality has shifted from gross disparities in access to more subtle differences, affecting the kind of education people receive and the qualifications they obtain. For sociologists who adopt a relational view of society,[1] educational inequality is not simply a malfunction of economic rationality: it is a consequence of wider social inequalities as well as a crucial factor in their reproduction between generations. These authors unpick the claim that education is a meritocratic system rewarding only ability and effort. As Jerome Karabel (2005, p. 550) writes in his study of admissions to elite American universities, 'those who are able to define "merit" will almost invariably possess more of it, and those with greater resources – cultural, economic and social – will generally be able to ensure that the educational system will deem their children more meritorious'.

Social class lies at the heart of persistent inequality. If we wish to understand the distribution of educational attainment in contemporary post-industrial societies, we need to recognize that these are *class* societies in which, as Basil Bernstein expresses it, class is 'the fundamental *dominant cultural category*' (Bernstein 1977a, p. 175). Although class is always mediated by race and gender, and the way in which it is lived has changed profoundly over the last century, it continues to structure the resources, experiences and subjectivities of the population.[2] Class influences many aspects of people's lives, including their income, health and educational attainment. Imogen Tyler (2015) writes that 'conditions of deepening economic and social inequalities urgently require class analysis if we are to comprehend the forms of exploitation that underpin the decomposition (and recomposition) of class relations under neo-liberal conditions' (p. 497). Inequalities may be symbolic as well as material, contributing to the 'hidden injuries' of class described by Sennett and Cobb (1972). In her study of working-class grammar school boys, Nicola Ingram (2011) questions whether it is possible to be perceived as working class *and* clever, noting that the development of working-class children can be hampered by pervasive assumptions of cultural and academic deficiency. In this kind of analysis, educational inequality is not merely a reflection of processes and struggles occurring elsewhere: education is a crucible of class, a place where class is *made*, both in moulding individual consciousness and in reproducing the class structure itself. This suggests that liberal theories tell only part of the story of education. Other stories can be told: for example the verdict delivered by Diane Reay in her book *Miseducation*:

> The working classes have never had a fair chance in education … and they definitely do not have one in a 21st-century England that is scarred by growing inequalities. The rhetoric of equality, fairness and freedom in education has intensified … but it has done so against a back-drop of ever-increasing inequalities, the entrenchment of neoliberalism and class domination.
>
> (Reay 2017, p. 185)

This book has two main aims: to examine the empirical evidence on social class inequalities in education and to discuss how these inequalities, and their persistence through periods of massive educational expansion, have been theorized. In its first aim, the book follows in the political arithmetic tradition (Heath 2000) of highlighting social injustice with quantitative evidence – a tradition which, in the sociology of education, dates back to the studies of access to secondary education by Gray and Moshinsky (1935) and Floud et al. (1956). Perhaps more importantly, it examines the concepts which underlie these and later studies, and enable researchers to translate questions relating to educational inequality into concrete hypotheses. Specific examples are drawn largely from the United Kingdom, but the book locates these examples within a broader context of international comparative studies. In its second aim, the book discusses the place of class – and related concepts, such as status – in accounts of educational inequality and stratification. The work of Pierre Bourdieu, Basil Bernstein and Raymond Boudon is discussed in detail – three thinkers who provide contrasting but complementary theorizations of class in education. The book also discusses a number of issues arising from Marxist educational theory. Although Marxism is now rather unfashionable in the sociology of education, these issues – such as the ideological role of education and the question of the relative autonomy of educational systems – are essential to an appreciation of contemporary debates.

The remainder of this chapter provides a backdrop to the main themes of the book. It begins with a general discussion of the concept of social justice, in which the possibility that both educational and wider social inequalities may in some sense be legitimate is critically examined. This discussion is followed by an outline of recent trends in educational expansion, both internationally and in the United Kingdom, which highlights the lack of a necessary connection with greater equality in education. The chapter then introduces the liberal theory of industrialism, a theory of declining educational inequality which has acquired a canonical status amongst policymakers and is frequently used as a touchstone by academic researchers. This liberal theory is then contrasted with recent patterns of change in the economy and employment, a reminder that inequalities of wealth and working conditions remain significant. In its final section, the chapter provides an outline of the structure of the book.

Social justice, opportunity and education

It is natural to begin with an obvious but not at all straightforward question: why should we care about educational inequality? Modern societies demand a range of educational outputs so that difference in education is inevitable and even desirable (Bynner and Joshi 2002). An educational system is *expected* to produce a distribution of attainment, with individual differences in dimensions such as type of institution attended, subjects studied and qualifications achieved. In this sense, we are all better off than if everyone received exactly the same education. However, it is more problematic if educational difference is associated with excessive inequality across the whole population, systematic inequality between social groups or both. At the population level, inequality in attainment may be so great that some children receive an education below the level required for them to function effectively in society, placing them in a state of *absolute* educational disadvantage (Bruckauf and Chzen 2016). Alternatively, *relative* educational disadvantage may be widespread (Thomas et al. 2001; Ferreira and Gignoux 2011), allowing basic forms of social participation but affecting the ability to compete in labour markets. Inequalities of this kind may lead to concern about their implications for individual well-being and social cohesion, even if they were felt to be justified by factors such as ability or effort.

Disadvantage in education, whether absolute or relative, is unlikely to be distributed equally across all social groups. Inequality of educational opportunity (IEO) refers to a systematic association between educational outcomes and certain social characteristics – usually corresponding to an ascribed status, such as class, race or gender, but potentially including other circumstances over which the individual has no control. Once again, this situation may cause concern, perhaps because it is considered to be unfair that a person's background should determine their chances of receiving a good education. However, whether inequalities are individualized or systematically associated with social characteristics, the point is that different people might not agree, either in their attitude towards educational inequality or on the underlying grounds for this attitude. Moreover, inequalities in education correlate with the distribution of other material and cultural goods, raising the question of whether *any* form of inequality can be tolerated. A discussion of educational inequality must therefore be located within broader debates on social justice.

Meanings of social justice

Ethical and moral norms are not absolute. In pre-industrial Europe, inequality was regarded as part of the natural order, and what we would now describe as a conception of social justice was tied closely to the maintenance and reproduction of this order. By the eighteenth century, the intellectual currents of the Enlightenment and the growth of individualism began to shift this conception, introducing the idea that people should have a rational share in the political, cultural and economic life of society. However, the basis of this rationality has always been highly contested, and how social justice should be conceived remains a challenging philosophical problem. For some authors, this is a question of how the benefits of society are shared out. As John Rawls (1999, p. 8) puts it, 'A conception of social justice ... is to be regarded as providing in the first instance a standard whereby the distributive aspects of the basic structure of society are to be assessed'. Social justice may also be conceived in terms of how people are treated and the structure of social relationships more generally (Winter 2018). Other versions of social justice focus on *participation* rather than distribution. For example, Bell (2016, p. 3) defines the goal of social justice as 'full and equitable participation of people from all social identity groups in a society that is mutually shaped to meet their needs'. However, distributive, relational and participatory justice cannot easily be separated and are connected in various ways by underlying relations of class, gender and race.

An uncompromising view of social justice is that it entails equality of outcome, the removal of any significant differences in people's conditions of existence. A slightly weaker position is that some inequality of treatment or resource allocation may be justified by *need*: people should receive what is required for them to live a fully human life. These understandings of social justice are captured by the famous Marxist doctrine 'From each according to [their] ability, to each according to [their] needs'.[3] In an attenuated form, needs-based justice underlies the idea of alleviating relative as well as absolute poverty or, in a specifically educational context, the Pupil Premium funding in England (Gorard 2015). Rawls (1999, p. 86) expresses this idea in a principle stating that undeserved inequalities call for redress: 'society must give more attention to those with fewer native assets and to those born into the less favourable social positions. The idea is to redress the bias of contingencies in the direction of equality'. Given that class is defined *in terms of* inequalities in power and condition, equating social justice with equality of outcome implies that there can be no socially just class system. However, other conceptions of social justice are possible and have been used to legitimize the class structure in various ways. In their book *Against the Odds*, Marshall et al. (1997) identify four principles which attempt to reconcile inequality of outcome with social justice. These are based on desert (or merit), legal entitlement, functional benefit to society and equal opportunity. The argument from desert proposes that those who are more able, work harder or have other valued attributes should be rewarded accordingly. Critics of desert point not only to the difficulty of identifying morally relevant attributes but also to the arbitrariness of their distribution. Is it not a matter of chance that I have a particular musical ability or that I was able to afford its development? Apparently intrinsic qualities can always be questioned in this way, and Rawls (1999) argues that it is simply not possible to 'deserve' one's place in the distribution of natural endowments.

The argument from legal entitlement is less circular but less obviously a basis for any claim to social justice. It asserts simply that I have a right to what is legally mine, whether I deserve it or not. From this perspective, inherited wealth, tax avoidance and purchasing private education for one's children are consistent with social justice. It is rights that are important, not merit, leading to the somewhat paradoxical situation that social justice becomes entangled with the coercive power of the state. However, a further possible justification for the unequal distribution of wealth lies in the argument of functional inequality: if an unequal society is more efficient and better able to care for its more vulnerable members than an equal one, then such inequality is acceptable. Rawls (1999) expresses this in terms of his *difference principle*: equality of outcome is preferable unless inequality makes all social groups better off. However, functional inequality raises questions of how much inequality is acceptable for how little benefit and the extent to which equality may be an end in itself.

In an attempt to transcend competing interpretations of social justice, David Miller (1999) proposes a contextual approach in which justice is related to different modes of human relationship. In communities with a high degree of solidarity between their members, need would constitute the main principle of justice, whereas in associations based on the achievement of specific goals justice would be based on merit. In society as a political entity, encompassing diverse needs, interests and abilities, Miller regards equality of status as the appropriate understanding of justice. The difficulty with a contextual theory of justice is that in actual relational systems, rather than the ideal types through which Miller develops his argument, several features may combine and conflict. In education, for example, different understandings of its aims and purpose entail different principles of justice: 'The instrumental perspective points towards differential treatment of children according to ability and performance; whereas if we start by considering children and adolescents as future citizens, we will want them to share a common experience' (Miller 1999, p. 38). As Gorard (2015) points out, contextual justice in education implies different, competing interpretations in which the treatment of students and the distribution of knowledge and resources are all at stake. Although it illuminates some aspects of the judgements involved, contextual justice simply pushes debates over inequality one step back rather than resolving them.

Equal opportunity

Equality of opportunity is often proposed as a way of reconciling inequality with fairness, although it is also advocated on the grounds of maximizing the talent available to society. It is necessary to distinguish between *formal* equality of opportunity, which refers to an absence of explicit barriers to achievement, such as legal or cultural prohibitions, and *substantive* equality of opportunity, which can be expressed in terms of life chances for different social groups.[4]

As a principle of social justice, equal opportunity in this sense requires that, whilst the rewards of different social positions may vary, the chances of achieving these positions must not differ systematically between social groups. Education has a critical part in this conception of social justice because of its mediating role in other life chances. However, equal opportunity glosses over a number of difficulties related to the intergenerational transmission of advantage. The socialist historian R. H. Tawney was a severe critic of attempts to separate opportunity and outcome:

> opportunities to 'rise' are not a substitute for a large measure of practical equality, nor do they make immaterial the existence of sharp disparities of income and social condition … The existence of such opportunities … depends, not only upon an open road, but upon an equal start … In the absence, in short, of a large measure of equality of circumstances, opportunities to rise must necessarily be illusory.
>
> (Tawney 1931, p. 111)

Supposedly egalitarian features of an education system, such as comprehensive schools or educational maintenance grants, should therefore be judged as a means to an end in light of the empirical evidence of their impact on educational outcomes. They constitute formal rather than substantive equality of opportunity, and their potential impact is limited by the conditions facing poorer families. There may also be unintended consequences of widening opportunities at higher educational levels: opening up some opportunities to poorer children may close down others, such as learning a trade. In an unequal society, increasing slightly the chances of working-class children obtaining middle-class jobs may reduce their chances of getting working-class jobs.

Even if substantive equality of opportunity could be achieved, it is not self-evident that significant residual inequality is acceptable. Atkinson (2015) proposes three reasons why inequality of outcome is still relevant, even if social background differences are eliminated. First, differences in condition matter, even when they can be attributed to individual failings or simply bad luck. Second, achieved social status is largely competitive: if one person gets a high-status job, other people do not. If the difference in rewards for different positions is long-lasting and relatively large, the lifetime penalty for misfortune or laziness can hardly be regarded as just. Finally, inequality of outcome directly affects equality of opportunity for the next generation: 'the beneficiaries of inequality of outcome today can transmit an unfair advantage to their children tomorrow' (Atkinson 2015, p. 11). Countries with higher levels of economic inequality tend to have lower social mobility and greater inequality in educational attainment than other countries (Jerrim and Macmillan 2015). Moreover, policies based on the redistribution of wealth appear to be more effective in tackling poverty than a 'social investment' model which prioritizes equality of educational opportunity (Solga 2014). It is simply not possible to disentangle equality of opportunity from equality of outcome.

It is clear, then, that there is no simple answer to the question posed at the beginning of this section. Some people may not care about educational inequality, regarding it as an inevitable byproduct of an efficient society or of people's right to deploy their resources for any legal purpose. Murphy (1990) goes further, regarding educational inequality as not inherently unfair but simply one form of difference in a culturally differentiated society. Others may care but for different reasons and with different conceptions of equality. In practice, social justice in education tends to be equated with equality of opportunity, although the notion of education *for* and *about* social justice is also encountered (Adams and Bell 2016). The idea of a 'socially just school' (Smyth 2004) proposes a holistic institutional approach involving practices which aim to mitigate the effects of disadvantage and foster critical social awareness. However, the conception of education for social justice has been critiqued – particularly by neo-Marxist scholars – as being grounded in a naïve attachment to transformative conceptions of education and a neglect of class as the primary dimension of inequality. For such authors, education for social justice involves a 'murky terrain' (Murray and Liston 2015) in which class inequality is just one amongst a competing array of injustices, undeniably real but serving to distract attention from the forces by which injustice is structured. Either way, it is clear that great care is needed in deploying conceptions of social justice to analyze educational inequality, particularly if the aim is to contest inequality through educational processes. Conceptualizing social justice in terms of removing 'barriers' to successful participation may overlook the possibility that these barriers are rooted in the interests of more powerful groups, who will not easily give up their advantage. This book focusses largely on outcomes rather than processes: if social justice in education is to have a substantive rather than a purely formal meaning, the distribution of educational outcomes requires the closest scrutiny.

Educational opportunity and social change

Since the early years of the twentieth century, there has been a dramatic expansion of educational opportunity. Before the Second World War the pace of change was generally slow, and in most European countries compulsory schooling ended at the age of 14 or earlier. There were wide variations in the availability of free secondary education, with Weimar Germany providing education free of charge to children up to the age of 18, whilst in many other countries fees were payable after the age of 14. In England, the proposal for free secondary education contained in the Spens Report of 1938 was considered a radical move, although it enjoyed widespread support. However, the postwar period saw more rapid change, and increases in the duration of compulsory schooling took place in the great majority of countries, with a minimum school-leaving age of 16 being achieved in several European countries[5] by the beginning of the 1970s. For children from more privileged backgrounds, participation rates in excess of 85 per cent for upper secondary education were not uncommon by the mid-1970s (Haim and Shavit 2013). Although social class differences in participation were substantial, increasing numbers of children from poorer backgrounds were able to complete secondary education. Expansion has continued into the present century, and in 2012 over 80 per cent of adults aged 25–34 living in member countries of the Organisation for Economic Co-operation and Development (OECD) had completed upper secondary education or above (OECD 2014a, p. 43). Appendix One shows more detailed recent trends across selected OECD countries.

In most countries, there has been a marked decline in the proportion of young people completing only lower secondary education and a significant increase in the proportion accessing tertiary (higher and higher vocational) levels. However, these overall trends conceal persistent differences between countries, with Italy and Spain in particular having relatively high non-completion rates for upper secondary education. In England, participation rates in full-time education for 16- and 17-year-olds increased from 44 per cent in 1988 to 82 per cent in 2016 (DfE 2017a). Figure 1.1 shows how this increase was dominated by growing numbers of students taking upper secondary qualifications, such as A/AS level and (more recently) other Level 3 qualifications, whilst the relative importance of lower-level qualifications and work-based learning declined.

Higher education has also expanded significantly across the globe, and mass participation has transformed what was once an elite privilege into an opportunity available to half an age cohort or more.[7] In Europe, average expansion rates

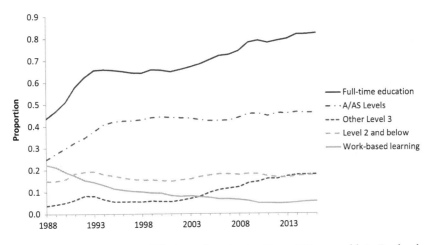

FIGURE 1.1 Participation in full-time education by 16- and 17-year-olds in England, 1988–2016, by qualification type.

Source: DfE (2017a).

of 125 per cent per decade were achieved as people born in the 1950s and 1960s entered tertiary education (Haim and Shavit 2013). Although growth rates are now less spectacular, between 1970 and 2013 tertiary education participation in Europe and North America rose from around 30 per cent of the age cohort to over 70 per cent (Chien et al. 2016). In Great Britain, during the five years leading up to the Robbins Report (NCIHE 1963), the number of full-time students had already increased by nearly 50 per cent, from 148,000 to 217,000. Within ten years, this number had more than doubled, and further increases followed as structural changes, driven by the policies of successive governments, expanded participation rates amongst young people (Boliver 2011; Whitty et al. 2015). By 2016–17, there were 1.8 million full-time students in UK higher education.

As Figure 1.2 shows, the expansion of higher education in Britain did not take place at a uniform rate, and periods of rapid growth in the 1960s, early 1990s and the five years on either side of 2010 have been interspersed with periods of relative stability.[8] However, the pattern of higher education expansion in Britain does not represent a series of sudden leaps forward in access to elite institutions; instead, expansion has been accompanied by curricular and institutional diversification. The two 'growth spurts' of the 1960s and early 1990s were achieved largely by the creation of a binary system in which polytechnics provided a second tier beneath the universities, followed by the Further and Higher Education Act of 1992, which recast polytechnics as less prestigious 'new' universities (Boliver 2011). A further distinction exists between universities and further education colleges, although higher education provision in

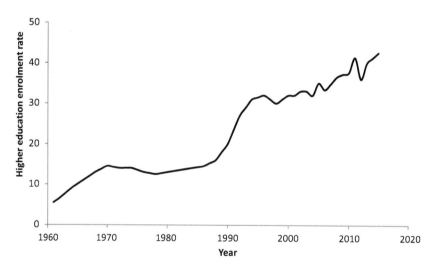

FIGURE 1.2 Higher education initial enrolment rate for young people in Great Britain, 1961–2015.[6]

Source: NCIHE (1997) for 1961–95; Boliver (2011) for 1996–98; DfE (2017b) for 2006–15.

these colleges has if anything declined. Currently, around 10 per cent of all higher education students in England are studying in colleges of further education (ETF 2017), compared with around 45 per cent at the time of the Robbins Report; the majority of these students are following courses below first degree level. A similar pattern of differentiation and stratification alongside expansion prevails in many economically advanced countries, where much of the increase in participation has been absorbed by second-tier institutions (Shavit et al. 2007). In Europe and North America, higher education students from disadvantaged populations are more likely to be enrolled part-time and in two-year colleges or short-cycle post-secondary programmes (Chien et al. 2016).

Throughout this period of expansion, increased participation rates have reflected a genuine demand for more education, whether for its own sake or for its labour-market value. Educational expansion has also been favoured by national governments as a means of increasing productivity and economic growth, leading to diffusion effects as less developed countries seek to emulate those where education is more established. Moreover, policymakers increasingly see expansion as an effective way of reducing social inequalities in education. The underpinning assumption is that, as participation rates increase across the whole population, children from low-participation groups will be drawn into the system, and therefore equality of opportunity must inevitably increase. It is certainly true that cross-national variations in the social class distribution of education result largely from variations in participation rates (Müller and Karle 1993; Paterson and Iannelli 2007a). There is also evidence that, in a given country, educational inequality reduces over time as education expands (Paterson and Iannelli 2007a; Blanden and Macmillan 2016). Expansion is therefore one of the few policy approaches known to be associated with lower educational inequality. However, its effectiveness in achieving *substantial* reductions in inequality is questionable, and the chief beneficiaries of new educational opportunities have been those classes already advantaged in economic and educational terms, at least until participation amongst these classes has matched demand (Raftery and Hout 1993; Haim and Shavit 2013).

Increased participation has also been stimulated by a lack of alternatives. Young people entering the labour market at the minimum school-leaving age tend to have few of the qualifications or skills valued by employers, and as a result their labour-market entry is concentrated in a relatively small number of industries and occupations. Although in the post-war period, employment in these industries was relatively buoyant, the decline of youth labour markets associated with the economic crises and deindustrialization of the 1970s and 1980s sharply reduced employment opportunities for school-leavers. Youth unemployment, always more sensitive to economic pressures than adult unemployment, rose substantially, falling back in the late 1980s but rising again in the early 1990s. Throughout this period, broader economic changes compounded the effects of recession, and labour-market restructuring continued into the 1990s and beyond. In the United Kingdom, this restructuring was particularly visible in localities where collective transitions from school to factory or mine had been commonplace, and youth transitions became more individualized and fragmented as employment shifted from manufacturing to the services sector. Apprenticeships declined markedly in Great Britain, from almost a quarter of a million in 1966 to 53,000 by 1990 (Gospel 1995). Although repeated promises have been made to revive apprenticeship as a mass participation route, this form of learning continues to suffer from low status and marginalization. By contrast, in countries such as Germany and Switzerland, where strong apprenticeship systems exist, concerns centre on the *diversion* of less advantaged students from general into vocational education and the lack of permeability between these routes.

In most industrialized countries, the policy response to youth unemployment has been to encourage young people to remain in or return to education. Greater educational opportunity is seen as both a route to economic success and a way of increasing social mobility. However, there is no guarantee that educational expansion will lead to either of these outcomes, particularly within societies characterized by high levels of inequality overall. Increased participation in education cannot be viewed in isolation from broader questions: what will be learned by whom, in what institutional contexts will learning take place and for what purpose? In England, this has been a contentious political issue since the struggles over the 1944 Education Act and the subsequent introduction of a tripartite system of secondary education. The minimum school-leaving age was raised to 16 only in 1972, although this had been promised in the 1944 Act. The eleven-plus examination, attempts to exclude secondary modern pupils from public examinations, and the lack of high-quality educational opportunities for 80 per cent of the school population provoked widespread resentment throughout the 1950s and 1960s (Simon 1991). There was particular concern over provision for pupils of average ability and below, leading to the Newsom Report (CACE 1963), whose title, *Half Our Futures*, was an eloquent plea for better opportunities for young people poorly served by the educational system. These struggles have continued in various forms, and long-standing issues, such as the division between academic and vocational studies, illustrate tensions between the democratization of educational opportunities, workforce development and the quest for positional advantage (Hodgson and Spours 2014). Educational expansion must therefore be seen in the context of persistent inequality and of the social and economic changes which, during the last 50 years, have produced a wholesale restructuring of participation in employment and education.

Liberal-industrial theories of education

The decline of social background as a factor in educational attainment has been predicted for many years by liberal theories of education, particularly those which take industrial development as a central factor. These liberal-industrial theories[9] emphasize the impact of technological progress and globalized markets on the recruitment and development of employees at all levels. Originating largely from authors familiar with the relatively fluid class structure of the United States, these theories propose that a fundamental trend of modern industrial societies is towards *universalism*: the adoption of objective systems of thought and social organization in place of localized affiliations of kinship, neighbourhood and class (Blau and Duncan 1967; Goldthorpe 1980). As a result, criteria for occupational selection are predicted to rely increasingly on principles of economic efficiency (Jackson et al. 2005). This should lead to increased social mobility, in which the expansion and reform of educational systems play a central role. Liberal-industrial theory therefore suggests three trends in the associations between social origins, educational attainment and class destination. First, the association between social origins and level of educational attainment should weaken over time. Second, the association between educational attainment and class destination should strengthen. This is because the qualities demonstrated by educational achievement should become the main criteria for selection in labour markets. Finally, these trends should combine to weaken the overall association between social origins and class destination so that social fluidity increases.[10] The social order therefore becomes increasingly meritocratic, and 'achievement' replaces 'ascription' as a determinant of life chances. This implies that the liberal theory of industrialism is also a theory of the decline of class, in which processes of class decomposition will outweigh those of class formation because of a continual interchange of families between classes (Goldthorpe 1996).

Liberal-industrial theory is related to human capital theory (Becker 1993), in which education is seen as an investment leading to greater productivity. Human capital refers to knowledge, skills and job-related attributes, and is assumed to be developed mainly through education and training. In many countries where interventionist industrial strategy has been displaced by neo-liberal assumptions about the power of market forces, large-scale investment in education is seen as one of the few areas in which state intervention is legitimate (Harvey 2005; Keep and Mayhew 2010). Education and other supply-side factors have therefore replaced alternative solutions to the challenges of globalization, an approach expressed in 1996 by the UK Labour party leader Tony Blair, who claimed that his three main priorities in government would be 'education, education and education'. Liberal-industrial theory can also be seen as an important ideology in legitimizing an unequal society. First, it presents current levels of inequality as belonging to a transitional phase rather than as an inherent aspect of class relations and so focusses on the future rather than the present. Second, by constructing meritocracy as an ideal, the inequality that remains is legitimized by arguments concerning individual talent and the demands of industrial efficiency. In a period of 'legitimation crisis' (Habermas 1976), when national governments can no longer guarantee rising living standards for all, promises of greater social mobility and meritocratic selection have become increasingly significant.

The term 'meritocracy' entered political debate following the publication of Michael Young's satire *The Rise of the Meritocracy* (1958), a dystopian vision in which a privileged elite perpetuates its advantage beneath a veneer of modernist rationality.[11] It was used in a more positive sense in *The Coming of Post-Industrial Society* by Daniel Bell (1976) to describe the creation of 'temporary elites' whose claim to a privileged position was based on expertise rather than hereditary power. More recently, the term's satirical origins have been largely ignored, and meritocracy has become 'one of the prevalent cultural and political tropes of our time, as palpable in the speeches of politicians as in popular culture' (Littler 2018, p. 1). In this political usage, meritocracy combines the social justice arguments of desert and functional inequality but with a specifically technocratic focus. Its popular appeal lies in the implicit contrast it evokes between societies based on inherited wealth and privilege, and a society in which privilege is deserved and benefits us all. For this contrast to be plausible, two conditions are essential: that everyone should have an equal chance of developing the expertise that carries high rewards and that merit – in the form of expertise – should be the sole arbiter of these rewards. The trends predicted by liberal-industrial theory are therefore crucial to meritocratic ideas. However, the 'promise' of meritocracy has been described as unachievable, even in principle, not only because of the lack of any neutral basis on which to agree a definition of merit but also because of practical inequalities in educational systems (Mijs 2016). In addition to arguments that meritocracy is a 'myth' (Reay 2017), it is also suggested that a fully meritocratic society would be no better than any other oligarchy: if only a small proportion of society receives high rewards, and according to narrowly economic conceptions of merit, how can this be compatible with social justice?

The liberal theory of industrialism has found only limited support from studies of educational attainment and social mobility, and there is considerable evidence that meritocracy, as a description of contemporary society, contains serious flaws. This evidence will be discussed in detail in later chapters; however, some brief remarks are worth making here. First, the degree of industrialization is only one factor in educational and social mobility. Other factors are also important, including wider social inequality, educational expenditure and the stage reached in educational expansion (van Doorn et al. 2011). Moreover, expansion has been associated with relatively modest changes in the underlying association between social origins and attainment. There is also evidence that the role of education in social mobility is not necessarily increasing in importance. Direct effects of social origins, in which social background influences class destination over and above educational attainment, continue to operate (Gugushvili et al. 2017). Whilst the disadvantages of being poorly qualified are evident, at higher levels the association between educational credentials and employment is arguably becoming looser and more unpredictable (Bukodi and Goldthorpe 2011). It therefore appears that liberal-industrial theory over-estimates the extent of decline in the association between social origins and destinations, partly because the influence of technological change has been considerably exaggerated. Although aspects of a knowledge economy can easily be discerned, their emergence has not eliminated low-skilled, manual or routine work; still less has it reduced material inequality and produced the affluent, leisure-rich society beloved of late twentieth-century futurologists. The claims of liberal-industrial theory need to be seen within the context of the reality of work in twenty-first-century economies.

Economy, work and society

The last 50 years have been a period of transformation in the economies of the United Kingdom and many other industrialized countries. As the processes of globalization have enabled heavy industry and other labour-intensive activities to be transferred to lower-cost locations, some traditional areas of employment have sharply declined, whilst others – for example coal mining in the United Kingdom – have all but disappeared. The description of these economies as post-industrial is therefore appropriate in terms of the extent of the changes that have occurred, particularly as they have affected certain regions and groups of workers. However, to describe a country as post-industrial does not imply a wholesale transformation to a digitized, decentred and knowledge-based economy or that a 'fourth industrial revolution' is radically changing working lives. Although the number of people it employs has declined since the 1960s, manufacturing remains an important industry, and activities such as construction have seen little change in their share of employment. Nor has unskilled work disappeared: millions of people operate supermarket checkouts, work in call centres, clean offices and serve in restaurants. In the United Kingdom, the largest private-sector employers are in retail and services, including supermarket chains; security providers; and other labour-intensive operations, such as catering and cleaning. Professional and technical employment has grown, but more routine occupations – sales, machine operatives and elementary occupations – continue to provide employment to large numbers of people, accounting for 7.9 million jobs in 2017 (ONS 2017a).

Figure 1.3 shows the changing pattern of employment in the United Kingdom over more than three decades. Perhaps the most notable feature is the sharp decline in the proportion of manufacturing jobs and the corresponding shift to health, education and administration, but the stability of employment in construction and in retail operations can also be seen. Overall, the impact of deindustrialization and the growth in service work are clearly evident: service jobs now account for 83 per cent of all jobs in the United Kingdom, compared with 64 per cent in 1978 (ONS 2017a). Similar processes have occurred elsewhere, and in many OECD countries there has been a substantial reduction

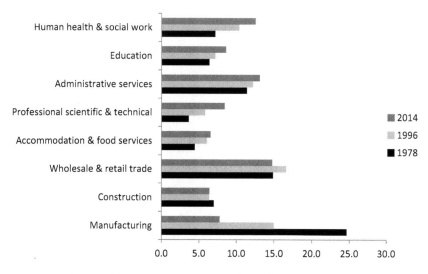

FIGURE 1.3 Largest UK employment sectors by industry and proportion of total jobs, 1978–2014.

Source: ONS (2017b).

in manufacturing employment, with job losses of 30 per cent or more in some manufacturing sectors over the period 1995–2015. The majority of sectors where growth has occurred are in financial and service industries (OECD 2017a, p. 96). However, although the percentage increase in employment in activities such as finance may be impressive, the actual numbers of people employed in these industries is relatively small.

In parallel with the shift to service work, the profile of occupations has also changed (what people do rather than what industry they work in). Figure 1.4 shows how the occupational structure of the United Kingdom differs between men and women, using the Standard Occupational Classification SOC2010, and how it changed between 2001 and 2017. Large and persistent gender differences are evident in skilled trades, manufacturing operations, secretarial work and caring services. However, some erosion of gender differences can be seen in professional and technical occupations, alongside an overall decline in skilled trades and secretarial work, factory work and the so-called 'elementary occupations.'[12]

A striking conceptualization of continuity and change in post-industrial society is provided by the concept of immaterial labour. In the *Grundrisse* [1857], Marx introduced a conception of knowledge as both an immediate productive force and a means by which social praxis – the practices and values through which we live our lives – is drawn into the forces of production (Marx and Engels 1987, p. 93). Neo-Marxist commentators, such as Antonio Negri and Maurizio Lazzarato, have developed these insights into an account of

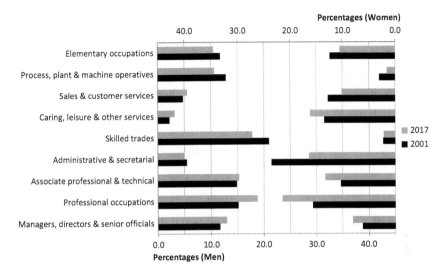

FIGURE 1.4 People in the United Kingdom in employment by occupation (men and women), 2001 & 2017. Percentages of all in employment for each gender.

Source: ONS (2017a).

immaterial labour: 'labour that produces the informational and cultural content of the commodity' (Lazzarato 1996, p. 133). However, immaterial labour can also be thought of in more mundane ways, including paid work in service industries and the unpaid emotional labour of caring and homemaking still performed largely by women (Fuchs 2016). Although terms such as emotional labour often refer specifically to paid care work, they also include the management of emotions – one's own and those of other people – in service work settings. In these occupations, behaviour and physical appearance are increasingly controlled, monitored and evaluated. Particularly for working-class men and boys, who in previous generations might have expected a life of material labour, these new forms of work challenge traditional identities (McDowell 2003; Nixon 2009). More generally, it has been argued that the growth of immaterial labour has produced a differentiated group of workers within what has been called 'knowledge' and 'affective' capitalism (Peters 2018), with some in relatively privileged positions, whilst others are immiserated and intensively exploited in ways similar to material labourers in production lines and sweatshops (Fuchs 2016, p. 371).

In recent years, evidence has accumulated for a significant degree of *polarization* within the labour market as deindustrialization has proceeded, and the use of technology to carry out relatively skilled but routine tasks has increased (OECD 2017a). Consequently, middle-skill jobs have disappeared and been replaced with jobs at the high-skill and low-skill ends of the occupational structure. The distribution of jobs is said to have assumed an hourglass shape in which jobs are predominantly 'lovely' or 'lousy', with little in-between (Goos and Manning 2007). Although this description is not entirely adequate, it nevertheless captures important structural transformations that have occurred in the labour market (Anderson 2009). Recent evidence on job polarization across the OECD shows that in most of Europe there was significant erosion of middle-skill jobs between 1995 and 2015, although in the United States and Japan changes at this level have been less dramatic. Lost middle-skill jobs have been largely replaced at both the low-skill and the high-skill ends, and in most regions more high-skill jobs have been created than low-skilled ones (OECD 2017a, p. 86). These changes broadly reflect the UK data in Figure 1.4, with job losses in occupations such as administrative and secretarial work, craft and skilled trades, and machine operation.

Claims of an occupational structure going 'pear shaped' – in that replacement of lost middle-skill jobs is predominantly at the low-skill end – are therefore not well founded, at least on average across the OECD. However, trends across large geographical areas do not reveal smaller-scale changes in employment, and in many cases rapid and localized deindustrialization has led to middle-skill job losses in a specific area, whilst high-skill job creation takes place elsewhere. Moreover, polarization in terms of skill is not the only story, and changes to the distribution of wages and employment conditions also need to be considered. Holmes and Mayhew (2012) and Salvatori (2015) find that wage polarization in the United Kingdom is less than might be expected, given the developments discussed earlier, and many jobs with middle wages persist alongside high- and low-wage work. However, several factors have contributed to an increase in low-paid employment: for example, the decline in trade union power since the early 1980s and increased labour-market participation by women. These factors have also combined with higher educational attainment amongst new entrants to the labour market to depress pay for White-collar work, and although job titles may suggest occupational upgrading, pay levels associated with these jobs have not increased (Holmes and Mayhew 2012).

The global financial crisis of 2008 and the subsequent recession refocussed attention on disparities in wealth and income, crystallized by the success of Thomas Piketty's book *Capital in the Twenty-First Century* (Piketty 2014). Income inequality has increased: between the early 2000s and mid-2010s most countries saw growing differentials between high and middle wages, and an increasing or stable gap between middle wages and the lowest paid (Salvatori 2015; OECD 2017a, p. 93). Greater inequality has not necessarily been accompanied by reduced living standards globally, and since the recession, most OECD countries have seen at least some increase in real earnings. However, there is considerable variation between countries. In the United Kingdom, real average weekly earnings reduced following the recession (Costa and Machin 2017) and were still below 2008 levels a decade later (ONS 2018). The picture of income inequality also needs to be seen in a longer-term perspective. In Europe between 1980 and 1995, the bottom half of earners saw their share of total national income decrease from around 22 per cent to 18 per cent. By 2008 this share had recovered to just over 20 per cent and was only slightly affected by the recession, remaining at 20 per cent in 2015 (WIL 2018, p. 45). The top 10 per cent of earners saw a slow but fairly steady increase in their share of national income, with only a slight dip following the financial crisis, from 32 per cent in 1980 to 38 per cent in 2015. The 'middle' 40 per cent of earners show trends closer to the bottom 50 per cent than to the top 10 per cent, suggesting that the gap between working-class and many middle-class occupations is more about conditions of employment than income. Many other countries, including the United States and Canada, show much more marked reductions for lower earners and greater increases for the top 10 per cent.

Wealth has a particular significance due to its persistence across generations and its affordance of a safety net against the vicissitudes that families may experience. Inequalities in wealth also tend to increase income inequality (Piketty 2014). Here also, a longer-term perspective is necessary, and although data is of lower quality than for income it is possible to trace some important trends. First, claims of ever-increasing inequality need to be set against significant declines in wealth inequality during the cataclysmic events of the first half of the twentieth century and into the 1970s. In the United Kingdom, over 90 per cent of personal wealth was held by the richest 10 per cent in 1913. This share had fallen to below 50 per cent in 1983, but it began to rise again – albeit modestly and somewhat irregularly – in the decades thereafter (WIL 2018, p. 208). A similar trend, but with a more marked recovery since the 1990s, is evident in the United States. These two countries are characterized by high levels of both wealth and income inequality compared to other countries (Bogliacino and Maestri 2016). Moreover, whilst countries such as Sweden, Finland and the Netherlands have relatively low income inequality, wealth inequality is high and has increased since the recession. Although the gross inequalities of the early twentieth century may now be limited to the richest 1 per cent, the economic resources to which poor and middle-income people have access are severely restricted compared to those enjoyed by the top 10 per cent. When household debt is taken into account, many people have no wealth at all.

As well as low pay, underemployment and job insecurity are common in many countries, and significant numbers of people experience in-work poverty. In the United Kingdom between 2004–05 and 2014–15, the proportion of adults in working households living in poverty grew from 12 per cent to 16 per cent, whilst 60 per cent of people of all ages living in poverty were in working households (Hick and Lanau 2017). Numerous studies have documented the lives of people, particularly in deprived areas, who 'churn' between various forms of insecure work, government training schemes and recurrent spells of worklessness (Shildrick et al. 2012). In recent years, 'zero hours' contracts and other forms of contingent work have become widespread in certain sectors of employment, whether based on digital platforms such as Uber or within labour-intensive conventional businesses – for example, firms providing courier, cleaning or warehouse services (Coyle 2017). Alongside contingent working, self-employment has also increased markedly. According to many commentators, much of this increase represents a deliberate strategy amongst employers to save costs by shifting employed workers to self-employed status, thereby avoiding financial commitments such as pension and National Insurance contributions. Such practices, and the restructuring of labour markets described earlier in this section, are part of the adaptation of capitalist societies to processes of globalization and technological change. Although they may intensify, or sometimes ameliorate, class processes, they have not resulted in fundamental changes to the basic economic relations within society that underlie the formation and maintenance of classes. The extent to which our understandings of class are adequate to contemporary circumstances is explored in the next chapter.

Structure of the book

The remainder of this book falls into three main sections. Chapter 2 provides an overview of debates on class and the different realizations of the class concept that are available to researchers. This chapter provides a foundation for both the empirical and theoretical discussions that follow. In the next two chapters, and in Chapter 9, quantitative evidence on educational inequality and social mobility is presented, together with discussions of the concepts underlying these quantitative studies. In the central section of the book, theorizations of educational inequality are discussed, with separate chapters devoted to Marxist educational theory, rational action approaches and the work of Pierre Bourdieu and Basil Bernstein. As well as providing an outline of the main features of these theories, each chapter considers how they conceptualize class and its relationship to inequalities in education. The conclusion draws together the themes of these three sections and considers their implications for conceptions of social justice and the theoretical work done by class in understanding educational inequality.

A book of this nature must of necessity be highly selective, and many important theoretical contributions have been excluded. The approaches discussed in Chapters 5–8 have been chosen not just for their significance in the history and current practice of the sociology of education but because they are, primarily and specifically, theories of class in education. They are also resolutely social and relational in their perspective. That is, they take any systematic differences between classes to be intimately bound up with social structures and processes, and in particular with class relations. These theories regard attributes such as values, dispositions and aspirations, not as explanations for inequalities in educational attainment, but as factors mediating the more fundamental workings of class. Their ultimate explanations are therefore sought at the level of society rather than the individual. Even cognitive ability, which some authors regard as of greater importance than socioeconomic factors (see Marks 2014), and which is unarguably implicated in *individual* attainment, is seen as essentially a product of social forces, expressing in its definition and measurement the interests of powerful groups. For these reasons, individualized explanations of educational attainment receive relatively little attention in this book; readers interested in such accounts will need to consult other works.

A further sacrifice to brevity is the quite condensed treatment of issues relating to race and gender in educational attainment, and the complete omission of important areas such as Critical Race Theory (Gillborn et al. 2018). However, it is hoped that sufficient references are provided for these issues to be followed up in more depth, and that the resulting closer focus on class will compensate for these omissions. Whilst the intersectionality of race, gender and class is an essential component of concrete studies of educational processes, within more abstract accounts there is still room for discussions that foreground class and see other dimensions of inequality as at least partly shaped by class processes. Bringing together in a single volume the contrasting approaches of Bourdieu, Bernstein and others presents an opportunity to understand not just their differences but also their common ground in providing sociological accounts of class in education.

Notes

1 A relational understanding of social phenomena is characterized by a focus on the connections, contradictions and oppositions of different social positions. It also has a deeper ontological meaning, in that explanations are sought in terms of the relationships between social positions rather than in their substantial properties. See Bourdieu (1984, pp. 159–160).

2 Of course, class is not the *only* cultural category of importance, and qualitative research provides rich and nuanced accounts of lived experience in terms of gender, race and class (see, for example, Skeggs 1997; Bhopal and Preston 2012; Simmons and Smyth 2018).

3 In his *Critique of the Gotha Programme* (1875), Marx proposed this slogan as appropriate to a developed, 'higher' phase of communist society.

4 Rawls (1999) refers to the latter as fair equality of opportunity.

5 France 1959; Sweden 1962; Netherlands 1969; Denmark 1971 (Garrouste 2010).

6 The enrolment rate refers to the percentage of the 'age group' entering higher education in each year. Because of differences in methodology, this age group varies between the sources cited as follows: 1961–95, under 21-year-old entrants as a percentage of all 18- to 19-year-olds; 1996–2015, under 21-year-old entrants as a percentage of all 17- to 20-year-olds. Participation rates for 1999 onwards are for England only, using the Higher Education Initial Participation Rate (HEIPR) for 17- to 30-year-olds. For 2006 onwards, rates for 17- to 20-year-olds are taken from the published HEIPR20 measure. The ratio of HEIPR20 to HEIPR rose slightly from 0.80 in 2006 to 0.82 in 2010 and more rapidly thereafter to 0.86 in 2015. For this reason, 1999–2005 rates for which no published HEIPR20 is available are estimated from the HEIPR using the ratio in 2006–07.

7 In 2016, there were 28 OECD countries where 40 per cent or more of 25- to 34-year-olds had completed tertiary education and seven countries with tertiary completion rates over 50 per cent (OECD 2017b, p. 44).

8 The sharp dip in 2012 evident in Figure 1.2 can be attributed to the increase in tuition fees from £3000 to £9000 per annum which took effect in that year.

9 Also described as functionalist or modernization theories.

10 The term 'social fluidity' refers to an individual's chances of achieving a different class destination from that of their class of origin relative to an individual from a 'reference' class. See Chapter 9 for a more detailed discussion.

11 The term had been used earlier, by Hannah Arendt in her 1954 critique of egalitarian education, 'Crisis in Education', and by Alan Fox in a 1956 essay, 'Class and Equality'.

12 Elementary occupations include labourers, hospital porters, bar staff, packers and shelf stackers.

2

CLASS IN POST-INDUSTRIAL SOCIETY

This chapter is concerned with the meaning of *class* in contemporary societies. In an era of profound social, cultural and economic change, the continued relevance of class to understanding the nature of inequality is often questioned, and the chapter begins by defending the class concept against claims that recent social trends have led to the 'death' of class. Debates on the meaning and purpose of class analysis are then discussed, together with the conceptual basis of class and its relationship with the foundational theories of Karl Marx and Max Weber, both of whom are critical to an understanding of the literature concerning class and education. Marxist class theory underpins many of the concepts used to theorize the production and reproduction of educational disadvantage as well as influencing more or less directly the work of authors such as Louis Althusser, Basil Bernstein and Paul Willis. Weber's theory of class has been taken in two quite different directions in contemporary research, both of which have an important bearing on educational inequality. Its emphasis on market relations in employment provides a basis for the influential classification schemes developed by John Goldthorpe and his colleagues; whilst Pierre Bourdieu describes the development of his distinctive approach to class as based on a rethinking of Weber's opposition between class and *Stand* [status group]. The chapter concludes with a discussion of the 'measurement' of social class.

Individualization, identity and class

For most people, the idea of class evokes a kaleidoscope of images representing wealth, education, language and consumption. How much we earn, where we were educated, and how we dress, speak and enjoy ourselves, signal to others the assumptions they might make about our background and how they might treat us. Traditionally, sociologists have taken the kind of work we do, or that our parents did, as determining the class we belong to. Other elements in the kaleidoscope – notably income and education but also cultural preferences – are to varying extents dependent on our employment situation and form relatively predictable patterns of behaviour amongst people in similar kinds of work. For traditional class analysts, these associations are explained by social relations inherent in the economic organization of society – whether relations of exploitation and domination as in Marxist understandings or the competitive relations encountered in labour markets for sociologists influenced by Max Weber. More recently, however, economic relations have increasingly been portrayed as irrelevant to the way that people conduct their lives. Accordingly, economic class has been seen as an outmoded concept with little value in understanding the situations of people in modern – or perhaps postmodern – societies. Identity politics have displaced class politics, and patterns of choice and consumption have to some extent become detached from traditional signifiers of social position. Whether one goes to Glyndebourne or to Glastonbury is seen as a matter of choice rather than class, and some people go to both. According to opinion polling after the 2017 UK general election, skilled manual workers were more likely to vote Conservative than to vote Labour, and the best predictors of voting preference were age, education and employment status (YouGov 2017). Perhaps most markedly, globalization, social media and the digital economy have multiplied the cultural and lifestyle choices available to most people, and made such choices increasingly difficult to predict in terms of occupation or family background. Apparently, individual identity has become more free-floating, and is no longer tethered to an economic base.

These trends have been evident to social scientists for many years, underpinned by a number of continuing political, social and economic factors. The loss of ontological security (Giddens 1991) characterizing the late modern age produced uncertainty, anxiety and feelings of powerlessness as many communities fractured and disintegrated. Globalization and deindustrialization, together with the predominance of neo-liberal policies in many Western democracies, have had a profound impact on the size, structure and condition of the 'traditional' working class, eroding collectivism and solidarity. In addition to these factors, Pakulski and Waters (1996) associate the 'death of class' with increased female participation in the labour market, greater differentiation and dispersion of power within corporations, and the embourgeoisement of manual workers. As the power of trade unions and other collective institutions has been systematically undermined, ideological assaults on working-class identities have presented an image of an increasingly classless society, in which whatever rewards we enjoy are seen as the products of hard work, good fortune or prudence rather than the outcome of class struggle and collective action (Snee and Devine 2018). However, reports of the demise of class identity are somewhat premature. Levels of class identification have remained surprisingly robust over the last 50 years, and relatively little change has occurred in perceptions of class conflict and the barriers between classes (Evans and Tilley 2017). Nor have individual identities necessarily kept pace with deindustrialization: there is evidence that in former industrial areas, forms of 'social haunting' occur in which identities and practices associated with long-defunct industries such as coal mining persist into later generations (Bright 2018). People also have more sophisticated understandings of inequality and their own place within the social structure than is often thought (Irwin 2018). Where class dis-identification has occurred, it may have more to do with the increasing political and economic marginalization of the working class than with changes in the degree of class consciousness *per se*.

Social and economic trends towards the differentiation of experience have been paralleled by currents in intellectual life. Writing in 1996, Neville Kirk observed that, although the explanatory power of class has been questioned since the nineteenth century, the period from the 1960s onwards was characterized by 'the sheer force, momentum and appeal currently exercised by ... anti-class trends' (Kirk 2017, p. 2). Theorists of late modernity argue that the traditions and certainties associated with industrial societies are being supplanted by the phenomena of individualization and reflexive modernization (Giddens 1991; Beck 1992; Lash 1992). According to these accounts, class, gender, religion and culture have ceased to provide templates of behaviour according to which the self can manage the multiplicity of risks and choices encountered in post-industrial societies. Ulrich Beck sees class, along with traditional social units such as the household, as a 'zombie category', a relic of nineteenth-century horizons of experience now supplanted by newer forms of knowledge and social organization (Beck and Willms 2004). However, these writers do not predict the end of inequality as such, arguing instead that inequalities will cluster around other, more culturally based divisions: 'Post-class societies will remain internally differentiated in terms of access to economic resources, political power and prestige ... The new cleavages that are emerging in post-class society may prove even more crippling and destabilizing than the old ones' (Pakulski and Waters 1996, p. 5).

Some people interpret reflexive modernization as describing a world of fluidity, mobility and choice in which identities are freed from the constraints experienced by earlier generations. However, a more convincing understanding is that late modernity presents new opportunities for capitalist accumulation. The success of companies such as Apple, Google and Facebook in extracting profit from expressions of identity illustrates the ability of capitalism to exploit varieties of selfhood. As Marx foresaw, immaterial labour now encompasses more than the conventional paid work of developing intellectual and cultural products; in the digital age, leisure activities such as participating in social media platforms generate data that can be exploited in various ways but also generate the very discourses on which these platforms thrive. Increased culturalization of the economy, the use of digital platforms to support 'gig' economies and flexible labour markets enable the exploitation of consumption and labour in both mundane and newly created ways. Rather than signalling an end to class-based inequalities, individualization and reflexive modernization are more appropriately viewed as features of capitalist development. The position in this book is that, whilst the debate concerning individualization needs to be taken seriously, class remains a fundamental organizing concept for understanding society. This is not to deny that the ways in which class relations are experienced and perceived have changed. Problems such as unemployment, ill-health and low pay are often seen in light of individual dispositions and failings, and people live out the complexity of social relations without necessarily formulating them in terms of class. However, processes of individualization have only obscured the ways in which social and economic structures shape our lives, not erased them completely. Class-based inequalities have remained remarkably stable in the transition from industrial to post-industrial society. In reality, 'social class hasn't dissipated or dissolved ... on the contrary, classificatory struggles have intensified. Inequality remains a matter of class, even when it is not understood as such by those who perceive or indeed experience inequality' (Tyler 2015, p. 498).

Questions of identity and class identification are often discussed in terms of a distinction between class as an objective category and class as a cohesive social and political group; what Marx described as a distinction between a class 'in itself' and a class 'for itself'. In *The Poverty of Philosophy*, Marx wrote that the 'mass of the people' achieves a conscious identity only through political action:

> The domination of capital has created for this mass a common situation, common interests. This mass is thus already a class as against capital, but not yet for itself. In the struggle ... this mass becomes united, and constitutes itself as a class for itself. The interests it defends become class interests. But the struggle of class against class is a political struggle.
>
> (Marx and Engels 1976a [Marx 1847], p. 211)

Weber makes a similar distinction, linking social action by the members of a class to general cultural and intellectual conditions as well as to subjective awareness of the causal links between class situation and life chances:

> For only then the contrast of life chances can be felt not as an absolutely given fact to be accepted... It is only then that people may react against the class structure not only through acts of intermittent and irrational protest, but in the form of rational association.
>
> (Weber 1978 [1922], p. 929)

Amplifying these points, Giddens (1973) distinguishes three levels of class consciousness, the first being simply a conception of class membership and therefore of society as being differentiated into classes. This is a lower level of consciousness than one which recognizes a conflict of classes based on opposing interests. However, Marx's idea of a class 'for itself' involves a further, *revolutionary* stage: a recognition that fundamental changes in the organization of society can be achieved through class action. Both Marx and Weber imply that higher levels of class consciousness require relative stability in class structures, to the extent that life chances are quite evidently associated with class position. High levels of social mobility and working-class embourgeoisement, such as occurred in the decades following the Second World War, may therefore lead to class dis-identification without any diminution of relative inequality. However, dis-identification may also be seen as a consequence of symbolic and political struggles over class in neo-liberal states, in which the universalization of middle-class identities and interests is an important strategy of social and economic control. Slogans such as 'we are all middle class now' are underpinned by long-term political projects involving the privatization of public assets and the retrenchment of welfare states. Values and behaviour which are taken for granted in public and private settings are discursively constructed in terms of *middle-class* norms, whilst working-class identities are increasingly marginalized and devalued. Indeed, some writers have argued that working-class disidentification may express an all-too-acute awareness of class relations and be performed as a way of resisting classification, a feeling that 'the classification [as working class] is a misrecognition of their value, for when it is applied to them it is usually used to condemn or express contempt' (Skeggs 2015, p. 214). The 'hidden injuries' of being working class (Sennett and Cobb 1972) reach beyond the economic realm into aspects of self and personal dignity. From this perspective, it is not surprising that class is perceived as an uncomfortable reality which many people prefer to avoid (Irwin 2015).

The conceptual basis of class

The concept of class presupposes the possibility of *classifying*: that individuals can be selected and categorized as belonging to such-and-such a class. In a remarkable essay on the origins of classification, Émile Durkheim writes of its function as a means to advance understanding: 'to make intelligible the relations which exist between things' (Durkheim and Mauss 1969 [1903], p. 48). The resulting systems of classification are not abstract and innate, but social. Things are not presented to us already grouped conveniently into classes: the existence of a classification is the outcome of socially embedded thinking, and social divisions are reflected in the principles of classification. Apparently objective schemes which claim to represent *social* class are no exception, and express relations of power and moral judgement as well as abstract intellectual considerations. As Pierre Bourdieu points out, systems of social classification contain a fundamental division between those who classify and those who are classified:

> Principles of division ... function within and for the purposes of the struggle between social groups; in producing concepts, they produce groups, the very groups which produce the principles and the groups against which they are produced. What is at stake ... is power over the classificatory schemes and systems which are the basis of the representations of the groups and therefore of their mobilization and demobilization....
>
> (Bourdieu 1984, p. 481)

From this point of view, any conceptualization of social class must be seen as part of a *theory of society* rather than as a purely technical matter of definition. This is perhaps most evident in the case of Marx, where class relations form part of a grand historical narrative in which the forces of production, class struggle and social change are inextricably linked. For Marx, class is categorical and relational: in capitalist societies, two qualitatively distinct classes, the bourgeoisie and the proletariat, are linked by relations of exploitation and domination. Other classes are either remnants of earlier social systems or defined in relation to the two main classes. There is little room for gradations of class, and fundamental differences of interest and condition characterize the class system. By contrast, Bourdieu envisages a *continuum* of class positions in a social space characterized by changing distributions of economic, cultural and social capital. From this perspective, class conflict is particularly intense at the boundaries between classes, in the form of struggles for distinction or superiority which take a cultural as well as economic form. In both approaches, class produces a stratification of society, but the nature of the stratification and the relationships between strata are significantly different.

Class analysis and class theory

The project of class analysis is based on the thesis that class has systematic consequences for people's lives and focusses on observed relationships between a class structure given *ex ante* and the distribution of different kinds of outcomes for individuals (Wright 2005). To some extent, this enables class analysis to stave off difficulties raised by competing theorizations of class and the objections of post-class theorists. In a similar typology to that of Giddens (1973), Breen and Rottman (1995) identify three broad types of class consequence: (1) unconscious or involuntary outcomes, such as inequalities in health or education as well as class differences in tastes and preferences; (2) differences in behaviour which are the result of conscious but not collective responses to class situations; and (3) explicitly class conscious behaviours which represent collective rather than individual responses. When conceived as a research programme, class analysis is fundamentally an empirical project, making few assumptions about the pre-eminence of class compared with other stratifying factors, or the nature of the causal relationships between class and life chances (Goldthorpe and Marshall 1992). However, as Breen and Rottman (1995) have pointed out, the link between classes and their consequences cannot be a purely empirical matter. A theory of class, they suggest, should demonstrate how the characteristics that are used to define class lead to observed patterns of life chances. This entails moving beyond a view of class analysis as starting from a class structure as a 'given' requiring no explanation to one in which the conceptualization of class can show, first, how class position gives rise to differential material conditions and, second, how class produces differences in cultural outcomes, such as education or patterns of consumption.

In traditional class analysis, the position people have within the field of economic production is seen as central to the causal explanations to be sought. Wright (2005, p. 22) expresses this succinctly in terms of two key claims: that what people *have* determines what they get; and that what people have also determines what they *have to do* to get what they get. The first of these claims asserts that people's rights and powers (if any) within the productive process influence their income and standards of living; the second, that these rights and powers also influence the strategies and practices people engage in to acquire their income. Other class consequences, including specific instances of the types enumerated by Breen and Rottman (1995), are then viewed as second-order effects of the two primary processes. As Wright points out, these claims entail no great commitment to a specific theory of class, although as will be seen later clear differences emerge when more detailed explanations are constructed. However, some critics of class analysis point to its excessive modesty in limiting its ambitions in this way. Thus, whilst Goldthorpe and Marshall (1992) make clear that their interpretation of class analysis does not require a commitment to problematic features of class theory such as class conflict, exploitation or class consciousness, this has led to accusations of theoretical exhaustion, fragmentation and minimalism (Bottero 2004), with calls for a 'renewal' of class analysis which involve a formulation of class in cultural terms (Devine and Savage 2000).

These debates have produced two complementary strands in the development of class analysis, each making a distinctive contribution to our understanding of class in post-industrial society (Bottero 2004; Crompton 2006). First, Goldthorpe and other traditional class analysts have continued to emphasize the structuring of life chances according to an economic conception of class, irrespective of whether people collectively or individually recognize classes in society or identify with any particular class. Goldthorpe (1996) argues that neither classical Marxist predictions of increasing class consciousness nor liberal theories of declining class inequalities are supported by the evidence on social change, so a theoretical approach is needed which explains persistent inequalities in outcome without recourse to assumptions about collective class behaviours. In the second strand of development, which has involved mainly qualitative research, the erosion or transformation of class identification is taken as a consequence of class processes worthy of investigation in their own right. Drawing on the cultural analysis of distinction and taste associated with the work of Pierre Bourdieu, numerous authors have broadened the notion of class to place greater emphasis on how it is enacted in the fields of cultural production and consumption. Although an emphasis on non-economic factors in the determination of social classes is not new (Poulantzas 1973), these approaches reflect ways in which shifts in the nature and functioning of capital have produced an intensification of its cultural expressions (Tyler 2015). Contesting Beck's idea of class as a 'zombie category', Reay (2006) argues that the analytical power of class is not confined to its traditional place in structuring life chances, but extends beyond this to constitute a vital aspect of contemporary social identities. She observes that class analysis is being reworked to 'focus on class processes and practices, the everyday workings of class, developing conceptualizations that move beyond the economic and exchange' (p. 289). Since the turn of the new century, studies inspired by this cultural form of class analysis have proliferated, and contexts such as 'reality' television programmes (Tyler 2015), the class resistance of social housing residents (McKenzie 2015) and social reproduction in the family (Crompton 2006) have taken their place alongside more traditional explorations of class in workplace or classroom.

The cultural reworking of class analysis raises a number of tensions with more traditional approaches. Although an attitude of 'positive pluralism' is possible, in which materialist and culturalist analyses are seen as complementary (Crompton 2006), one might question whether the class concept is sufficiently elastic to accommodate both viewpoints. It is certainly true to say that class can be conceptualized in different ways. However, if class is reinterpreted in terms of an individualized hierarchy, in which people position themselves by comparing their own social and cultural practices with those of other people and groups (Bottero 2004; Reay 2005), this blurs the distinction made by Max Weber between class and status. It also entails a shift towards a continuum of positions and therefore – as Bottero (2004) recognizes – a fundamental break with class categories. Culturalist approaches also differ amongst themselves in terms of their use of traditional components of class theory as reference points. Authors such as Skeggs and Reay continue to emphasize the role of power and exploitation in class processes, so that the material and the cultural remain intertwined, whilst for Bottero (2004) processes of hierarchical distinction need not be characterized in terms of class conflict or exploitation. For class processes to be consequential, 'All that is required is for specific cultural practices to be bound up with the reproduction of hierarchy' (Bottero 2004, p. 989). However, Flemmen (2013) argues that purely cultural analyses are unsatisfactory *as class theory* because they neglect the 'key insight' that capitalist societies are organized around class divisions integral to the workings of their economies. The extent to which cultural dimensions of class can be autonomous from their economic context is therefore a critical consideration and will be returned to on numerous occasions elsewhere in this book.

Marxist class theory

The location of class and class relations within the dynamics of historical and economic circumstances is central to Marx's theory of society. In a letter of 1852 to Joseph Weydemeyer, Marx wrote that whilst 'bourgeois' historians and economists had written of classes and class struggle, the distinctive contribution of historical materialism was to show that the existence of classes is bound up with particular phases in the development of production, and that class struggle will lead first to a 'dictatorship of the proletariat' and ultimately to a society in which classes no longer exist. For Marx, class is more than an analytical tool: a class society 'is not simply a society in which there happen to be classes, but one in which class relationships provide the key to the explication of the social structure in general' (Giddens 1973, p. 127). The nature of class is also historically specific, connected with the dominant mode of production at a given time. Each mode of production entails particular forms of social relation, stemming from the immediate context of production but extending to other aspects of life. These relations include the rights and powers that people have over the means of production and over what is produced. When these rights are unequally distributed, so that control over resources and products is restricted to certain groups of people, the social relations of production are referred to as *class relations* (Wright 2005, p. 10). A mode of production may therefore be defined as a specific combination of ownership, possession and use of the means of production. The small producer, who is owner, worker and beneficiary of the means to produce a certain item, is contrasted with the capitalist, who owns and benefits from the means of production but employs others to operate and manage them, and with the wage labourer, whose only asset is labour power itself. The resulting differentiation between people, not as individuals but according to their position within the relations of production, is a key part of the constitution of classes and the ideology that surrounds them:

> Social relations are closely bound up with productive forces ... The hand-mill gives you society with the feudal lord; the steam-mill, society with the industrial capitalist. The same men who establish their social relations in conformity with their material productivity, produce also principles, ideas and categories, in conformity with their social relations.
>
> (*The Poverty of Philosophy*, Marx and Engels 1976a
> [Marx 1847], p. 166)

For Marx, the economic structure of society provides the 'real foundation' of social consciousness, acting in a famous metaphor as the base which underlies a political, cultural and ideological superstructure. Social change of a profound nature – for example, the transition from feudalism to capitalism, or the socialist transformation Marx predicted would follow – arises from contradictions between the development of this economic base, in particular burgeoning increases in productive power, and the ideologies embodied in a superstructure which lags behind economic development.

In a fragment at the end of Volume III of *Capital* (Marx and Engels 1998 [Marx 1894], p. 870), Marx echoes Adam Smith's division of society into three orders to identify 'three big classes' of a society based on capitalist production: wage labourers, capitalists and landowners. Marx saw a process of development in which the means of production is progressively concentrated in the hands of capitalists, transforming more and more categories of labour into wage labour, and in which landowning is increasingly drawn into the capitalist mode of production. Ultimately, then, capitalist social structure has a tendency to polarize around two fundamental classes, capitalists and the 'working class'.[1] In *The Principles of Communism* (Marx and Engels 1976a [Engels 1847], p. 100), Engels writes that all other classes are being gradually swallowed up by the two main classes of capitalism: the bourgeoisie, who almost exclusively control the means of production, and the propertyless wage labourers or proletariat. However, the idea of Marx as a proponent of a demonstrably false, two-class model of society is a distortion of his ideas: as a claim about real societies the 'two-class' model was a rhetorical device deployed in a political context, and a model of society in which the only classes are the bourgeoisie and the proletariat should more properly be regarded as an idealization. In any concrete society, modes of production other than capitalism will persist so that 'the stratification of classes does not appear in its pure form' and intermediate strata blur the sharp edges of the main classes (Marx and Engels 1998 [Marx 1894], p. 870). There is no doubt that Marx recognized the existence of intermediate classes not merely as decaying remnants of the old petty bourgeoisie but as inherent adjuncts to capitalist production.

In capitalist societies, class relations embody a distinctive form of *exploitation*, a concept which Wright (2005) regards as pivotal to Marxist class analysis. Exploitation provides a causal account of the processes through which income inequalities are generated by emphasizing the implications of class relations for the distribution of material goods. In this sense, exploitation designates an interdependent but unequal relationship between people, in which the advantage of the exploiter cannot occur without disadvantage to the exploited. In Marxist theory, this is precisely what is involved in capitalist production: the wage labourer has no rights over the means of production, and as part of the unequal relationship between capitalist and wage labourer, the former has the right to alienate the product from the worker. According to Marx's famous theory of surplus value, the source of revenue for the capitalist is the difference between the value of the final product and the price (wages) paid for the labour that produced it. The key to surplus value lies in the distinction between the exchange value of labour power – the 'market rate' the worker can expect – and its use value or productive power in modern industrial processes:

> the [exchange] value of labour power, and the value which that labour power creates in the labour process, are two entirely different magnitudes, and this difference ... was what the capitalist had in view, when he was purchasing the labour power.
> (*Capital* Volume 1, Marx and Engels 1996 [Marx 1887], p. 204)

In this account, the interests of capitalists and wage labourers are not merely different but antagonistic: profit depends on depriving the worker of the surplus value generated in the labour process. Nevertheless, capitalist and wage labourer remain interdependent. The interests of capital are served by measures to increase the use value of labour power (such as automation or the intensification of labour) whilst depressing wage costs. However, the reproduction of the labour force is an essential part of the relationship, which must provide for at least a minimum level of health, well-being and education. As will be seen in later chapters, it is the need to maintain and reproduce both the labour force and the social relations of capitalism that provides the foundation for a Marxist theory of education.

The global economic crisis of 2008 stimulated renewed interest in Marx's writings on crises in capitalism (see, for example, Gamble 2009; Blacker 2013; Harvey 2014). In Volume III of *Capital*, Marx describes a general tendency in capitalist production for a decreasing rate of profit on capital, and the intensification of internal contradictions as attempts to counteract this tendency – such as increased output, greater efficiency or reduced wages – lead to a self-defeating cycle. The same tendency is responsible for creating a 'reserve army of labour' consisting of wage labourers made surplus to requirements by investment in more advanced industrial processes. These trends can be partly offset by the creation of new markets as capitalism 'continually generates new "needs"; commodities that in time seem indispensable to our daily existence' (Rikowski 2004, p. 568). However, the inescapability of multiple contradictions (Harvey 2014) means that crisis is a *normal state* of capitalism rather than an extreme situation. Recurrent crises 'are always but momentary and forcible solutions of the existing contradictions. They are violent eruptions which for a time restore the disturbed equilibrium' (Marx and Engels 1998 [Marx 1894], p. 248). For scholars writing in the twenty-first century, these ideas provide an insight into processes in which new settlements between neo-liberal states and their populations are legitimized, settlements in which boundaries are redrawn between public and private ownership, the role of the state is redefined, and the reserve army of labour is reconstituted to discipline the remaining workforce (Gamble 2009; Ainley 2013). Recent crises have also been seen as accelerating the reconstitution of class itself. Guy Standing (2011), drawing on Marx's notion of the *lumpenproletariat*, the 'dangerous class' created by idleness and poor living conditions, identifies the precariat as a new class comprising people who, whilst not being long-term unemployed, lack basic forms of job and income security. However, unlike Marx's *lumpenproletariat*, these are not people on the fringes of society: as discussed in Chapter 1, precarious work is the normal condition for many thousands, if not millions, of men and women who are central to the modern service-based economy. However, whilst it may be true that the old industrial working class has been systematically eroded and redistributed, it is questionable whether precarious employment can be seen as heralding a new *class*. Much working-class employment has always been insecure and associated with variable and unpredictable levels of income; it is perhaps preferable to see these phenomena as representing new forms of exploitation involving the degradation of working conditions, albeit at different rates and intensities across the class structure.

Weber's theory of class

Weber's writings on class are relatively brief. However, they indicate several important differences from Marxism. Whilst recognizing the importance of the economic sphere, Weber rejects the claims of historical materialism and the primacy of economic relations. Although such relations are an important factor in social action,

> the degree of this influence varies widely ... at some point economic conditions tend to become causally important, and often decisive, for almost all social groups, at least those which have major cultural significance; conversely, the economy is usually also influenced by the autonomous structure of social action within which it exists.
>
> (Weber 1978 [1922], p. 341)

In *The Protestant Ethic and the Spirit of Capitalism*, written explicitly as a polemic against economic determinism, Weber reverses what he calls the naïve historical materialist position that ideas are subordinate to the mode of production. On the contrary, he attempts to show that capitalism was itself a product of the mind, that the spirit of capitalism prefigured the capitalist order (Weber 2001 [1930]). The relative autonomy of ideas that this implies finds expression in Weber's distinction between the economic order and the social order, and the resulting differentiation of class, status group and party. Although all three are manifestations of the distribution of power within society, none of them is reducible to the others. Classes are rooted in the sphere of production and acquisition, whilst status groups are defined in relation to consumption and style of life. Parties, and to a certain extent status groups, are voluntary associations or aggregates of people, whilst membership of a class is a matter of one's position in production relations rather than of choice. Classes are therefore economically rather than culturally determined and identified through specific kinds of causal connection between the market situation of individuals and their life chances: 'the kind of chance in the *market* is the decisive moment which presents a common condition for the individual's fate. Class situation is, in this sense, ultimately market situation' (Weber 1978 [1922], p. 928).

Weber's definition of classes assumes that differences between people in their possession of property and other marketable resources, including knowledge and skills, will lead to differences in class situation – defined as the typical probability of acquiring goods, attaining a position in life and finding inner satisfactions. A 'class' is then understood as comprising all people in the same class situation – that is, having similar life chances. Although this understanding might seem to allow a multitude of classes, Weber goes on to define a *social class* as 'the totality of those class situations within which individual and generational mobility is easy and typical' (Weber 1978 [1922], p. 302). The central concerns of modern class analysis – the patterns of association between class and life chances on the one hand, and patterns of social mobility on the other – are built into Weber's understanding of class from the outset. Four social classes are identified: the working class, the petty bourgeoisie, the propertyless intelligentsia and professionals, and 'the classes privileged through property and education' (p. 305). Weberian class dynamics are somewhat different to those in Marx: there is no essential tendency for classes to polarize around the bourgeoisie and proletariat, and the increasingly bureaucratic and scientific organization of society is more likely to strengthen the intermediate classes rather than push them into the working class. Exploitation, in the sense of the extraction of surplus value, is not an inherent feature of class relations; rather, individuals bring different resources and abilities to the labour market, inevitably producing differences in material rewards. In a 'fair' market, whether regulated by law or social convention,[2] transactions between people in unequal positions will not necessarily lead to conflict. Where it does occur, class conflict is typically expressed through competitive struggles within the labour market or as wage disputes, and is likely to involve clashes between those in immediate and direct contact with each other, such as workers and managers, rather than large-scale confrontations between proletariat and capitalists. Weber rejects the idea of class as a group or expressing a collective consciousness, and criticizes Marx for proposing that whilst an individual class member may be in error about their interests, the class as a whole is infallible in this respect. Although classes result from social action, they are not an expression of collective action or consciousness, but derive from relationships of power and exchange within specific arenas of economic life, such as the labour and commodities markets and the capitalist enterprise. Weber does not agree that consciousness is determined by the mode of production; however, he believes that two basic categories underlie all class situations: property and lack of property (Weber 1978 [1922], p. 927).

Weber regards class as only one mode of stratification within society. Whilst class situation is determined purely by economic criteria, the analogous concept of status situation refers to another causal relationship – between the social estimation accorded to a person and their life chances. A status group comprises all people within the same status situation; although usually amorphous in nature, a status group does in fact constitute a group in that its members are conscious of belonging and may on occasion act collectively. Status involves a range of possible types of claim to esteem, including style of life, formal education, occupation and hereditary prestige (Weber 1978 [1922], p. 305). These claims are not arbitrary, but are rooted in social conventions; indeed, Weber observes that status groups are 'the specific bearers of all conventions' (p. 936). Status is not solely determined by class situation, and Weber notes that determinants of class such as money and property do not in themselves imply a particular status. Conversely, status may be acquired without necessarily being underpinned by wealth, provided education and upbringing create a particular style of life. However, class and status are connected in obvious ways, and there is likely to be considerable alignment between the two. Weber is under no illusions about the relationship between status and power: 'Every definite appropriation of political powers and the corresponding economic opportunities tends to result in the rise of status groups, and vice-versa' (p. 306). Nevertheless, class and status are *logically* distinct, and their interrelation is the contingent product of specific historical circumstances. Contemporary interpretations of Weber's approach to class and status differ in terms of the extent to which they separate the two concepts (Archer and Orr 2011); for Bourdieusian theorists, class and status become intertwined within a continuum of hierarchical distinctions, whilst traditional class theorists have tended to maintain the distinction as different dimensions of the stratification of life chances (Chan and Goldthorpe 2007).

Intermediate classes and the 'new' middle class

Much of the debate on educational inequalities centres on explaining working-class failure or disaffection. How working-class kids get working-class jobs (or, more recently, no jobs at all) is often explained in terms of low achievement, resistance to schooling and a lack of aspiration. At the same time, the relationship of middle-class families to schooling – and particularly the White middle class – is often normalized and either rendered invisible or constructed as a neutral backdrop against which working-class families are found wanting (Hollingworth and Williams 2010). These trends reflect broader processes in which the working class has become increasingly marginalized in economic, political and cultural terms. Savage (2003) suggests that by the end of the twentieth century the working class had been 'eviscerated', creating a social and cultural vacuum which was colonized by a middle class busy constituting itself as a new 'particular-universal' class:

> That is to say, although it was in fact a particular class with a specific history, nonetheless it has become the class around which an increasing range of practices are regarded as universally 'normal', 'good' and 'appropriate' ... the practices of the middle class have increasingly come to define the social itself ....
>
> (Savage 2003, p. 536)

There is increasing interest amongst class researchers in looking beyond these processes of normalization to investigate the structure and practices of the middle classes. Stephen Ball suggests that the middle class constitutes an ideological roadblock around which working-class families must negotiate: 'They are worthy of attention because they are there ... But further they are of particular importance ... because their actions produce or contribute to the perpetuation, inscription and reinvention of social inequalities both old and new' (Ball 2003, p. 5). However, any discussion of the middle class (or classes) must begin with its identification. The pre-capitalist middle class, so called because it stood between the landowning aristocracy and the working masses, was transformed and fragmented in the transition from feudalism to capitalism. One segment became Marx's bourgeoisie, the class of capitalist property owners. Another segment, comprising the old petty bourgeoisie (shopkeepers, small producers and small farmers), has declined in size but has not disappeared. However, this remnant has been supplemented by a burgeoning 'new' middle class, which owes its existence to large-scale industrial production and the growth of the state. The new middle class performs the professional, managerial and technical functions essential to complex modern societies and relies largely on educational credentials rather than the inheritance of property for its reproduction. This is an increasingly global class,[3] and whilst the growing middle classes of India, China and other 'new' economies may stimulate economic growth, competition for middle-class employment has intensified (Brown et al. 2011).

The identification of the middle class has posed particular difficulties for Marxist class theory. The economic position of many salaried employees – their lack of significant property and reliance on earned income – would appear to place them within the working class, albeit as a relatively privileged stratum. However, authors such as Poulantzas (1973) and Carchedi (1977) regard them as a separate class or classes, with their own specific class interests. They argue that political and ideological relations must be taken into account in class determination. Although technical and managerial workers share many of the economic relations characterizing the working class, their *ideological* position is to exercise knowledge and authority in the production process. The dominance of this function justifies placing them as a fraction of the middle class, distinct from the traditional petty bourgeoisie of small producers and shopkeepers as well as from the established professions. Poulantzas (1973) suggests that their relatively privileged position in relation to capital inclines these groups to ideological traits such as individualism, attraction to the status quo and a belief in aspiration and social mobility. These arguments have been critiqued and developed by Milios and Economakis (2011), who reject the idea of a homogeneous ideological position within such an economically diverse class, preferring to see ideological differences between different fractions of the middle class according to their economic interests.

The changing nature – and often downgrading – of White-collar work may support the view that many formerly middle-class occupations are being proletarianized, so that we should talk of a new working class rather than a new middle class (Ainley 2013). However, such a new class would still be ideologically distinct from the 'old' working class. Occupational downgrading merely reinforces class strategies aimed at maintaining differentials with working-class attainment and achieving the more desirable middle-class positions. Nevertheless, the extension of market rationality to agencies of symbolic control such as education and social services has created new tensions and insecurities amongst the middle class, and privatization is eroding ideological distinctions between public- and private-sector professionals (Bernstein 2001). Anxiety, rather than complacency or comfort, is a term often used to describe the outlook of this class fraction. As it struggles to maintain a position separate from and above the working class, but continually under pressure from the increasing scope of capitalist accumulation, the middle class as a whole remains 'a class-between, a class beset with contradictions and uncertainties' (Ball 2003, p. 4).

Middle-class relationships to education have been the subject of intensive research in recent years. In their study of White middle-class identities and urban schooling, Reay et al. (2011) illustrate the effect of growing insecurity on the educational strategies of middle-class families. Whilst idealized images of 'middle classness' in terms of liberal values combined with independence and aspiration still persist, these authors describe a less constrained individualism in which self-interest has begun to dominate: 'It appears that what is being progressively marginalized in White middle-class identity formation is civic commitment and a sense of communal responsibility' (Reay et al. 2011, p. 6). Thus support for public services or sending one's children to a local comprehensive school may be interpreted in altruistic terms but may also represent a wish to maintain professional employment opportunities or to develop valuable interpersonal skills. Studies of this nature present a diverse picture of a skilful and agile middle class, determined in difficult circumstances to secure upward social mobility for their children, or at least the reproduction of existing class positions. In this project some families are willing to take risks but know that the risk can be managed by drawing on economic and cultural resources not available to less privileged families; others invest these resources in traditionally exclusive strategies such as private education. Although the premise that working-class children fail at school, whilst middle-class children succeed may be crude (Power and Whitty 2002, p. 598), Stephen Ball's characterization of the middle class as a roadblock to working-class educational success seems particularly apposite.

Mapping the class structure

The history of social classification systems in the United Kingdom is usually traced back to the Registrar General's classification developed by the statistician T.H.C. Stevenson in 1913. This development was a response to concerns about the distribution of infant mortality raised almost 30 years earlier, which had initially been dealt with on the basis of geographical variation rather than social class. During the late Victorian period, various social classification schemes had been proposed by anthropologists and social reformers, including Francis Galton and Charles Booth. These schemes were based not only on type of occupation and income but also on factors such as moral behaviour, living conditions and the ability to employ servants.[4] Szreter (1984, p. 525) suggests that Galton's work in particular embodied assumptions about heredity and natural ability, and 'introduced an explicit moral evaluation into the classification of occupations, whereby the professional class was held up as the desirable standard'. Those who believed that environment, rather than heredity, was the chief determinant of individual abilities and dispositions had therefore to tread carefully in devising social classifications. Ultimately, however, Stevenson became convinced that an occupationally based system was superior to others and used this approach in his analysis of infant mortality in the 1911 census (Stevenson 1913, p. xli). The Registrar General's classification survived, with some modifications, to the 1971 census. Its final version is shown in Table 2.1.[5]

Social classification schemes typically attempt to construct a stratification of society which is a good predictor of outcomes such as health, education or

TABLE 2.1 Social class based on occupation
(Registrar General's classification)

I	Professional occupations
II	Managerial and technical occupations
III	Skilled occupations
	(N) Non-manual
	(M) Manual
IV	Partly skilled occupations
V	Unskilled occupations

Source: Rose et al. (2005, p. 8).

social attitudes. Following Weber's distinction between class and status, we may distinguish between stratification on the basis of class, understood as a structure grounded in the relations of economic life, and stratification based on a status order derived from an individual's social position. Empirically, it appears that inequalities in economic life chances tend to reflect stratification by class, whilst differences in cultural consumption are associated more strongly with status (Chan and Goldthorpe 2007). The Registrar General's classification (now referred to as SC) was an example of the second kind of stratification, a status hierarchy based on the social standing and skill levels supposed to be associated with different occupational types. Although it correlated quite well with inequalities in health, education and income, it was justifiably criticized for its intuitive, a priori nature and lack of a coherent theoretical base. These deficiencies became problematic as the nature of occupations changed, with the category of 'manager' and the distinction between manual and non-manual work posing particular problems. A more sociological classification scheme, known as Socio-economic Groups (SEG), was introduced alongside SC in 1951, and took into account employment status and the size of the employing organization as well as occupation. Although SEG was generally regarded as an improvement on the earlier classification, criticisms that it lacked a theoretical underpinning continued. However, attempting to found a system of social classification on a clear theoretical basis means adopting a position on the concept of class itself, leading back into the disputes discussed earlier. The neo-Weberian approach of John Goldthorpe and his colleagues in the CASMIN project has perhaps been the dominant solution to this problem, although other perspectives – for example Erik Olin Wright's explicitly Marxist class schema (Wright 1997) and the Cambridge Social Interaction and Stratification (CAMSIS) scale (Prandy 1990) – have also been influential.

Wright's approach has a rather different theoretical basis to Goldthorpe's, being based on the concept of exploitation rather than Weberian market relations. However, they both give primacy to the economic sphere and lead to distinct class categories. Indeed, Wright (2005, p. 27) has acknowledged that at a practical level there is no great difference between these approaches, particularly for questions concerning the impact of class on the lives of individuals. By contrast, the CAMSIS scale is based on the assumption that the unequal distribution of resources is reflected in people's relationships within social, political and economic networks. Although occupation is still found to be the most significant indicator of location in the overall structure of advantage and disadvantage, it is the patterns of relationship – across social, cultural, political and economic spheres – between individuals with different or similar occupations that define their position within a single continuous measure of social stratification. These alternative approaches are of great theoretical and practical interest, with their own research agendas and literatures. However, they have not been extensively applied in research on educational inequality:[6] for this reason, the main focus in this chapter will be on Goldthorpe's approach and its relationship to the current official system used in the United Kingdom, the National Statistics Socio-economic Classification (NS-SEC).

The Erikson-Goldthorpe classification

The idea that employment relations are central to understanding and describing the class structure of modern societies has provided the conceptual basis for a wide range of empirical research in a broadly Weberian project of class analysis. Originally developed in the context of the Oxford mobility survey (see Chapter 9), the resulting classification was refined to enable comparative studies across countries with varying economic structures. The long history of this programme has led to the coexistence of a number of slightly different schemas, variously referred to as EGP (Erikson, Goldthorpe and Portocarero; see Erikson et al. 1979), Goldthorpe (1980), and Erikson and Goldthorpe (1992). Their common approach is based on the nature of the employment relation, rather than the status of occupations or the attributes of individual people, distinguishing first between employers, the self-employed and employees. For employees, a crucial distinction is made between two kinds of relationship with the employer. In a labour contract relationship, employees are paid for specified amounts of labour, whether in terms of hours worked or tasks completed (piece-work rates). These employees are normally subject to a considerable degree of monitoring and control, and have little room for autonomy other than what is essential to the performance of their allocated tasks. In a service contract relationship, employees are remunerated for a more broadly defined role with more elastic hours of work. In return for an annual salary; a formal career structure; and other benefits, such as pensions, the employee has considerable autonomy and discretion, exercising authority on behalf of their organization or deploying specialized knowledge and expertise (Rose et al. 2005). The employment conditions associated with labour contract and service contract relationships are therefore qualitatively different, both in terms of the returns to labour and in the dispositions required of the employee. Whilst a service contract relationship is designed to encourage the development of a moral commitment to the employing organization, a labour contract requires little more than compliance with procedures. The distinction between these two contract relationships implies differences in a range of specific features with the potential to generate inequalities in economic outcomes, such as stability and security of employment, long-term prospects and psychological satisfaction from one's work. People in a service-contract relationship are often referred to as members of the *service class*.

There has been considerable debate over the appropriate unit of analysis for classification systems. Erikson and Goldthorpe (1992) argue that members of the same family share the same 'class fate' so that determining class position by father's occupation is justified (assuming the father to be the main earner in the family). Although this assertion was vigorously contested during the 1980s and 1990s (see Beller 2009), a consensus emerged that the Erikson-Goldthorpe approach did not produce any serious misrepresentation of class trends compared to individual-level determinations of class. Moreover, children must be assigned a class origin in research on social mobility or educational attainment, for which a single, family social class has conventionally been used. Whilst there can be significant advantages in a joint determination of family social class which takes into account the individual class positions of both parents in a two-parent family (Beller 2009) the conventional approach continues to dominate class analysis.

The conceptual structure of the Erikson-Goldthorpe class schema is shown in Table 2.2, which shows both a seven-class variant (I-VII) and the full eleven-class schema produced by subdividing Classes III, IV and VII. The principles of these subdivisions are different in each case: within Class III, higher and lower grades of routine non-manual work are distinguished, partly to take into account differing patterns of non-manual employment between men and women.[7] However, in Classes IV and VII, the main distinction is between the industrial and agricultural sectors. Chan and Goldthorpe (2007, p. 51) note that, whilst the schema primarily describes a structure of inequality, the classes it contains should not be seen as falling into a simple hierarchical order. This is particularly true of the 'intermediate' Classes III, IV and V, which offer different balances of advantage and disadvantage regarding job security, income stability and long-term prospects, and cannot easily be ranked. The

TABLE 2.2 Conceptual structure of the Erikson-Goldthorpe class schema. Positions within the full 11-class schema are shown in brackets at the end of each set of branches

Employers	Large (**I**)			
	Small	Industry (**IVa**)		
		Agriculture (**IVb**)		
Employees	Service	Higher grade (**I**)		
	contract	Lower grade (**II**)		
	Intermediate	Routine non-manual	Higher grade (**IIIa**)	
			Lower grade (**IIIb**)	
		Lower technical and manual, supervisory (**V**)		
	Labour	Manual	Industry	Skilled (**VI**)
	contract			Non-skilled (**VIIa**)
			Agriculture (**VIIb**)	
Self-	Industry (**IVa**)			
employed	Agriculture (**IVc**)			

Source: Erikson and Goldthorpe (1992).

Erikson-Goldthorpe classification has been extensively critiqued, particularly from those involved in developing the CAMSIS scale (Prandy 1990). Its initial focus on male employment has caused difficulties in adapting it to the changing economic situation of women, and its claims to be a categorical rather than hierarchical classification have been questioned. It has also been argued that the economic context of production cannot be separated from consumption and social interaction, and that the concept of employment relations does not necessarily lead to sharp distinctions between classes and homogeneity within them (Prandy 1990, 1998). Nevertheless, Erikson-Goldthorpe has formed the basis for an extensive body of comparative research on social mobility as well as providing the theoretical foundation for the official socio-economic classification in the United Kingdom, the NS-SEC classification used by the Office of National Statistics (Rose et al. 2005).

The National Statistics Socio-Economic Classification

The NS-SEC retains the conceptual basis of the Erikson-Goldthorpe schema but has modified its approach to take into account the changing nature of work, particularly in patterns of male and female work, the growth in employee positions and the increasingly bureaucratic nature of large enterprises. It is possible to show that the classification relates to observed structures of inequality, and 'causal narratives' can be produced to account for these structures in terms of the employment relations measured by the class variable (Rose 1998, p. 757). Although a lively debate was conducted following its introduction (Prandy 1998; Rose 1998), the NS-SEC is now established as the main social classification system in official UK statistics.

The full NS-SEC classification is extensive and unwieldy: for the purposes of social research, it is usually collapsed into simpler systems with fewer categories, most commonly the 'eight class' version shown in Table 2.3. The broad division between service contract and labour contract relationships is outlined in this table, and also gradations within these types of contract. The eight-class NS-SEC includes employers in two ways: large employers are classified with higher professionals and managers, and small employers are classified with own-account workers (non-professional self-employed people). The treatment of large employers provides some conceptual difficulties, particularly because in modern economies these employers tend to be organizations and institutions. Although some large employers are individuals, constituting around 0.1 per cent of the population, their numbers are too small to distort the higher professional class. Nevertheless, the NS-SEC (and the Goldthorpe schemas before it) do not easily capture any notion of a capitalist 'ruling class'.

Although NS-SEC has been in use for a relatively short time, it is possible to use earlier class schemas to estimate the change in the NS-SEC class structure over a longer period (Goldthorpe 2016). Figure 2.1 shows this change for

TABLE 2.3 The 'eight class' version of the NS-SEC, together with their defining features and examples of occupations falling under each class

NS-SEC analytical class (eight-class version)	Defining features and example occupations
1 Higher managerial and professional occupations	Service relationship employment: senior managers; medical and legal professionals; architects
2 Lower managerial and professional occupations	Attenuated service relationship: teachers, youth workers, nurses, physiotherapists
3 Intermediate occupations	Positions intermediate between a service relationship and a labour contract: secretaries, clerical officers, technical maintenance
4 Small employers and own-account workers	Employer with fewer than 25 employees. Self-employed workers such as market traders, builders, carpenters
5 Lower supervisory and technical occupations	Supervisory or technical positions with a modified form of 'labour contract': motor mechanics, plant operatives
6 Semi-routine occupations	Slightly modified labour contract: checkout operators, scaffolders, sheet metal workers, receptionists
7 Routine occupations	Basic labour contract: Packers, canners, assemblers, cleaners, HGV drivers, welders
8 Never worked and long-term unemployed	Positions which entail exclusion from the labour market

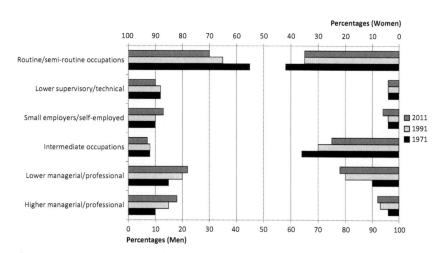

FIGURE 2.1 Estimated NS-SEC class distribution (percentages) of economically active men and women in Great Britain, 1971–2011.

Source: Adapted from Goldthorpe (2016).

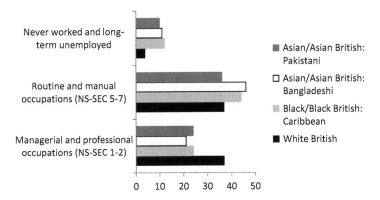

FIGURE 2.2 NS-SEC class distribution for men in England by ethnicity, showing selected groups within the NS-SEC (Rose et al. 2005, p. 38). Eight-class NS-SEC categories given in brackets.
Source: 2011 census. Dataset DC6206EW.

both men and women between the census years 1971 and 2011; the gender difference in class structure is particularly evident in the intermediate occupations, but smaller differences are also seen across other classes, including the under-representation of women in the higher managerial and professional class. Whilst some equalization has occurred over time, the pattern of class differences by gender remains very similar to the situation in 1971. Overall, changes in the class distribution, particularly the growth in the professional and managerial classes over this period, reflect the changing patterns of employment shown in Figure 1.4. Differences in socio-economic structure according to ethnic background can also be observed. Data from the 2011 census shows that, apart from those of Indian and Chinese backgrounds, men from all other ethnic groups are less likely to be found in managerial and professional occupations than White British men, and are substantially more likely to be long-term unemployed.

These differences are particularly noticeable for men from Black and Bangladeshi backgrounds, who are also more likely to be in routine or manual employment than other ethnic groups (see Figure 2.2). These points will be returned to in Chapter 3, in the context of eligibility for free school meals.

Notes

1 The identification of the working class is a contested area in Marxist class theory. There is broad agreement that not all wage-earners are working class – for example salaried professionals and managers. However, some authors further restrict the working class to those directly engaged in producing surplus value (Poulantzas 1973).

2 Weber refers to this state of affairs as *formal* equality, of the kind suggested by the phrase 'equality before the law'.

3 Koo (2016) points out that the term 'global middle class' conceals diverse social categories in varied economic and cultural conditions. However, it has two broad meanings. It can refer to the totality of people in middle-class occupations across the world, or to an affluent and globally mobile segment within this totality. The former meaning is intended here. For a discussion of the educational orientations of the globally mobile middle class, see Ball and Nikita (2014).

4 The social classification used in Booth's poverty maps of London included as its lowest class the city's 'vicious, semi-criminal' inhabitants. The next class are described as 'shiftless, hand-to-mouth, pleasure loving, and always poor; to work when they like and play when they like is their ideal' (Booth 1887, p. 329)

5 The Registrar General's classification also forms the basis of a social classification used in market research, which uses the categories A, B, C1, C2, D, and E.

6 Bukodi et al. (2014) and Barone and Ruggera (2018) use the CAMSIS scale as an alternative measure to Erikson-Goldthorpe class.

7 Crompton (2008, p. 62) notes that this distinction emerged from feminist criticisms that earlier versions of the classification failed to recognize that, for women, clerical work is often a 'dead end'. When applied to women, Class IIIb is treated as Class VII.

3

PATTERNS OF INEQUALITY
IN EDUCATION

This chapter presents quantitative evidence on patterns of inequality in educational opportunity, drawing on research from the United Kingdom and
on international comparative studies. The chapter begins with a discussion of
how educational inequality is to be conceived and measured, followed by an
overview of research findings based on this conceptual framework and relating
particularly to the transitions between lower secondary, upper secondary and
higher education. Although it is mainly concerned with class-based inequality,
the chapter discusses the use of eligibility for free school meals (FSM) as a social
background variable. Debates on the relationship between cognitive ability,
educational attainment and social background are also briefly outlined. The
chapter concludes with a discussion of educational inequalities related to gender
and ethnicity.

Measuring inequality of educational opportunity

In his book *Education, Opportunity and Social Inequality*, Raymond Boudon
(1974, p. xi) makes the following definition:

> By inequality of educational opportunity (IEO) I mean the differences in
> level of educational attainment according to social background ... Thus a
> society is characterized by a certain amount of IEO if, for instance, the prob-
> ability of going to college is smaller for a worker's son than for a lawyer's.

This definition can be extended in obvious ways to inequalities of race and
gender. However, it is incomplete without specifying how attainment and social
background should be measured. There is no single answer to this question,

and the practicalities of data collection and analysis will influence how IEO is made operational in a particular piece of research. More fundamentally, decisions about how to capture attainment and social background may be grounded in a conception of social justice, as well as taking into account factors such as policy concerns and objective features of the educational systems being studied. To allow for 'credential inflation', a relative rather than absolute measure of attainment may be used (Sullivan et al. 2011). A further consideration is the disciplinary context within which researchers work and the problems that occupy them most intensely. For example, economists have tended to measure social background in terms of income or other *attributional* properties, whilst sociologists have preferred to work with *relational* properties such as social class or status. These distinctions are by no means fixed, and for both theoretical and practical reasons various social background measures may be used in addition to or in place of social class and income, including parental education, FSM eligibility , neighbourhood or school location, and measures of cultural environment (Ferreira and Gignoux 2011; Blanden and Macmillan 2016). In some studies, a single continuous measure of socio-economic status (SES) is constructed from several individual measures. Because educational inequality may evolve in different directions according to different measures of these, some researchers use a multidimensional approach, in which a number of these measures are used both singly and together (Bukodi and Goldthorpe 2013). However, for traditional class analysts there is a crucial distinction between class and properties such as income or residential location. Any association between attributional properties and educational attainment would be seen as an *epiphenomenon*, driven by class as an underlying causal factor. From a sociological point of view, the causal efficacy of categories such as class and status provides a distinct advantage when representing social background.

An example will help to illustrate the decisions and compromises required by a combination of research question and availability of data. In Figure 3.1, the aim is to show how attainment at age 16 differed between social classes in England in the decade following the introduction of the GCSE examination in 1988. Complete information on social class was not available for the school populations concerned. It was therefore necessary to use survey research – in this case the Youth Cohort Study of England and Wales (YCS), a series of longitudinal data sets covering 16 cohorts between 1985 and 2007. In the period shown, social class was represented by the Socio-Economic Group (SEG) classification (see Chapter 2). Attainment is captured by the proportion of young people in each social class achieving five or more grades A*-C at GCSE. The significance of this measure derives partly from its use as a threshold for progression to upper secondary education (see Demack et al. 2000 for a discussion of this point), and also from its institutionalization in national school performance measures.

In Figure 3.1, it is clear that class differences in attainment rates exist, with a noticeable divide between children from manual and non-manual

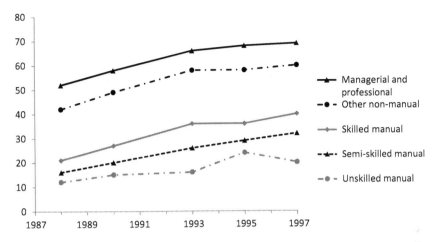

FIGURE 3.1   Achievement of 5+ grades A*-C at GCSE in England 1988–97 by social class (SEG). Percentages.

Source: DCSF (2008).

Note: The A* grade was introduced in 1994; the highest grade available until then was A.

backgrounds. A fairly steady increase in attainment over time for all classes apart from unskilled manual is also evident, whilst the attainment gaps are relatively constant. It appears that, although attainment increased overall – or, more precisely, this threshold was achieved by a higher proportion of children in each social class – inequalities in attainment showed little change. However, in periods of expansion, it can be more appropriate to consider the *proportionate gap* between social groups: that is, the ratio between the attainment gap and the overall rate of participation or achievement (Gorard et al. 2001; Sullivan et al. 2011). Thus a raw gap of 10 percentage points is very substantial in relation to an attainment rate of 20 per cent; the same gap would be less significant if overall attainment were 60 per cent, although one might still question why such a gap had persisted. In Figure 3.1, the raw gap in attainment between children from the managerial/professional class and children from skilled manual backgrounds changes very little. However, the proportionate gap declines from around 1.0 to 0.6, suggesting some equalization.

Odds ratios

Educational expansion typically follows an 'S'-shaped curve with a low initial rate of growth, a period of high growth-rate in the middle and, if the expansion persists for long enough, the return of low growth when very few people remain who have not been educated to the level concerned. This pattern of expansion, known as a *logistic curve*, means that the rate at which attainment is increasing depends on the stage of educational expansion that has been reached.[1]

If two social groups are at different stages in a process of expansion, percentage gaps may widen or narrow without there necessarily being any change in the underlying association between social background and attainment. Measures of inequality based on percentage or proportionate gaps would not capture this unchanging association, and researchers investigating over-time changes in inequality have tended to use an alternative measure which is not sensitive to educational expansion. This measure, known as the *odds ratio*, indicates the relative chances of achieving certain outcomes between different social groups, and shows whether the achievement gap has changed by more or less than would be expected on the basis of a logistic curve (Heath et al. 1992). An odds ratio of unity implies equality between different social groups.

The simplest case where odds ratios can be defined is when there are just two social groups or classes C_1 and C_2, and a single dichotomous outcome based on participation in a given educational level. This corresponds to a 2 × 2 table containing the participation rates (or probabilities) of people from each group. Frequencies (the actual numbers of people rather than probabilities) may also be used (see Table 3.1). In general, if the probabilities of children from classes C_1 and C_2 satisfying a particular educational criterion are respectively p_1 and p_2, the odds ratio for class C_2 relative to class C_1 is given by

$$r_{1,2} = \frac{p_1 / (1 - p_1)}{p_2 / (1 - p_2)}$$

An important property of odds ratios is that they do not change if the row or column frequencies in the 2 × 2 table are multiplied by a constant.[2] These operations correspond to a change in the relative size of one class without changing its participation rate (row multiplication), or a change in participation rates which affects both classes in the same proportion (column multiplication). The odds ratio is therefore invariant if educational expansion proceeds in either of these ways.

Figure 3.2 shows two logistic curves representing attainment or participation rates over time for a 'higher' and a 'lower' social class. Although the curves look quite dissimilar, the only difference in the underlying mathematical relationship is that the curves have different starting points, so that initially the higher-class participation rate is 15 per cent, whilst that for the lower class is 3 per cent. Because of this initial difference, over time the gap in participation rates first

TABLE 3.1 Contingency table showing the proportions and total numbers of people from two social groups who participate at a given educational level

Social group	Participating	Not participating	N
C_1	p_1	$1 - p_1$	n_1
C_2	p_2	$1 - p_2$	n_2
N	$n_1 p_1 + n_2 p_2$	$n_1(1 - p_1) + n_2(1 - p_2)$	$n_1 + n_2$

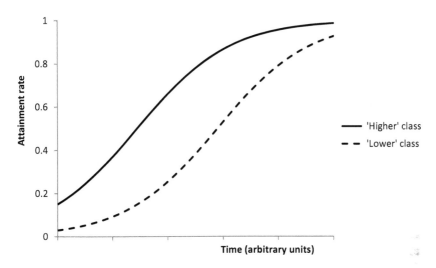

FIGURE 3.2 Logistic growth curves representing educational expansion with a constant odds ratio between two social classes.

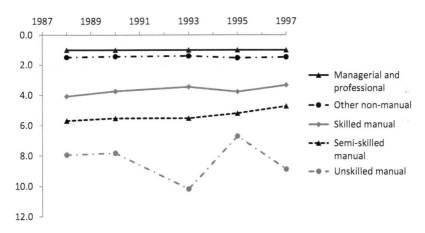

FIGURE 3.3 Achievement of 5+ grades A★-C at GCSE in England 1988–97 by social class (SEG). Odds ratios referred to managerial/professional class.
Source: DCSF (2008).

widens and then narrows. However, these changes are purely the result of expansion: inequality as measured by the odds ratio remains the same throughout the period shown in the graph. Changes in the participation gap beyond those caused by expansion would imply a different participation-time relationship for the two classes, and this would generate a change in the odds ratio.

The use of odds ratios is illustrated by Figure 3.3, which shows class differences in the attainment of five or more grades A★-C based on the same data as in Figure 3.1, but using odds ratios relative to the managerial/professional class as the measure of inequality. It can be seen that these odds ratios remain largely unchanged over time, with the exception of pupils from unskilled backgrounds where considerable fluctuations occur.[3]

Educational inequality in comparative perspective

The analytical framework outlined in the previous section has been extensively applied, including detailed national studies, such as Paterson and Iannelli (2007a), Boliver (2011) and Sullivan et al. (2011) in the United Kingdom, and Blossfeld et al. (2015) in Germany, as well as cross-national comparisons of a small number of countries such as Jerrim and Vignoles (2015). Several large-scale international comparative studies using nationally representative data sets have also been conducted, providing opportunities to apply a consistent methodological framework to the question of how inequality differs between countries and changes over time. Many of these studies use some version of the Erikson-Goldthorpe class schema to represent social background; however, national studies tend to be less consistent, either interpreting a class schema in different ways or using other variables – such as parental education – as a proxy for social background. For example, the UK studies mentioned earlier use 5-class, 3-class and 2-class versions respectively of either the Erikson-Goldthorpe or NS-SEC schemas, whilst Blossfeld et al. (2015) use parental education. Although some studies are mainly descriptive and use measures such as proportionate gaps to assess the extent of inequality, the majority construct statistical models of the association between social origins and attainment. These models allow the extent and development of inequality to be understood but also enable the relative importance of different social background factors to be identified. The specification of the models themselves has undergone some change over time, as increasing participation has shifted the focus from inequalities expressed in terms of years of schooling, to inequalities in access to higher levels of education (Breen and Jonsson 2005). However, since the work of Robert Mare in the 1980s, it has been recognized that models based on simple probabilities of making a transition from one educational level to the next conflate the effects of educational expansion with the underlying association between social origins and attainment. Models based on the odds[4] of children from each social origin category making a particular transition do not suffer from this problem, and the estimates of association they give are invariant with respect to educational expansion (Mare 1981). Such models claim to give a 'true' picture of how inequality changes over time, although this claim has been contested (see Lucas 2001).

The first major comparative study to use the Mare model was based on analyses of 13 industrial countries, drawing on data sets which, although probably the best available at the time, were nevertheless variable in quality.

Reflecting its title of *Persistent Inequality* (Shavit and Blossfeld 1993), this study indicated that the effects of social origin on educational attainment had remained stable over a significant period, with only Sweden and the Netherlands showing a reduction in the strength of association. However, subsequent analyses questioned this finding, and it became clear that inequality had reduced in several countries, particularly at lower transition points and during the years between 1930 and 1970 (Erikson and Jonsson 1996a; Breen and Jonsson 2005). At later transition points, such as entry to upper secondary and tertiary education, inequalities remained largely unchanged. More recent research has provided an increasingly detailed picture of continuity and change (Shavit et al. 2007; Pfeffer 2008; Haim and Shavit 2013). However, comparisons between studies are often difficult to make because of methodological differences, including variations in sample size, data collection methods and how social background and educational attainment are represented. For this reason, the work of Breen et al. (2009) is particularly valuable in providing a relatively uniform analysis of cohorts born in the first two-thirds of the twentieth century across eight European countries, using EGP social class. This study found substantial reductions in educational inequality, largely for children born in a 30-year period in the middle of the century. This finding reflects the educational reforms taking place across Europe at the time, including increases in the minimum school-leaving age. Although Breen et al. (2009) were not primarily concerned with distinguishing between different educational transitions, a comparative analysis of eight countries using more recent birth cohorts indicates that in most countries the effect of social background decreases sharply between the transition to upper secondary education and the transition to tertiary education (Jackson 2013). More recently, Barone and Ruggera (2018) have extended the work of Breen et al. (2009) to cover trends in 26 countries for people born between 1930 and 1980, with similar findings of declining inequality in the post-war decades. The decline is robust against different measures of social background, with downward trends apparent for EGP social class, parental education and parental status measured by an international variant of the CAMSIS scale. However, there is considerable variation between different countries, with Britain and Germany having the smallest reduction in IEO[5] (apart from Romania and Bulgaria), whilst the greatest reductions were in Finland and Sweden. In the most recent cohorts, trends towards equalization weakened considerably, suggesting that 'the "golden age" of educational equalization [may be] already behind us' (Barone and Ruggera 2018, p. 22). In general, greater reductions in IEO have been found when social background is measured by class rather than by parental education. A persistent, and even strengthening, effect of parental education is reported by Bukodi et al. (2018), which they trace in part to the nature of educational systems and the ability of parents to navigate their intricacies.

Social class and measures of disadvantage

The use of administrative data on school attainment offers a number of advantages over survey research. It covers the great majority of the school population, is routinely collected year-on-year and is normally available within a year or so after its collection. An increasing number of research studies have used administrative data to investigate questions of educational inequality (for example, Chowdry et al. 2012; Gorard 2015; Crawford et al. 2017a). However, political sensitivities over class, together with the practicalities of data collection and concerns over the prospects of the most deprived sections of society, have led official statistics to focus on specific aspects of socio-economic disadvantage rather than the more fundamental concept of class. Circumstances such as low family income, living in poor neighbourhoods and having been in care are often more accessible to measurement as well as being more directly related to national or transnational policies on disadvantage. These circumstances are all associated to some extent with social class; however, they are by no means close proxies for the class location of individual families. Administrative data on educational achievement according to eligibility for FSM is a case in point. Although FSM eligibility cannot be straightforwardly identified with low social class, it indicates a population group which is significantly disadvantaged in educational terms. Figure 3.4 shows the relationship between FSM eligibility and achievement of five or more GCSE passes at grades A*-C, including English and mathematics, covering a more recent period than Figures 3.1 and 3.3.

Entitlement to FSM has been used to capture social disadvantage in a range of countries, including the United States, Sweden and Japan. In the United

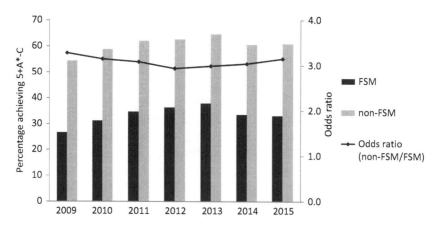

FIGURE 3.4 Achievement of 5+ grades A*-C at GCSE (including English and mathematics) in England 2009–15 by eligibility for free school meals (FSM). Percentages and odds ratios.

Sources: DfE (2014, 2015, 2016).

Kingdom, systematic data on FSM eligibility has been available since 1989, and a number of studies have analysed the relationship between FSM and educational attainment (Shuttleworth 1995; Ilie et al. 2017; Taylor 2018). In official statistical publications, eligibility for FSM has become a standard indicator of social disadvantage when monitoring educational attainment, and annual updates are provided on FSM and achievement at GCSE, A-level and access to higher education. Although the largely income-based criteria have varied to some extent over time, eligibility for FSM provides a relatively stable, clearly defined indicator of disadvantage (Taylor 2018). FSM-eligible pupils are amongst the most disadvantaged in the population, not only in terms of income but also according to a range of other indicators. In England, over three-quarters of such pupils have parents with qualifications below A-level, nearly two-thirds have parents who are unemployed and a similar proportion live in social housing (Ilie et al. 2017). However, as a binary category, eligibility for FSM cannot fully capture the nuances of the income distribution or of variability within FSM or non-FSM groups of children. Many disadvantaged children do not receive FSM and are therefore not included in the statistics, even when the inclusion criteria are relaxed to cover any period of eligibility in the preceding five years.[6] Although there is no doubt that children eligible for FSM are much more likely to be in the lowest income households, the benefits on which eligibility depends push their families up the income scale, so that many families not included in the FSM statistics are actually poorer (Hobbs and Vignoles 2010). In England and Wales, slightly less than half of children living in poverty are recorded as eligible for FSM, and although around half of FSM-eligible children live in the most deprived areas, the remainder are distributed across richer neighbourhoods (Ilie et al. 2017; Taylor 2018).

Whilst FSM eligibility is an important measure of disadvantage, it may be unreliable as a proxy for social class. Because eligibility is mainly income based, any circumstances which significantly curtail family income could result in a pupil becoming eligible, whatever their parents' occupation. Nearly half of FSM-eligible pupils are from single-parent families, and this may restrict earnings potential even for parents in high-status occupations. Over extended periods, temporary unemployment could draw children from more advantaged households into the FSM category. Table 3.2 shows the proportion of pupils from each NS-SEC class eligible for FSM at any time in the five years before sitting their GCSE examinations. As might be expected, children from professional and managerial households are considerably less likely to be eligible than those from semi-routine, routine or long-term unemployed backgrounds. However, there is a gradient rather than a sharp divide between classes and over one-third of children with parents in routine occupations have not been FSM-eligible. The table also shows the proportion of all FSM-eligible pupils accounted for by each social class, indicating that nearly 20 per cent of eligible children are from families in NS-SEC Classes 1–3 compared with around

TABLE 3.2 Eligibility for free school meals in England by social class. Sample of 12,678 pupils who were eligible for free school meals at any time in the five years prior to taking GCSE examinations in 2006

	Proportion of pupils in each class who were eligible for FSM (per cent)	Proportion of all FSM-eligible pupils accounted for by each class (per cent)
Household occupation (NS-SEC)		
Higher managerial and professional	3.7	1.9
Lower managerial and professional	9.4	10.7
Intermediate occupations	16.1	6.9
Small employers and self-employed	19.1	8.2
Lower supervisory and technical	25.7	10.4
Semi-routine occupations	41.8	20.9
Routine occupations	62.9	18.7
Never worked/long-term unemployed	90.6	22.3

Source: Ilie et al. (2017, p. 262).

60 per cent from Classes 4 to 7. If the intention is to differentiate between children from different class backgrounds rather than family income levels, eligibility for FSM is rather a blunt instrument. However, as an indicator of potential educational disadvantage, FSM eligibility is relatively effective. Although parental occupational class and parental education are the best predictors of pupils' attainment at GCSE, explaining a higher proportion of the variance between pupils than other indicators, they are only marginally better than FSM eligibility (Ilie et al. 2017).

Access to higher education

Over the last 60 years, there has been a significant expansion of higher education provision in most industrialized countries (Liu et al. 2016; Mountford-Zimdars and Harrison 2016). However, inequalities in access to higher education have been remarkably persistent throughout this period of expansion. In their classic study *Origins and Destinations*, Halsey et al. (1980) showed that university participation rates for working-class students more than tripled for cohorts born between 1913–22 and 1943–52, from 0.9 per cent to 3.1 per cent. However, in the same period participation by students from service-class backgrounds also more than tripled, from 7.2 per cent to 26.4 per cent, so that the gap in participation rates between these classes increased by far more than the growth in participation by working-class students. Significant levels of inequality according to family background continue to be found in many countries (Shavit et al. 2007; Crawford et al. 2017a). Although comparisons are often difficult – for example because of differences in educational systems and class structures – various attempts have been made to construct international rankings of inequality in access to higher education. Using parental education as a social background measure, OECD data for 27 member countries shows some degree of inequality in all cases but considerable variation between countries (OECD 2012, Table A6.1). In this ranking, the United Kingdom is one of the least unequal countries, with Germany, France and the United States amongst countries with greater inequality.[7] However, the relationship between social background and access to higher education is too complex to capture by participation rates alone. Shavit et al. (2007) identify three groups of questions concerning social inequality in higher education: the overall relationship between inequality and expansion; the relationships between expansion, institutional differentiation, and selectivity; and the effects of marketization and privatization. The last two of these questions will be discussed in Chapter 4, whilst the remainder of this section focusses on changes in access over time and their relationship with expansion.

In the United Kingdom, many studies of higher education expansion are based on survey research such as the British Household Panel Survey (BHPS), which provides a long-term perspective on trends in access between the 1940s and the late 1990s (Paterson and Iannelli 2007; Boliver 2011). Between 1960 and 1994, increased participation was not associated with significant reductions in class-based inequality (Boliver 2011). During two periods of expansion, in the 1960s and 1990s, odds ratios between service and working-class positions decreased only in the first expansion period, and then only slightly. Odds ratios between service and intermediate classes decreased markedly in the expansion of the 1990s, although they remained significant. For more recent cohorts, longitudinal surveys such as the Youth Cohort Study of England and Wales (YCS) and the Longitudinal Study of Young People in England (LSYPE) have also been used. Using YCS data and the NS-SEC measure of social class, Iannelli (2007) demonstrates a slow but not uninterrupted decline in inequality for cohorts in England and Wales between 1989 and 2001. A similar pattern occurred in Scotland, but in all three countries the expansion which occurred following the 1992 Further and Higher Education Act coincided with an increase in odds ratios in 1993, possibly because professional classes were quicker to take advantage of these new opportunities.

Administrative data from higher education admissions and funding bodies provide a further insight into recent trends. Figure 3.5 shows the change over time in two official measures of social inequality in higher education participation in England. Introduced in 2007 but applied to cohorts entering higher education between 2003 and 2009, the FYPSEC[8] measure was based on parental occupation using the eight-class version of the NS-SEC classification. Omitting the category of long-term unemployed, it distinguished between two broad groupings: Classes 1–3 and Classes 4–7. For each grouping, the

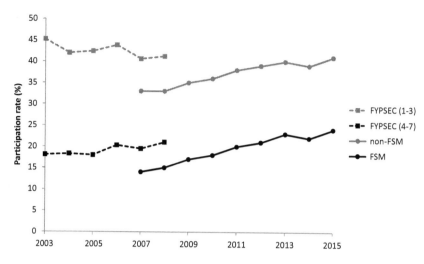

FIGURE 3.5 HE participation of younger students in England by FYPSEC and FSM measures, 2003–15.

Sources: BIS (2010); DfE (2017c).

measure expressed the number of young people who entered full-time higher education between the ages of 18 and 20 as a proportion of all young people in this age range. However, FYPSEC suffered from a number of weaknesses affecting its accuracy and consistency, and from 2011 it was replaced by the FSM measure, which expresses the proportion of young people progressing to higher education at age 18 or 19 according to whether or not they had received FSM. Both the FSM and FYPSEC measures are dichotomous, and therefore lack the sensitivity of analyses according to social class, even collapsed versions such as that used by Boliver (2011). However, the broad trends illustrated in Figure 3.5 suggest that, since the beginning of the twenty-first century, any reductions in inequality have been modest.

Entry to higher education comes at the end of a series of transitions, and participation rates are strongly influenced by the distribution of prior attainment across different social groups. It is therefore important to determine to what extent differences in participation can be explained by differences in academic performance rather than other factors, such as the diversion of people from certain social groups into vocational education or the labour market.[9] In some countries the association between prior attainment and entry to higher education – at least in terms of access across all types of institution – is quite weak. For example, in the United States only 60 per cent of the gap in participation rates between different social groups is explained by prior attainment, 55 per cent in Australia, and 30 per cent in Canada (Crawford et al. 2017a). Depending on the measure of social background that is used, in England this figure is over 80 per cent (Crawford and Greaves 2015, p. 34), and some studies claim that almost all of the gap in participation rates is accounted for by differences in prior attainment (Gorard 2008; National Audit Office 2008). Using a measure of SES that combines eligibility for FSM and various neighbourhood measures of deprivation, Crawford et al. (2017a) show that in England, all of the difference in participation rates between the top and bottom fifths of the socio-economic distribution can be explained by attainment at age 16, and almost all can be explained by attainment at age 18.

Attainment, cognitive ability and social background

The largely social origin of educational inequalities is contested by some scholars, who argue that liberal-industrial theory is correct in its predictions of declining inequality (see, for example, Marks 2014). As universalism increases, any remaining social background inequalities would, they argue, be the result of systematic differences in cognitive ability rather than social processes operating over and above cognitive skills. It is certainly true that significant class differences exist in cognitive ability, even when measured at an early age. For example, using data from the British Cohort Study (BCS), Feinstein (2003) found a 13 percentage-point difference at the age of 22 months in average cognitive performance between children from high- and low-SES groups[10]. Other studies have found similar differences and have attempted to trace the evolution of social background gaps in cognitive ability as children grow older (Crawford et al. 2017b). Clearly, these differences could have social origins, even where infants are concerned. However, a key question for those who assert the primacy of cognitive ability is what happens afterwards. If the relative importance of cognitive ability stays the same, or even increases, it could be argued that social processes are of relatively minor importance in education. Conversely, if social background becomes more important, and in particular if initially high-achieving poor children fall behind, it would be difficult to contest the importance of social processes in generating educational inequality.

In this debate, the work of Leon Feinstein (2003) has achieved a certain notoriety. In addition to demonstrating the existence of social background gaps in early cognitive ability, Feinstein also suggested that the trajectories of children from different social backgrounds were radically different. By the age of seven, children from low-SES backgrounds who had been amongst the most high-attaining children from all backgrounds had (on average) fallen behind significantly. Even more striking was the finding that these children had been overtaken by high-SES children who had initially been in the lowest-attaining group. Feinstein's paper was seized upon by politicians from all parties and influenced policies such as the Sure Start preschool programme and other educational interventions. However, a critique of his work by Jerrim and Vignoles (2011) suggested that the 'crossover' between high-ability, low-SES children and low-ability, high-SES children may have been a statistical artefact.

Controversy over these findings continues, but it now appears that extreme changes in the position of high- and low-SES children in the distribution of cognitive ability are not robustly supported by the evidence (see the debate in Feinstein et al. 2015). Nevertheless, even critics of Feinstein have demonstrated significant *and widening* inequalities in attainment as children progress through most of their school career. For example, using school administrative data, Crawford et al. (2017b) show that the gap in average attainment between the least and most advantaged pupils is around 16 percentage points at age seven, widening to around 29 percentage points by age 16. The gap declines slightly after this, to approximately 26 points in higher education.[11]

In other research, Bukodi et al. (2014) have found that, in Britain and Sweden, parental class, status and education have significant, independent effects on educational attainment after controlling for early cognitive ability. The combined effect of class, status and education is substantial: for children in the highest quintile of early cognitive ability, these social background factors taken together generate a difference of at least 30 percentage points between the most and least advantaged in the probability of high attainment at the end of secondary school. The idea that cognitive ability is in some way a fixed individual characteristic is in any case highly questionable, and there is considerable debate over the relative importance of environment and heredity in cognitive development (Feinstein et al. 2015; Bukodi and Goldthorpe 2019, pp. 109–110). A dualistic distinction between these factors is increasingly seen as outdated (Heckman 2007; Nielsen and Roos 2015), and a model of educational careers in which cognitive and non-cognitive abilities are provisional, alterable and moulded by social as well as individual factors appears to provide the most solid foundation for investigating educational inequalities.

Inequalities of class, gender and ethnicity in education

Class does not account for all differences in outcome between different groups, and patriarchal and racist structures also shape the patterns of inequality encountered in contemporary societies. The educational performance of ethnic minority and female students must be seen within the context of these historically determined structures, which in their most overt form have entailed exclusion from all or certain parts of the educational system. In the United States, the formal provision of education for African-Americans was either non-existent or profoundly limited until late in the nineteenth century (Green 2013, p. 196), and segregated schooling – whether *de jure* up to the landmark ruling of the US Supreme Court in 1954 or *de facto* since then – has persisted. *De facto* racial segregation can also be found in Europe, for example in the emergence of White- and South Asian-dominated schools in the North of England, and the segregation of Roma children in some Central and Eastern European countries. On a global scale, the education of women and girls is still by no means universally established. Although in the United Kingdom the exclusion of women from higher education ended with the creation of segregated institutions such as Girton College[12] (founded in 1869), in many developing countries the adult literacy rate for women is only around half that of men. However, exclusion, segregation or other overt forms of discrimination are not the only factors responsible for inequality: just as with class, ostensibly neutral or meritocratic processes can produce educational disadvantage, particularly when structured social disadvantage is also present. These processes have been described as constituting *institutionalized* forms of racism and sexism, in which practices originally established to serve the needs of a relatively homogeneous normalized group (such as White middle-class males) become entrenched within changing social circumstances. As a result, they not only fail to take account of the needs of other social groups but may also actively work against their interests. Educational inequalities may therefore persist long after the removal of any formal barriers to participation.

Changing gender inequalities and the 'new gender gap'

There is an extensive literature documenting a decline in gender inequalities in developed countries throughout the twentieth century, particularly inequalities affecting earlier transitions (Buchmann et al. 2008). Although there was considerable variation between countries, the educational disadvantage of women reduced dramatically and for the generation born around 1960 a 'new gender gap' in favour of women began to emerge at all levels below upper tertiary education (Breen et al. 2010). Various explanations have been proposed for this trend, primarily concerning changing patterns of employment and social attitudes, and relating to gender-specific differences in non-cognitive abilities and their impact on school success (Breen et al. 2010; Blossfeld et al. 2015). In higher education, gender inequalities initially followed the pattern of logistic expansion discussed earlier. Until about 1965, average participation rates worldwide were about 2 per cent for men and 1 per cent for women. As participation began to increase, men were able to take greater advantage of the new opportunities made available and the participation gap increased to around 3 percentage points. However, after 1970 this gap began to narrow, and by 1990 women had achieved parity with men in overall participation rates; by 2000 the gap had reversed to around 6 percentage points in favour of women, compared with a global average enrolment rate of just over 25 per cent (Schofer and Meyer 2005; Shavit et al. 2007). In England and Wales, parity was achieved in the mid-1990s (a little earlier in Scotland), and by 2015–16 the participation gap between female and male first-time students in England had increased to 12 percentage points in a total participation rate of 49 per cent (Iannelli 2007; DfE 2017c). Most of this gap can be explained by gender differences in prior attainment, particularly at age 16 (Crawford and Greaves 2015).

The existence of a new educational gender gap in certain countries does not necessarily mean that female disadvantage has been eradicated; increased participation by women at a particular level of education is often accounted for by enrolment in lower-status courses and institutions, or by credentialism affecting traditional areas of women's employment, such as nursing and teaching. At the most selective universities in England, the gender gap is much smaller than for higher education in general, and after controlling for prior attainment participation by male students is slightly higher than for females (Crawford and Greaves 2015). Moreover, comparatively little is known about how changes in gender inequality have been distributed across the class structure. Breen et al. (2010) conclude that the decline in class-based educational inequality which occurred in a range of countries over the twentieth century showed no systematic differences between men and women, although in some classes there was evidence of differential parental investment in the education of boys and girls. However, Becker (2014) suggests that as well as greater labour-market opportunities, increased access of women to higher class positions over time has also been a factor in reversing the gender gap.

Inequalities in the attainment of ethnic minority groups

Concerns over the educational attainment of ethnic minority communities in the United Kingdom date back many years, and a review of research by Tomlinson (1981) referred to 33 studies of children from Black Caribbean backgrounds and 19 of children from Asian backgrounds. These studies showed systematic educational disadvantage, with immigrant children from the Caribbean having the lowest attainment of any ethnic group, ethnic minority children born in the United Kingdom performing better than immigrant children, and all these groups having lower attainment than White British children. Craft and Craft (1983) also found evidence of educational disadvantage, but in a complex pattern of quantitative and qualitative inequalities in which interactions between class and ethnicity (gender was not considered) were prominent. A notable feature of these patterns was that participation in post-compulsory education was greater for all other ethnic groups than for White British; however, this was often in lower-level programmes rather than prestigious A-level courses. Although progress since the early 1980s has been mixed, the inequalities referred to in the Swann Report (1985) have reduced and over successive generations average attainment amongst ethnic minority groups has improved. However, whilst certain groups now outperform White British students, others – particularly Black Caribbean pupils – continue to have significantly lower average attainment.

The scale of inequalities according to gender and ethnicity for 16-year-olds in England is illustrated in Figure 3.6, which also compares these inequalities with differences between pupils eligible for FSM and other pupils, using official

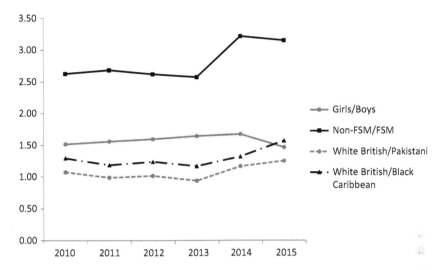

FIGURE 3.6 GCSE attainment of pupils in England by free school meal (FSM) eligibility, gender and ethnicity 2010–15. Odds ratios for achieving 5+ A*-C grades between non-FSM and FSM pupils, female and male pupils, and White British compared with selected ethnic groups.

Sources: DfE (2014, 2015, 2016).

Note: Due to changes in methodology the underlying attainment rates for 2014 and 2015 are not directly comparable with earlier years. Underlying data for 2015 include only pupils attaining grades A*-C in English and mathematics.

data published annually by the UK government. Gillborn et al. (2018) rightly warn of the dangers associated with quantitative measures of inequality, which must inevitably be based on *classification* in the Durkheimian sense discussed in Chapter 2. Choices related to recording and representing ethnicity, such as which groups to include, which to subsume within other groups and which to exclude, are made by those who classify rather than those who are classified. The resulting imbalance of power can reinforce as much as challenge racist attitudes and practices. The ethnic groups shown are selected as representing particularly disadvantaged groups in relation to White British pupils: those not shown include pupils from Chinese and Indian backgrounds, who perform better on average than White British pupils; Bangladeshi-background pupils, whose performance is broadly comparable with those from Pakistani back-grounds; and pupils from mixed White and Black Caribbean backgrounds, whose performance is quite similar to that of pupils from Black Caribbean families. Pupils from Traveller and Gypsy/Roma backgrounds are also not in-cluded; these pupils are on average the most educationally disadvantaged ethnic group in England (Wilkin et al. 2009).

Recalling that an odds ratio of unity represents equality between groups, a significant feature of Figure 3.6 is the substantially greater scale of inequality according to eligibility for FSM, which was not only consistently larger than inequalities according to gender and ethnicity[13] before 2014 but increased as the focus shifted to traditional academic subjects. However, there are complex interaction effects between class and factors such as geography,[14] ethnicity and FSM eligibility. As noted in Chapter 2, people from certain ethnic groups – Black and Bangladeshi in particular – are more likely to be long-term unemployed or in routine occupations than those from White British backgrounds and less likely to be in managerial or professional employment. Other evidence suggests that Muslim men (and women) are amongst the most disadvantaged groups in labour-market terms (Khattab and Modood 2018). The lower income, and less secure employment, that this implies increases the likelihood that children from certain ethnic backgrounds will be eligible for FSM. This is likely to increase interaction effects; for example, in 2015 the GCSE attainment rate (5+ A*-C including English and mathematics) for all Bangladeshi pupils (62 per cent) was greater than that for all White British (57 per cent), partly because the attainment rate for Bangladeshi pupils eligible for FSM was twice the corresponding rate for White British pupils (DfE 2016).

The differential effects of curriculum change may also be seen in Figure 3.6. Following changes in school performance indicators which gave greater weight to traditional academic subjects than to vocational qualifications, inequalities of gender and ethnicity (as measured by odds ratios and also by raw percentage gaps) increased sharply in 2014. By contrast, the gender gap in favour of girls, which had been substantially larger than the ethnic gaps shown in the figure, declined following the restriction of the 5+ A*-C benchmark to pupils who had achieved grades A*-C in English and mathematics. Nevertheless, girls outperformed boys in all the ethnic groups shown and amongst pupils eligible for FSM, with raw gaps generally around 8–10 percentage points in an average attainment rate (including English and mathematics) of 57 per cent for all pupils. The behaviour of these inequalities under changing methodologies suggests that, for both gender and ethnicity, qualitative differences within an educational level are significant and analysis of overall inequalities needs to be supplemented by scrutiny of different types and measures of attainment.

Similar patterns of inequality are evident in access to higher education in England. A gender gap in favour of women of around 6–9 percentage points in participation rates amongst younger students has been consistently observed since 2000 (DfE 2017b), compared with a gap between FSM and non-FSM students of 19 percentage points in 2006–7 and 17 per cent points in 2014–15 (DfE 2017a; see Figure 3.5). Whilst some ethnic groups have lower average performance at age 16 relative to White British pupils, higher education participation rates are greater for all ethnic groups than for White British (Crawford and Greaves 2015). To some extent this can be attributed to changing educational decisions, with an upsurge in the desire to attend university in some groups formerly associated with 'low aspirations' (for example, Black Caribbean boys). However, access to high-status universities shows considerable variation between ethnic groups, with less than 5 per cent of young people from Black Caribbean backgrounds entering the most selective universities between 2005 and 2010, compared with around 10 per cent of White British and 20–25 per cent of Indian young people (Crawford and Greaves 2015). These differences were largely (but not exclusively) due to socio-economic background factors and to attainment at age 16, indicating that the underlying causes relate to more general educational and social inequalities rather than to specific aspects of higher education entry.

In political and academic debates arising from these patterns of inequality, White working-class boys are often constituted as a group 'left behind' by globalization and neo-liberalism and contrasted with other social groups in terms of aspiration and educational achievement. McDowell (2003) writes of a 'crisis of masculinity' characterized by anxieties over the behaviour, attainments and future prospects of working-class young men in Britain, and the implications of deindustrialization and other social forces for gendered educational identities and performances have been intensively researched (for a recent contribution and summary, see Stahl 2018). However, whilst it is clear that White working-class boys are a significantly disadvantaged social (not ethnic) group, and that patterns of disadvantage are mediated by ethnicity and gender, the similarities between different working-class groups are as important as the differences. Using FSM-eligibility as a measure, substantial social background differences in attainment at age 16 exist for virtually all ethnic groups, for girls as well as boys (DfE 2016). Moreover, the attainment of Black Caribbean boys eligible for FSM is little different to that for White British pupils. It is also clear that aspiration has a limited role in shaping patterns of access compared to other factors: for example, although only half of White British working-class boys expressed a desire to participate in higher education, this was twice the proportion that actually does so (Berrington et al. 2016).

The complex interactions between class, ethnicity and gender make it necessary to use statistical modelling to investigate the relative contribution of these factors. In a series of studies using data from the nationally representative Longitudinal Study of Young People in England (LSYPE), Strand (2011, 2014a, 2014b, 2016) has explored the interactions between SES,[15] ethnicity and gender as well as the effects on attainment gaps of school-specific factors. As indicated earlier, gender, ethnicity and SES do not combine in simple additive ways, and substantial interactions occur. The most significant interactions at age 16 were between ethnicity and SES, and a less marked but still significant interaction between ethnicity and gender (Strand 2014a). The ethnicity-SES interaction is manifested in different SES gradients for different ethnic groups. Whilst low-SES pupils from almost all[16] other ethnic groups have higher attainment than low-SES pupils from White British backgrounds, high-SES boys and girls from White British backgrounds outperform high-SES pupils from most other ethnic groups. The lowest-attaining ethnic group amongst high-SES pupils is Black Caribbean – particularly male pupils. The disadvantaged position of Black Caribbean boys is also reflected in educational progress from age 11 to age 16, where medium- and high-SES Black Caribbean boys with high prior attainment make significantly less progress than comparable pupils in other ethnic groups. The ability of social class – or, more precisely, SES – to explain ethnic gaps in educational attainment is therefore limited. Although it can account for attainment gaps between certain ethnic groups, other factors must also be important, in the case of Black Caribbean pupils at least. The existence of direct effects of race, in addition to those mediated by class and gender, cannot be excluded (see also Strand 2011, 2016).

Maximally maintained inequality

The evidence presented in this chapter demonstrates the complex relationship between inequality and educational expansion. Although in general inequalities have diminished, equalization has been limited to certain periods and transitions, whilst substantial inequalities remain. In fact, there is no necessary connection between expansion and equalization. Educational expansion can occur without *any* reduction in the association between participation and social background, if changes in the composition of society increase the relative size of groups with a high propensity to remain in education. In this case, overall participation rates will increase unless provision fails to keep pace with demand. For example, Halsey et al. (1980) showed that all of the growth in attendance at selective secondary schools between the 1920s and the 1950s was due to a redistribution in the class structure of precisely this kind. More importantly, even during periods of 'true' educational expansion higher social classes may benefit most, because they are better placed to take advantage of new opportunities. *Maximally maintained inequality* (MMI) refers to the persistence of inequality under these conditions, in which the association between educational attainment and social origins only begins to decline once the effects of compositional change and demand from higher social classes have been absorbed (Raftery and Hout 1993). More specifically, MMI describes any of three cases: (a) expansion keeps pace with increased demand due to population growth or change in the class structure: in this case participation rates show little change over time, and odds ratios remain constant; (b) provision grows faster than this basic level of demand: participation rates increase for all social classes, but odds ratios remain constant or even increase because of more rapid growth in educational demand amongst higher classes; (c) demand from higher social classes approaches saturation (very high participation rates): in this case participation rates amongst lower social classes increase faster than in higher classes, and odds ratios decrease (Raftery and Hout 1993).

The MMI hypothesis has been tested extensively using international data, and it appears to provide a reasonable description of the earlier stages of expansion, particularly of case (b) in which there is persistent inequality in spite of an overall increase in participation rates (Shavit et al. 2007). However, there is conflicting evidence for a decline of inequality only when 'saturation' is reached for more advantaged classes. First, there is disagreement over what constitutes saturation. For Raftery and Hout (1993) it implies participation rates nearing 100 per cent. However, Lucas (2009) argues that on this basis MMI is ill-defined because of the behaviour of odds ratios as probabilities approach unity, whilst arbitrarily taking a lower level of participation as 'saturated' would simply be an ad hoc fix. Nevertheless, other authors have taken around 80–90 per cent as marking the onset of saturation for a given social origin group, either from plateaux in the corresponding participation rates (Paterson and Iannelli 2007; Boliver 2011) or from a priori definition (Haim and Shavit 2013). Thomsen et al. (2017) have found varying situations in the Nordic countries between 1985 and 2010: in Norway and Finland inequality reduced before saturation was reached, whilst in Sweden, with initially lower levels of inequality, more privileged groups retained their advantage. It has also been observed that MMI seems not to apply in former state socialist countries, where inequalities in access to higher education reduced before demand from more advantaged groups was saturated (Shavit et al. 2007).

Notes

1 In a logistic curve, the formal mathematical relationship between the participation or attainment rate (p) and the time (t) is given by the equation $p = e^{kt} / (A + e^{kt})$, where $1 / (1 + A)$ is the participation rate at time $t = 0$ and k is a constant related to the rate of expansion.

2 If the table contains proportions rather than frequencies all rows and columns must also be multiplied by a renormalization constant to preserve the overall population size.

3 It is likely that these fluctuations are due to the small size of this category in the YCS cohorts. See Demack et al. (2000).

4 More precisely, the natural logarithm of the odds, expressed as $\ln\left[p / (1 - p) \right]$ where p is the probability of making the transition.

5 Using a single summary measure of IEO rather than the full set of odds ratios between class categories.

6 Gorard (2012) explains that initially pupils known to be FSM-eligible and those actually taking the meals were tracked separately. However, as FSM eligibility became more closely associated with school performance management, regulations changed so that only those pupils actually receiving free meals were reported.

7 See Crawford et al. (2017a, p. 17) for a more detailed discussion of this data.

8 Full-time young participation by socio-economic class. For a discussion of the importance of older students in higher education expansion, see Souto-Otero and Whitworth (2017).

9 In the literature, this distinction is often expressed in terms of the primary and secondary effects of social stratification. See Chapter 8 for a discussion of these effects.

10 In this study, SES was based on the occupation of both parents at the time of the child's birth (Feinstein 2003, p. 83).
11 The methodology of this study includes assigning estimated rankings to young people who do not participate in education after the age of 16.
12 Women were not admitted to degrees at Oxford University until 1920 and not until 1948 at Cambridge.
13 Inequalities between the highest-performing ethnic group (Chinese) and the lowest performing groups (such as Black Caribbean) are comparable with the FSM/non-FSM inequality. However, it seems more reasonable to consider the scale of inequalities between a given ethnic group and the majority population.
14 An example of interactions between geography and ethnicity is that greater proportions of ethnic minority pupils are found in areas – notably London – with better-than-average school performance (Crawford and Greaves 2015).
15 In these studies socio-economic status is defined using a range of measures including NS-SEC class, parental education, FSM-eligibility, home ownership and neighbourhood deprivation.
16 Low-SES Black Caribbean boys have only slightly higher attainment than low-SES White British boys.

4

STRUCTURE AND STRATIFICATION IN EDUCATIONAL SYSTEMS

In the previous chapter, patterns of inequality within and between countries were examined without enquiring closely into the institutional context of these countries: that is, the internal structure of their educational systems, the relationships between the different parts of these structures, and the connections between education and the world of work. The aim of this chapter is to consider these institutional contexts on a macroscopic level, first classifying educational systems in terms of factors such as the degree of stratification they contain, then exploring the relationship between systemic features and educational opportunity. The chapter concludes by discussing evidence pertinent to an important institutional debate within the English school system: the question of the impact of grammar schools on educational inequality.

The comparative analysis of educational systems

Educational systems are frequently analysed using a two-dimensional typology based on the concepts of standardization and stratification (Allmendiger 1989; Kerckhoff 2001; Bukodi et al. 2018). *Standardization* is the extent to which the processes of education meet the same standards nationwide. The presence of a national curriculum and teaching standards, a universal school funding formula and centralized examinations would indicate a high degree of standardization. Although countries where regional autonomy is high, such as the United States, are likely to be less standardized than those with centralized political systems, coordination on a national level may reduce the diversity associated with federal or devolved government (Dollmann 2016). Greater standardization may offset the effects of social background, for example, by reducing opportunities for more affluent parents to use social networks, time and financial resources to lobby for favourable treatment (Bukodi et al. 2018).

Stratification is normally used to describe the differentiation of an educational system through 'tracking' within educational levels[1] in terms of either formally distinct institutional types or different curriculum tracks within the same institution (Allmendiger 1989; Van de Werfhorst and Mijs 2010; Iannelli et al. 2016). In countries where stratification is high, for example in Germany, Switzerland and the Netherlands, there is early separation into tracks differing significantly in their curricula, typically specializing in general or vocational education, and some tracks may be 'dead ends' offering no formal possibilities of progression or transfer to higher-status tracks (Pfeffer 2008). In countries with less stratified education systems, such as the United Kingdom, the United States and Australia, formal curriculum differentiation is introduced at a later stage; however, internal differentiation may occur earlier through processes such as streaming or subject-specific ability grouping (setting). A third typological dimension may also be used: the degree to which education is *commodified*, either provided by the state as a public good or purchased as a private good in a marketized system (Bukodi et al. 2018). This dimension can be measured by combining indicators such as the share of a country's GDP devoted to public provision of education, the prevalence of private education, and the level of tuition fees for tertiary education. Table 4.1 classifies 19 countries on the basis of their standardization, stratification and one aspect of commodification (Pfeffer 2008). The evolution of these dimensions since the 1950s has been analysed in Great Britain, Sweden, Germany and Italy by Bukodi et al. (2018). Only Germany has maintained a highly stratified system, with the three other countries showing substantial reductions in stratification. In Great Britain, standardization was low until the 1990s, but since the 1988 Education Reform Act this dimension has been comparable with the other countries. Commodification has shown a more complex picture, with education as a public good peaking in the 1960s or 1970s in all four countries, but declining significantly thereafter except in Sweden.

A more descriptive typology of upper secondary education systems has been developed by Green and Pensiero (2016), and is helpful in understanding the various combinations of factors and their relationship with other social and

TABLE 4.1 Stratification, standardization and privatization of education. Countries in bold have a comparatively high prevalence of private education

Standardization	*Stratification*		
	Low	*High*	*Very high*
Low	Canada, **Great Britain, USA**	**Belgium, Northern Ireland**, Slovenia	
High	**Denmark**, Finland, Ireland, New Zealand, Norway, Sweden	**Chile**, Czech Republic, Hungary, Italy, Poland	Germany, Switzerland

Source: Pfeffer (2008).

economic institutions. This typology identifies four types of system in which the analytical concepts introduced earlier are combined in different ways, illustrating the complexity of institutional arrangements across industrialized countries. The most strongly tracked education systems have high levels of differentiation across multiple dimensions, including institutions, curricula and qualifications. However, such systems may be viewed as one extreme of a continuum in which less strongly tracked or 'linked' systems share common elements but retain some degree of differentiation. At the other extreme, 'integrated' or 'unified' systems have no distinct tracks (Green and Pensiero 2016). Status differentiation may also occur, in which nominally equivalent institutions have markedly different standing and reputations; this kind of stratification may arise from differences in academic selectivity, resources or social selectivity, and quite commonly from a combination of all three (Boliver 2015; Croxford and Raffe 2015).

The *selectivity* of a stratified educational system refers to the dominant modes of organizing and regulating the transition from earlier untracked phases of education into the available tracks, including the extent to which individuals' choices and actions influence this process. In a more selective system, the transition to a particular track or school type is largely based on prior achievement, with parental or individual choice playing only a minor role. In less selective systems there is greater freedom of choice for children and their families, and consequently performance in the earlier stages of schooling is – formally at least – less important. Educational systems with a lesser degree of stratification and selectivity may be described as comprehensive systems. However, Burger (2016) argues that other factors are also important constituents of a comprehensive educational system. These include the extent of preschool provision, the prevalence of private schooling and the quantity of instruction received in a school year. The social selectivity of a school system, determined by the degree of social segregation between different institutions, is also relevant. Although most schools in England are nominally comprehensive, Gorard (2015) notes that allocation to schools by parental choice and residential location has maintained significant disparities between schools in average academic attainment and the social background of their pupils. At the most obvious level, the social composition of a school is likely to influence its aggregate performance and therefore its standing compared with other schools. However, the impact of school composition may extend beyond this effect, generating differences over and above what might be predicted from the socio-economic characteristics of students at an individual level. Although its reality is contested (Marks 2015), this *compositional effect* is predicated on the assumption that the social composition of a school, by exposing children to a particular peer group and its mix of cultural and social capital, can shape educational performance independently of a student's initial ability and socio-economic status (SES). Poor children in a high-SES school, for example, may perform better than they would in a school with similar institutional features but a low-SES intake (Dumay and Dupriez 2008; Burger 2016). Indeed, an association between attending largely middle-class primary schools and achieving entry to grammar school was noted many years ago by Jackson and Marsden (1962) in their classic study *Education and the Working Class*.

Institutional context and educational opportunity

National institutional arrangements on educational inequality may affect both the distribution of attainment over the whole population and equality of opportunity. There are clearly potential interactions between *quality* of education, in terms of the number of students within a population reaching certain levels of knowledge and skill, and the degree to which a system provides *equality* of opportunity. However, the two concepts are logically distinct and whether a connection between the two exists is an empirical question (Pfeffer 2015). Evidence on the relationship between the distribution of attainment and the nature of educational systems is mixed, with some studies suggesting that highly differentiated systems have greater dispersion inequality in a range of attainment measures, whilst others find that the distribution of attainment is not significantly affected by differentiation (Van de Werfhorst and Mijs 2010). By contrast, evidence on equality of opportunity is more consistent, and repeated studies since the 1960s have pointed to larger social background effects in systems where early selection occurs (Van de Werfhorst and Mijs 2010). In the United Kingdom, there has been extensive research on the impact of internal forms of differentiation or 'ability grouping', such as streaming or setting. Boaler (1997) draws attention to the contradictions between the assumptions of fixed 'ability' inherent in the notion of streaming, and psychological research which demonstrates attainment to be fluid and changeable. In stratified educational systems, the extent of mobility between different curriculum tracks is therefore an important consideration. Where tracking is based on institutional differentiation, mobility – particularly in an upwards direction – is likely to be extremely low. In other circumstances, mobility may be higher, for example where a single institution provides a range of tracks, or where specific institutional forms exist to promote access to higher tracks.[2] However, most studies of internal differentiation point to a negative impact on equality of opportunity, partly because of social background differences in allocation to curriculum tracks but also because differences between tracks in factors such as the quality of teaching and curriculum content tend to fix low attainment within lower tracks (Gamoran 2010; Francis et al. 2017).

Although international comparisons of the impact of internal differentiation are difficult, a number of recent studies confirm that social background inequalities are magnified by external differentiation, that is, by institutionally stratified systems (Van de Werfhorst and Mijs 2010). Institutional stratification and its indirect effects, such as social segregation, have a significant impact on the intergenerational transmission of opportunity, and in highly stratified systems an effect on expectations appears from quite an early age (Buchmann and Park 2009). Early tracking has been found to reinforce the effects of family background (income, parental education) on years of schooling and the probability of completing tertiary education (Brunello and Checchi 2007). Very highly stratified systems (such as Germany and Switzerland) have lower rates of educational mobility between generations than the great majority of other countries, and this tendency is also found – although with greater cross-national variation – amongst other stratified systems (Pfeffer 2008). Conversely, educational mobility is greater in countries with a comparatively low degree of stratification. Rather than a trade-off occurring between educational quality and equality, there is some evidence of a positive association between the two, so that systems with a lower degree of institutional differentiation provide greater equality of opportunity and also perform better on measures of educational quality (Pfeffer 2015).

The impact of institutional arrangements depends on broader socioeconomic factors, and significant interactions may occur which reinforce or offset the social processes leading to educational inequality (Bukodi et al. 2018). For example, the effect of weaker stratification may be counterbalanced by growing social and economic inequality, reducing the apparent effect of such reforms. More generally, across a number of economically advanced countries income inequality is positively associated with educational inequality, with particularly strong effects in relation to university graduation (Blanden 2013; Jerrim and Macmillan 2015). There is also some evidence that education tends to be more commodified in countries with greater income inequality, receives a lower proportion of national wealth and is associated with greater use of private education (Jerrim and Macmillan 2015). Perhaps surprisingly, the prevalence of private education appears to have little impact on equality of opportunity (Burger 2016), possibly because of other private investments in education and the prevalence of social segregation within public sector education.

Vocational education and the diversion thesis

Most educational systems make some form of distinction between academic and vocational education, particularly from the upper secondary stage onwards. Although qualification structures and institutions vary considerably, academic programmes tend to prepare students for higher education, whilst vocational education is focussed on more or less immediate entry into the labour market. The class structure of vocational education is complex, and although in many countries school-leavers following vocational programmes are more likely to be from disadvantaged backgrounds, the identification of vocational students as working class is not necessarily valid (Thompson 2009a; Hupkau et al. 2017). *Vocational specificity* refers to the availability of curricula designed to prepare students for particular occupations and which lead to vocationally specific credentials (Kerckhoff 2001). At one extreme is the German 'dual system' of apprenticeships, which the great majority of young people enter in their mid-teens, and which combines authentic work experience, schooling designed to provide occupation-specific theoretical knowledge and upper-secondary general education in core subjects such as mathematics and German language (Solga et al. 2014). Less vocationally specific systems, such as in Britain and France, tend to have a dominant general education sector and looser ties between vocational learning and specific occupations. These systems are often associated with lower parity of esteem between academic and vocational education, and overall participation may be heavily skewed towards academic programmes, whilst a relatively small number of lower-attaining students are clustered in vocational provision (Green and Pensiero 2016).

In principle, vocational education provides opportunities to acquire knowledge and skills relevant to specific occupations, thereby facilitating the school-to-work transition and preparing a new generation of productive workers. This human capital orthodoxy has underpinned much of the national and international policy discussion on vocational education and training for many years, for example as expressed in the United Kingdom by government reports such as the Post-16 Skills Plan (BIS 2016), and in international reports which include *Skills Beyond School* (OECD 2014b) and the European Skills Agenda (European Commission 2016). In addition, vocational education – particularly at the secondary level but also in post-secondary or 'higher' vocational education (Bathmaker 2017) – can provide a 'safety net' for those who have been less successful at school (Shavit and Müller 2000; Di Stasio 2017). However, in many countries vocational education suffers from low status and can often be an irreversible choice which limits opportunities, particularly in terms of progression to higher education. As a result, vocational education may be viewed by middle-class families as for 'other people's children' (Richardson 2007, p. 411) and is considered by some scholars to divert working-class students from the academic route. Rejecting the human capital approach, they argue that students' social origins are highly predictive of the types of schools they attend, with students from lower social classes less likely to be found in academically oriented schools and having lower expectations of progression to higher education or high-status occupations (Buchmann and Park 2009). The academic-vocational distinction therefore operates as a mechanism for the reproduction of social inequality in which students are allocated to vocational tracks according to class background rather than on the basis of ability or aptitude. In this sense, vocational education is a part of the 'making' of class, through which young people are differentiated into qualitatively distinct and hierarchically ordered groups. However, dismissing vocational learning as simply a diversion from more worthwhile forms of education has been argued to express middle-class educational norms and to underestimate its potential value to working-class young people in avoiding unemployment or very low-paid work (Shavit and Müller 2000). Engaging in vocational rather than academic education therefore entails lower overall risk for a working-class young person, albeit at the cost of reducing their chances of longer-range social mobility (Hillmert and Jacob 2003). For lower-attaining students, vocational curricula may be more effective in developing literacy and promoting further training and adult competences. Moving to a more comprehensive post-16 system may increase intergenerational mobility in education, but without compensation for the specialist strengths of vocational tracks this could disadvantage those left behind (Brunello and Checchi 2007).

Vocational education could be considered a diversion if, other things being equal, its graduates attain less desirable occupations than those following academic tracks. Conversely, it could provide a safety net if risks such as unemployment and low-paid employment are less than those associated with other tracks. Shavit and Müller (2000) propose that these two criteria are linked through the nature of a country's educational system and labour-market organization. In vocationally specific systems, there is a close alignment between credentials and occupational requirements; in these systems, vocational qualifications signal to employers the possession of specific knowledge and skills. In countries with less vocationally specific systems, vocational awards signal general attributes in a similar way to academic qualifications but with lower credibility. Much of the explanation for between-country variations in the role of vocational education therefore lies, not in the nature of vocational education *per se*, but in the structure of the labour market and the way employers use qualifications in selection processes (Wheelahan and Moodie 2017). Whilst in most countries secondary vocational education reduces to some extent the chances of unemployment and low-skilled work, these advantages are most pronounced in countries where highly specific vocational education systems are closely aligned with labour-market structures. However, the disadvantages of vocational education in relation to higher education access and occupational attainment are also greatest in this kind of system: thus vocational education and training can provide a safety net and restrict progression opportunities at the same time.

Effectively maintained inequality

Educational systems will not necessarily respond elastically to demand; moreover, educational policies can be volatile, self-contradictory and likely to produce unintended consequences. Reflecting this complexity, Paterson and Iannelli (2007a) propose a version of maximally maintained inequality (MMI) with four stages of expansion, including an initial elite phase with low overall participation and high inequality, followed by periods of 'tracked' and 'untracked' merit selection. In a tracked system, disadvantaged students gain access to higher levels of education through separate, selective institutions or streams within a single institution. As a result, there are moderate reductions in inequality and moderate increases in average attainment. By contrast, untracked merit selection is based on aptitude within a broadly comprehensive system, with no selection to different institutions. This results in a large rise in average attainment, but may not deliver corresponding reductions in inequality as more advantaged groups continue to increase their participation. Paterson and Iannelli (2007) suggest that resourcing continued expansion for these groups may be a political precondition for reconciling middle-class families to the end of selection. Only in a final, 'universal' stage, when a level of attainment is reached by the great majority of an educational cohort, does the saturation condition of MMI apply, although changing political circumstances may lead to a reassertion of earlier stages until the level of attainment becomes literally universal.

This perspective highlights the importance of class strategies aimed at establishing or maintaining qualitative differences *within* educational levels as well as quantitative inequalities based on participation or achievement rates. Lucas (2001) proposes a theory he refers to as *effectively maintained inequality* (EMI), in which qualitative differences within a level of schooling are conceptualized in terms of a set of categories such as curricular tracks or institutional types, ordered in status and relatively insulated from each other. The allocation of individual students to these categories is assumed to depend on three factors: the state of development of the level in terms of overall participation rates; the individual's social background; and the extent to which qualitative differences within the level can be exploited:

> Effectively maintained inequality posits that socioeconomically advantaged actors secure for themselves and their children some degree of advantage wherever advantages are commonly possible. If quantitative differences are common the socioeconomically advantaged will obtain quantitative advantage. If qualitative differences are common the socioeconomically advantaged will obtain qualitative advantage.
>
> (Lucas 2001, p. 1652)

According to EMI theory, if a particular level of schooling is not yet saturated, more advantaged families will take a disproportionate share of the opportunities at that level. However, once the level approaches saturation, competition will occur around the *type* rather than the quantity of education obtained: more advantaged families will begin to exploit qualitative differences, taking a disproportionate share of the most advantageous categories within a level. These two processes may occur together: if qualitative differences are worth exploiting before an educational level becomes saturated, advantaged families will attempt to secure both quantitatively and qualitatively more beneficial educational outcomes. The crucial difference between EMI and MMI theories, therefore, is that under MMI the effects of social background on educational attainment decline to zero once a particular educational level becomes near-universal, whilst under EMI these effects remain, although they are expressed in more subtle ways.

The general pattern predicted by EMI may be produced by a variety of potential mechanisms, of which Lucas (2001) emphasizes those which draw on the greater knowledge and experience of the education system possessed by higher socio-economic groups, alongside their capacity for and willingness to engage in strategic educational behaviour. Being placed in, and remaining within, desirable educational tracks throughout a school career may require continual engagement and decision making by parents. However, some decision points are more critical than others, and Lucas regards the ability of middle-class parents to marshal resources and focus them on these critical points as an important factor in EMI. This may include attempts to subvert bureaucratic procedures, such as challenges to decisions over tracking or allocation to specialist programmes, in which the chances of success are likely to differ according to social background. They may also include *collective* class behaviours in which parents act together to maintain or reform school procedures in ways advantageous to their own children. Green and Pensiero (2016) suggest that the impact of EMI can be mitigated by factors which offset stratification to some extent, such as greater parity of esteem for vocational and academic tracks. However, as the history of post-16 educational reform in England shows, opposition to comprehensive initiatives of this nature is precisely one of the class strategies that are employed to maintain the possibility of advantage (Kerckhoff et al. 1997; Hodgson and Spours 2014). It can be argued that a combination of urban residential segregation, neo-liberal market reforms and educational expansion has created social and institutional spaces in which EMI can flourish: we now turn briefly to an examination of specific examples of these spaces.

Marketization, schooling and social segregation

Over the last few decades, neo-liberal educational reforms have become the new orthodoxy in a number of countries. Paralleled by public management reform in other sectors, such as health and social services, these countries have diversified their schools, colleges and universities and introduced market (or pseudo-market) forces into their educational systems. Such reforms place a greater premium on parental knowledge and experience of education, and thereby increase some of the advantages already enjoyed by middle-class families. They also institutionalize a new set of assumptions about the relationship between families and education, in which school choice becomes another aspect of cultural consumption but one with high stakes for future success. Even the move from selective to comprehensive schools has been associated with struggles for class advantage: Kerckhoff et al. (1997) describe tactical resistance and manipulation amongst middle-class families in England, as some have fought to preserve grammar schools, whilst others have created enclaves of advantage in the comprehensive system. In this environment, information management, utilization of social networks and the time and material resources necessary to maximize one's options are all important factors in producing the critical consumers assumed by market models of education. Pierre Bourdieu (1984, p. 264) contrasts different 'modes of appropriation' of art and other cultural practices between fractions of the middle class, in which these practices are evaluated and responded to on the basis of the return they offer on investments of economic and cultural capital – precisely the kind of strategies rewarded by marketized education systems. The working-class response, Bourdieu argues (p. 33), is more functional, constrained by more limited economic and cultural resources. Moreover, positive qualities of working-class communities may be devalued by education markets. Simmons and Smyth (2018, p. 9) highlight traditions of authenticity, solidarity, attachment to place and a commitment to public and community institutions: these are not traditions likely to sit comfortably with 'shopping around' for the best school; strategic church attendance to secure a place at a faith school; or other competitive practices, such as private tuition. As noted in Chapter 2, these considerations have led to a renewed interest in the role of middle-class behaviours in social reproduction, with authors such as Ball (2003), Power et al. (2003) and Reay et al. (2011) conducting powerful analyses of middle-class educational strategies. They have also led to concerns about the impact of market reforms on the social composition of schools, concerns which are motivated partly by the possibility of compositional effects on performance and partly by the impact of socially segregated schools on social cohesion (Coldron et al. 2010).

The notion of a 'social imaginary' (Taylor 2004), which expresses the ways in which people imagine their existence and regulate their social interactions, has been extensively used to understand middle-class practices and their discursive origins. Although in some respects social imaginaries describe the common-sense practices that underpin most people's lives, they also refer to deeper normative principles and images underlying these practices, and in particular visions of certain social groups that begin from the class interests of elite groups but later spread throughout society. Thus Reay and Lucey (2007, p. 1191) describe the educational implications of middle-class imaginaries which construct 'invidious representations of inner-city comprehensives as unruly places, characterised by poor performance and bad behaviour'. These constructions are not merely discursive moves aimed at establishing the superiority of one's own family; they have practical consequences in terms of stigmatization and social segregation within the school system. Anthony Giddens (1998) writes in his book *The Third Way* of voluntary middle-class exclusion as a strategy likely to damage the quality of public provision overall, whilst in a specifically educational context, the depiction of comprehensive schools in working-class areas as places to avoid can be seen as depriving these schools of social and cultural capital (Reay and Lucey 2004). In this sense, school choice has consequences for others as well as benefits for those well versed in strategic behaviours.

Social segregation may be defined as the clustering of children from similar social and economic backgrounds[3] within the same schools (Gorard 2016). However, whilst there is widespread agreement that social segregation in education is potentially harmful in a number of ways, its relationship with market reforms is complex and other factors are also important. For example, the selectivity of education is particularly significant and countries with strongly tracked systems such as Austria, Germany and Hungary have relatively high social segregation compared with England and the United States, whilst the Nordic countries and Scotland have relatively low segregation (Jenkins et al. 2008). In countries such as England where admission to oversubscribed schools is based on criteria such as proximity to school, educational segregation is also likely to be associated with residential segregation, in which differences in the material and cultural resources available to families from different class backgrounds will tend to be an underlying factor.

The investigation of patterns of change in social segregation and their relationship with market reforms have given rise to what Allen and Vignoles (2006) call a 'lively debate' over appropriate ways of measuring segregation (see also Gorard 2009). This debate stemmed from a widespread expectation that marketization of the kind that occurred in England following the 1988 Education Reform Act would increase social segregation. However, this proved not to be the case, and Gorard (2016) shows that segregation according to FSM-eligibility actually reduced slightly between 1990 and 1994. Although it increased again in later years, in 2014 it was below its 1989 level. In interpreting this finding, it needs to be remembered that English education was a historically segregated system, whether because of the provision of different types of school for working-class and middle-class pupils or later because of selection. Marketization therefore *initially* provided an opportunity for some working-class parents to seek places in more middle-class schools; however, the approximate stability of segregation since then suggests that the broader factors discussed earlier have blocked any greater fluidity in school admissions. Gorard (2016, p. 143) argues that, in such circumstances, 'Almost any diversity is a problem', and state-sponsored diversification of new school types is tantamount to funding inequality and social segregation.

The grammar schools debate

In twenty-first-century England, grammar schools carry a political significance out of all proportion to their numbers. For some commentators, particularly those on the right, grammar schools are the forgotten engine of social mobility, a beacon of opportunity for bright working-class children; for others, grammar schools are the remnant of an elitist and outdated system, one which excluded most working-class children from high-quality education. During the 2017 general election campaign, the issue of selective education returned to prominence when the Conservative Party manifesto promised to end the ban on new grammar schools instituted by the 1998 School Standards and Framework Act. Although this commitment was dropped following the Conservatives' failure to win an overall majority, grammar schools remain a contentious issue. However, their social and educational significance has changed considerably over the last 60 years, and before discussing evidence relevant to the current situation it is necessary to review briefly the development and decline of the selective system of which grammar schools formed a part.

Following the Education Act of 1902, the great majority of children in England and Wales were taught in Elementary Schools, which provided education of limited quality for the working class. Originally, most of these were 'all-age' schools catering for pupils of both sexes between the age of five and (from 1922) fourteen, although in later years some elementary schools were able to provide for older children. A parallel system of fee-charging, selective secondary schools provided for sections of the middle class and for some elementary school children who were able to secure scholarship or 'free' places in these schools.[4] In 1938, free places accounted for just under half of secondary school places (Simon 1991). A substantial proportion of secondary school pupils left school at 15 or 16, although many stayed until the age of 18. Over and above the elementary and secondary (grammar) schools were those catering to the most advantaged classes: the direct grant grammar schools, largely derived from endowed grammar schools associated with the ancient universities; the public schools; and a range of other private schools. In 1938, around 83 per cent of 11- to 14-year-olds attended elementary schools, and 11 per cent attended secondary schools (Board of Education 1938).

The restriction of educational opportunity enshrined in the pre-war system was a target of criticism for many years. During the Second World War, a radical education movement crystallized around proposals for the abolition or assimilation of the public schools, free secondary education for all over the age of 11, a school-leaving age of 16 and a common code of school regulations. However, the 1944 Education Act left untouched the system of public and other independent schools. The implementation of a 'universal' secondary school system in the decade following the 1944 Act entrenched earlier divisions in a tripartite system based on the classification of young people into an academic minority, an intermediate technician class, and a working class who would have little use for academic learning. For the 'non-academic' majority of children, secondary modern schools provided a limited curriculum, and initially were strongly discouraged from preparing their pupils for external examinations. For children deemed more able but of a practical bent, technical high schools were provided in some authorities. The grammar schools were preserved for children – presumed relatively small in number – capable of benefiting from a fully academic education and destined for higher-level employment. There was no evidential basis for this tripartite system, either in its essential ideas or in the relative proportions of its component parts. Commenting on the Norwood Report which promulgated the tripartite idea in 1943, the historian S.J. Curtis wrote:

> Seldom has a more unscientific or more unscholarly attitude disgraced the report of a public committee ... The suggestion of the committee seems to be that the Almighty has benevolently created three types of child in just those proportions that would gratify educational administrators.
>
> (Curtis 1952, p. 144)

One of the outcomes of the post-war period was a highly selective system in which the divisions between grammar and secondary modern schools were to persist well beyond the comprehensive reforms of the 1960s and 1970s. A 'chasm' existed in the quality of provision between grammar and secondary modern schools, and until the introduction of the low-status Certificate of Secondary Education in 1965 the latter 'offered two-thirds of children virtually no opportunity for within-school qualifications and ... was not able to support a broad set of further education and training qualifications' (Hart et al. 2012, p. 24).

The grammar school system – it is seldom referred to as the 'secondary modern system' – reached its peak in the mid-1960s, although the number of children attending comprehensive schools was already significant. However, shortly after the Labour general election victory in 1964, it became Government policy to reorganize secondary education along comprehensive lines, and although Circular 10/65 to this effect was withdrawn by the incoming Conservative government in 1970, the proportion of pupils in grammar schools fell to 10 per cent by the mid-1970s and has been around 5 per cent since the end of that decade (Bolton 2017). The 1997 Labour government's ban on new grammar schools formalized this situation, and an uneasy truce prevailed until the publication of the Green Paper *Schools That Work for Everyone* by Theresa May's Conservative administration in September 2016. There are currently 163 grammar schools in England, catering for 167,000 pupils or 5.2 per cent of the maintained school population (Bolton 2017). However, the presence of grammar schools in a local authority does not imply the existence of a wholly selective secondary school system: only 10 out of 151 local authorities have such a system,[5] whilst a further 26 authorities have one or more grammar schools within a mixed system. Although less well publicized and increasingly converting to academies, there were 120 secondary modern schools in 2017.

Given the historical background and continuing political tensions over the existence and expansion of grammar schools, it is not surprising that selective education has been the subject of extensive research in recent years. Two questions have been central. First, what is the social impact of academic selection – who gains access to the grammar schools, and how do social selection and segregation differ between selective and non-selective systems? Second, what is the impact of grammar schools on pupil performance? For example, do similar pupils perform better or worse in selective systems, and how are any differences in performance distributed across pupils from different social backgrounds and prior attainment? Unfortunately, as Coe et al. (2008) explain in an exhaustive literature review, there are serious conceptual and methodological difficulties involved in providing definitive answers to these questions. Schools are complex institutions, and disentangling the effects of selection from other factors is a difficult task, involving both pupil-level and school-level data. Moreover, it is clearly insufficient to consider the impact of selection on the selective school itself: the effects of 'creaming' and the potential ability of a grammar school to attract staff and other resources will affect nearby schools, which may be situated in other local authorities. There is also a dilution effect caused by the small scale of the present selective system, so that creaming and other effects are shared between a relatively large number of schools, thereby reducing individual school effects and making them more difficult to observe. Nevertheless, certain broad conclusions may be drawn. In terms of access, grammar schools are amongst the most socially selective state schools in the country, and the chances of pupils from poorer backgrounds attending one are considerably lower than for other pupils. Using a continuous scale of SES based on a combination of individual-level (FSM) and neighbourhood measures, Burgess et al. (2017) show that rates of grammar school entry are low for all but the most affluent families. In selective areas only 9 per cent of those at the 20th SES-percentile and 17 per cent of those at the 40th percentile attend grammar school, compared with 51 per cent of those at the 90th percentile.[6] These relative chances result in a high level of social segregation (Gorard and Siddiqui 2018): only a very small proportion of pupils in grammar schools are eligible for FSM, compared with pupils in other schools.[7] This is partly because FSM-eligible pupils have lower attainment overall. However, social selectivity is not just a question of ability: significant differences remain even when comparing pupils with similar levels of prior attainment and when other characteristics likely to affect grammar school entry are taken into account.

There is substantial evidence that high-ability pupils from poor backgrounds are less likely to attend a grammar school than more advantaged pupils with similar performance (Atkinson et al. 2006; Cribb et al. 2013; Burgess et al. 2017). In the most recent of these studies, Burgess et al. (2017) show that two children in selective authorities, both performing at the upper end of the Key Stage 2 attainment distribution but placed in the poorest and most affluent SES quintile respectively, have a 45 percentage point difference in their chances of access to grammar school. A significant non-meritocratic element therefore exists in relation to grammar school entry; Cribb et al. (2013) suggest that this may be partly due to compositional effects in the primary schools attended, the costs of travelling to a grammar school, and competition for places from children who attended fee-paying primary schools. However, selective schools do not have a monopoly on segregation, and some of the most socially and academically selective schools in the country are high-performing comprehensives (Coe et al. 2008). As EMI predicts, affluent parents appear to be adept at seeking out qualitative advantages wherever they can be found.

There is certainly evidence that some pupils benefit from attending grammar schools, although this is partly offset by worse outcomes amongst those who do not attend. Coe et al. (2008) conclude that it is likely that pupils in grammar schools perform better than pupils of equal ability in comprehensives, although the size of this effect is uncertain and may be sensitive to school compositional effects. These authors found no consistent answer to the question of which specific groups benefit from attending a grammar school, although there was some evidence that FSM-eligible pupils and those on the borderline of grammar school entry derive greater advantage than the highest-attaining pupils (see also Harris and Rose 2013). This may be due in part to the significant resourcing and academic disadvantage found in some secondary modern schools (Levacic and Marsh 2007). On the broader question of which type of school system performs better at a local authority level, Coe et al. (2008) again found no clear answer in the literature. However, their own analysis of national data showed that pupils in grammar schools perform better than pupils in other schools by just over one-half of a GCSE grade after controlling for pupil-level characteristics. The problem with assessing this evidence is that grammar schools are very different kinds of school, with a concentration of performance-enhancing factors such as having a sixth form. After controlling for school-level characteristics, the additional performance of grammar schools in this study reduced almost to zero. More recently, Gorard and Siddiqui (2018, p. 13) draw similar conclusions, and are uncompromising in their assessment of the implications for policy:

> Dividing children into the most able and the rest from an early age does not appear to lead to better results for either group, even for the most disadvantaged … The policy is a bad one and, far from increasing selection, the evidence-informed way forwards would be to phase out the existing 163 grammar schools in England.

The contribution to social mobility of expanding the grammar school population therefore promises to be slight at best. At worst, the impact of such a policy would be to increase social segregation and intensify the negative effects of grammar schools on neighbouring institutions. The relationship between school type and social mobility will be returned to in Chapter 9.

Notes

1 It may also refer to the distribution of students across different levels, and across tracks within levels.
2 For example, the vocational upper secondary schools which provide access to some forms of tertiary education for students initially placed in vocational tracks (Schindler 2017)
3 Measures of segregation usually require a binary classification of socio-economic background, for example high or low SES. In England, eligibility for FSM is often used. Segregation by ethnicity is also of great importance, but the focus here is on socio-economic background.
4 Referred to as 'Special Places' after 1933.
5 Defined as containing a high proportion of selective schools, rather than being exclusively selective (Bolton 2017, p. 5).
6 The political significance of the range between the 20th and 40th percentiles is that it corresponds to the 'just about managing' group highlighted by Theresa May's Conservative government.
7 The proportion of grammar school pupils recently eligible for FSM is consistently given as around 2–3 per cent compared with 13–14 per cent nationally. See Coe et al. (2008); Cribb et al. (2013); Andrews et al. (2016); Gorard and Siddiqui (2018).

5

SOCIAL REPRODUCTION

Schooling and class society

The notion of education as a pathway to greater equality has obvious attractions. Those of us who have experienced the educational system as *individually* transformative might be forgiven for finding such a prospect intuitively appealing. However, the contrary viewpoint – that education is an oppressive system which exists to reinforce inequality rather than promote social justice – has been expressed just as powerfully. This viewpoint has a complex history, drawing on Weberian and Marxist accounts of class and status and inspiring a diverse group of theoretical perspectives. The British political arithmetic tradition has always highlighted distributive injustice, particularly in education, and in the United States Randall Collins (1971) provided a penetrating neo-Weberian critique of liberal-industrial theories of educational stratification. Subsequently, the idea of schools as sites of social reproduction rather than transformation has become an important theme within the sociology of education, and theories of *cultural* reproduction associated with Pierre Bourdieu and Basil Bernstein have acquired a dominant position. Although both Bourdieu[1] and Bernstein owe a great deal to Marx, their dominance is partly the result of the demise of an explicitly Marxist educational theory. The focus in this chapter is a discussion of the now-unfashionable neo-Marxist[2] critiques of education which gathered momentum as part of a general resurgence of interest in Marxism during the late 1960s and early 1970s. The discussion draws on three currents in Marxist thought on education: the structural Marxism of Louis Althusser; the correspondence principle of Bowles and Gintis; and the resistance theory of Paul Willis. The chapter concludes by examining some reasons for the decline in Marxist educational theory and briefly discussing recent contributions to the field.

Class society and social reproduction

Marxist critiques assert that an important social function of education is to *maintain* the capitalist system and that working-class educational failure is an inherent part of this function. Even so, Marxists have also recognized the transformative power of education when separated from bourgeois ideology. Speaking in August 1869, Marx[3] captured succinctly the tension between the twin potentialities of education: 'On the one hand a change of social circumstances was required to establish a proper system of education, on the other hand a proper system of education was required to bring about a change of social circumstances' (Marx and Engels 1985, p. 398). Some 50 years later, Lenin also emphasized the role of education in the revolutionary class struggle as opposed to its conservative function in bourgeois society: 'the working people are thirsting for knowledge because they need it to win ... they see how indispensable education is for the victorious conclusion of their struggle' (Lenin 1965 [1918], p. 87). This revolutionary view of education persists in movements such as Freire's liberation pedagogy. However, in Marxist education theory the potential of education for social transformation has taken second place to a vision of education as a central pillar in maintaining the capitalist system.

Any theory of class must explain how class society is perpetuated within and between generations. In the first volume of *Capital*, Marx writes: 'The maintenance and reproduction of the working class is, and must ever be, a necessary condition to the reproduction of capital' (Marx and Engels 1996 [Marx 1887], p. 572). The working class of today must be the working class of tomorrow, or at least approximately so, and must carry forward its dependence on capital from parent to child. This requires both the reproduction of the working class as a set of individuals available to fill certain class positions, and of the relations of production which determine these positions. Marx describes what this means for the capitalist mode of production:

> Capitalist production ... reproduces and perpetuates the condition for exploiting the labourer ... [it] produces not only commodities, not only surplus value, but it also produces and reproduces the capitalist relation; on the one side the capitalist, on the other the wage labourer.
>
> (Marx and Engels 1996 [Marx 1887], pp. 576–577)

From a purely structural perspective, it matters little who occupies the class positions thus reproduced: high levels of mobility within and between generations would satisfy the requirement for exploitable labour, provided sufficient individuals are available to meet the needs of capital. At the level of class consciousness, the stability of an individual's class position and its transmission between generations are more significant. Marx saw clearly the importance of social mobility in processes of class formation, stability and decomposition

(see Goldthorpe 1980, pp. 4–9). A fluid class structure, in which mobility between widely separated positions is common, may hinder the development of
a specific consciousness implied by the notion of a 'class for itself', or even to
allow the empirical identification of a 'class in itself'. However, the importance
of intergenerational stability as a factor in class formation is contested and may
be more relevant to working-class rather than middle-class identities. Patterns
of inequality and social mobility suggest that recruitment to the working class
is largely from within, whilst the new middle class is more heterogeneous in
origin. Savage (2000, p. 84) suggests that middle-class formation 'involves a
dynamic relation to time, in which middle-class people expect prospective
rewards, and in which work lives are embedded around ideas of individual
progress and advancement'. It is the end point of mobility, rather than its starting point, which is significant in forging middle-class identity. Nevertheless,
it would be a mistake to think of a working class with no inward movement.
Even during the upgrading of the occupational structure which took place after
the Second World War, a 'sunken middle class' provided an important aspect
of working-class identity, with aims and values shaped by the class experiences
of more affluent relatives as well as previous generations (Jackson and Marsden
1962). The heterogeneous identities resulting from class mobility highlight an
important difference within Marxist approaches. Whilst the humanist Marxism
associated with scholars such as E.P. Thompson emphasizes identity, human
agency and the contingencies of class struggle, structural Marxism focusses at
a more abstract level on class positions rather than their occupants. For structural Marxists such as Louis Althusser, it is the general forms through which
capitalist relations of production are maintained that are the object of interest.

Education and the State

How are the relations of production reproduced over time? It is clear that this
reproduction must occur at the societal level rather than at the individual workplace. Institutions critical to the capitalist mode of production, such as private
property, can be guaranteed only by the state. Furthermore, the complexity of
the division of labour diffuses the responsibilities for maintaining and reproducing the labour force throughout a society. What is at stake here is not the supply
of labour to any particular unit of production or conformity to the requirements
of a specific occupation or industry, but submission to the relations between
capital and labour. Put more generally, the stake is human consciousness itself, as
produced by the social relations of the existing mode of production. In a much-
quoted passage,[4] Marx writes of the shaping of consciousness by these relations:

> The totality of these relations of production constitutes the economic
> structure of society, the real foundation, on which arises a legal and
> political superstructure and to which correspond definite forms of

> social consciousness ... It is not the consciousness of men that deter-
> mines their existence, but their social existence that determines their
> consciousness.
>
> (Marx and Engels 1987 [Marx 1859], p. 263)

Using the base-superstructure metaphor introduced in this quotation, Louis
Althusser conceptualizes the state as part of the superstructure of society, an
assemblage of institutions whose function is to maintain the rights of capitalists over the means of production and to perpetuate the social relations of
capitalism. To use a phrase characteristic of the Marxist theory of the state,
the superstructure is determined 'in the last instance' by the economic base,
but in Althusser's view it has *relative autonomy* and may even exert a reciprocal action on the base (Althusser 2001 [1971], p. 91). As will be discussed
later, the extent of this autonomy – and even the coherence of a concept in
which autonomy is relative – is a subject of dispute. In a continuation of the
quotation above, Marx himself seems to allow the superstructure at least
some autonomy:

> it is always necessary to distinguish between the material transformation
> of the economic conditions of production ... and the legal, political, re-
> ligious, artistic or philosophic—in short, ideological forms in which men
> become conscious of this conflict [between technological development
> and entrenched interests] and fight it out.
>
> (Marx and Engels 1987 [Marx 1859], p. 263)

Building on the insights of Gramsci, Althusser argues that *cultural* institutions
operating at the level of ideology are just as much a part of the state as institutions such as government, the law and the police. He therefore divides the
state into two levels of operation: the repressive State[5] apparatus of classical
Marxist theory and a number of *ideological State apparatuses* (ISA), which include
institutions such as the Church, the educational system and the trade unions
(pp. 95–96). This terminology, however, does not imply a complete functional
separation of the two levels: the 'repressive' institutions operate partly through
ideology, supplementing or even replacing overt coercion with symbolic constraints on behaviour and thought, whilst ISAs make some use of coercion
and punishment to underpin their ideological functions – for example, expul-
sion and other sanctions which form part of the disciplinary regime in formal
schooling.

For Althusser, ideology exists in material form as well as in the mind; it is
embodied in the physical fabric, people and practices of an ISA. In a system of
education, the buildings and infrastructure of educational institutions, their
teachers, and the rituals and practices of education (including curricula and
examinations), are the realization of a particular ideology of schooling and its

relationship to the rest of society. The significance of ISAs lies in their rein-forcement of, and to some extent their functional substitution for, the repres-sive institutions of the state. Put loosely, a little ideology goes a long way, and a continuous, largely invisible struggle for 'hearts and minds' can reduce the need for overt repression. In this struggle, the ruling class has an overwhelming advantage: as Marx points out in *The German Ideology,*

> The ideas of the ruling class are in every epoch the ruling ideas, i.e. the class which is the ruling *material* force of society, is at the same time its ruling *intellectual* force. The class which has the means of material produc-tion at its disposal, has control at the same time over the means of mental production....
>
> (Marx and Engels 1976b [Marx 1845], p. 59)

This intellectual dominance does not occur without contestation; however, the perpetuation of a certain form of society makes ideological control es-sential. Althusser argues that 'no class can hold State power over a long pe-riod without at the same time exercising its hegemony over and in the State Ideological Apparatuses' (Althusser 2001 [1971], p. 98). However, ideological institutions such as the educational system are more than the object of class struggle: because of their relative autonomy they are more than likely to be the *site* of the struggle itself, as different class interests use institutional structures to vie for control. This is all the more important in the case of education because, Althusser argues, the educational system is the *dominant* ISA, having privileged access to the minds of children from an early age and over many years.[6] This conception of education parallels Durkheim's analysis of the Jesuit education system, in which the 'education of the will' was a central part in the formation of the Christian citizen, a way of ensuring that knowledge of classical civiliza-tion posed no danger to faith or the interests of the Church (Durkheim 1977 [1938], p. 265ff). Althusser holds an essentially functionalist view of education, but one differing significantly from the liberal functionalist theories discussed earlier: contradicting liberal claims to meritocratic selection and the reproduc-tion of politically neutral knowledge and skills, Althusser's functionalism sees education as inherently class-biased and existing largely to serve the interests of the bourgeoisie.

The idea of the *subject* is central to Althusser's discussion of ideology. The effect of ideology, he argues, is that the great majority of people accept the 'real' conditions of their existence because they appear right and just, or at least inevitable. Ideology does not – indeed, cannot – conceal these conditions, but constructs within the individual subject an 'imaginary relationship' to them (Althusser 2001 [1971], p. 109). With the exception of a small proportion of recalcitrants for whom the repressive State apparatus becomes necessary, people 'work by themselves', channelled by the ideologies realized in concrete form in the institutions and practices of ISAs. This effect, Althusser observes, can be described through the ambiguity of the term 'subject': on the one hand denoting 'a free subjectivity, a centre of initiatives, author of and responsible for its actions' whilst also indicating 'a subjected being, who submits to a higher authority, and is therefore stripped of all freedom except that of freely accepting his submission' (p. 123). The fundamental task of ideology is to reconcile these two meanings within consciousness: to constitute a subject from an individual, one who lives and acts within ideology and therefore perceives their subjection as natural. Ideology does not prevent people from perceiving that they are exploited or lack material and symbolic resources: rather, it represents these conditions as inevitable and unchanging, either arising justly from the values, rights, and actions of free subjects or, if unjust, as imposed by irresistible forces. How ideology accomplishes its task is a different matter, and Althusser's account of this is less than compelling.[7] However, it supplements our understanding of material forms of coercion with the impact they have on consciousness; for example, not just the disciplining of labour by the threat of unemployment, but the subjection associated with such threats as consciousness becomes moulded to fit.

Althusser's account of education was almost immediately disputed by writers concerned less with a 'scientific' analysis of capitalist society than with a programme for radical action. Its influence on teachers was described as 'crushing'. Whilst providing a critical alternative to the liberal-industrial conception of education, it seemed to offer no basis for a corresponding praxis: 'Its message not only leaves the teacher completely flattened and speechless but it is likely to reinforce the idea that radical change is beyond his frame of reference' (Erben and Gleeson 1975, p. 122). For many scholars, a turn away from Marxism to Michel Foucault's conceptualization of power and the state was more attractive. Foucault argues that power cannot be dissociated from resistance, and can only be exercised over free subjects: 'At the very heart of the power relationship, and constantly provoking it, are the recalcitrance of the will and the intransigence of freedom' (Foucault 1983, pp. 221–222). Nor is the state an entity, existing above and outside individuals: the state is a mode of integration, a sophisticated structure in which the condition for being 'inside' is that one's individuality should take a specific form. The state is not something given outside power struggles and ideology, but constituted by them:

> power must be understood ... as the process which, through ceaseless struggles and confrontations, transforms, strengthens, or reverses them ... [and] as the strategies in which they take effect, whose general design or institutional crystallization is embodied in the state apparatus, in the formulation of the law, in the various social hegemonies.
>
> (Foucault 1978, pp. 92–93)

Althusser's structural Marxism has been the subject of more general critiques, perhaps most bitingly from the historian E.P. Thompson. In *The Poverty of Theory*, Thompson (1978) argues that Althusser's work is ahistorical, substituting an unchanging corpus of ISAs for historical processes played out in specific ideological arenas. This static and abstract approach, he continues, constructs the proletariat as idealized passive subjects rather than active agents. Thompson contrasts Althusser's work with an 'open, exploratory, self-critical Marxist tradition' (p. 228) which attempts to unravel the processes in which affective and moral consciousness is formed and disclosed within historical class struggles. However, such criticisms are perhaps slightly unfair to Althusser, who warns that his account of ISAs must lead to an incomplete picture if they are considered abstractly, separated from their realization in concrete situations. He emphasizes that the state and its constituents have no meaning outside the class struggle, and that this implies a proletariat with agency rather than mere passivity: 'There is no class struggle without antagonistic classes. Whoever says class struggle of the ruling class says resistance, revolt and class struggle of the ruled class' (Althusser 2001 [1971], p. 125). What ISAs represent is the structural form in which ideologies are realized; however, the *origin* of ideologies lies in the social classes themselves, and these classes are found, not merely in abstract conceptualizations, but engaged in class struggle. Althusser (1969, p. 111) writes that Marx has given us 'two ends of the chain' linking the economic base of society (the forces and relations of production) and the superstructure (the state and its repressive and ideological apparatuses). One end of this chain is the principle that, 'in the last instance', the superstructure is determined by the economic mode of production; the other end is the principle that the superstructure has relative autonomy: that is, its various domains are not *completely* determined by the base. In order to understand the particular form and effect of a domain such as education, the space between these two ends of the chain needs to be filled by a close study of how it has been shaped by material and cultural forces.

The concept of relative autonomy has been subject to many critiques from within the sociology of education. Fritzell (1987) points out that relative autonomy is often interpreted in simplistic ways, as implying a certain *quantity* of autonomy rather than specific kinds of relationship between systems. These relationships can be structural, referring to the possibility of empirically deriving properties and social relations in one system from corresponding features in a different system, or functional, in which one system may contribute to the reproduction of another. Gordon (1989) argues that relative autonomy operates with an undifferentiated notion of the state which does not acknowledge competing interests within and between its structures. She suggests that, although sociologists have recognized the need to provide the detailed studies of the state and education that would fill in some of the links in Althusser's chain, in practice few have actually done so. Such criticisms and the attempts to repair them have led to a focus on the alleged logical incoherence of the relative autonomy concept. Thus it is argued that economic determination in the last instance either means nothing or contradicts the notion of autonomy, whilst (notwithstanding Fritzell's explanations) the idea that autonomy can be 'relative' is too imprecise to be of value. However, the appeal of relative autonomy was always perhaps more practical than theoretical. For many educators, it suggested possibilities for combining a radical critique of education with a transformative educational praxis. Rikowski (1997, p. 558) argues that this is attempting to have one's cake and eat it, combining a lifeline to traditional Marxism with a view of education as a space for student resistance, teacher politics and radical pedagogic practice. Relative autonomy, Rikowski (1997, p. 561) concludes, involves the 'dissolution of Marxism' for the sake of an apparently more inclusive politics. However, Rikowski sees the only solution to this dilemma in a 'scorched earth' policy which completely reformulates Marxist educational theory. Whilst relative autonomy continues to be used within the Bourdieusian tradition, where it appears most effectively in the detailed analysis of specific fields, Marxist scholarship has had little further creative engagement with the concept.

The correspondence principle and *Schooling in Capitalist America*

In the United States, Marxist thought was largely moribund during the McCarthy era. However, the civil rights movement and the resurgence of an 'academic left' during the 1960s brought renewed attention to Marxism and a major development in its application to the field of education. Gottesman (2016) describes how the publication of two controversial studies, the Coleman Report (1966) on equality of educational opportunity and the Jencks Report (1972) on social inequality more generally, generated intense debate on the impact and cost-effectiveness of the education system. Whilst the Coleman Report appeared to ignore structural economic inequality and was read by some as endorsing the view that the values and family structures of poor (particularly Black) communities were more important than material factors, the Jencks Report placed economic structures at the heart of unequal outcomes in adult life. However, it cast doubt on the relevance of education to social transformation, arguing that inequality was largely determined by forces operating outside the educational system:

> None of the evidence we have reviewed suggests that school reform can be expected to bring about significant social changes outside the school. More specifically, the evidence suggests that equalizing educational opportunity would do very little to make adults more equal.
>
> (Jencks et al. 1972, p. 255)

Both the Coleman report's marginalization of structural inequality and the effective irrelevance of education to social outcomes proposed by Jencks were contested by two economists, Samuel Bowles and Herbert Gintis, in their seminal work *Schooling in Capitalist America* (Bowles and Gintis 1976). In a critique of the Coleman report (Bowles and Levin 1968), Bowles and his co-author had earlier argued that the report's conclusions were undermined by methodological flaws, and that equality of opportunity could not be achieved without changes to the structural relations on which schooling is based. But whilst accepting the importance of economic structures, Bowles and Gintis (1976, p. 248) argued against Jencks that, if education was ineffective as a way of tackling structural inequality, this was precisely *because of* the existing relations of production which give rise to inequality in the first place. Although accepting the basic thesis that schooling reproduces a structure of economic inequality originating in capitalist production relations, they also noted that education has a crucial role in legitimizing the allocation of individuals to economic positions on the basis of supposedly objective considerations of merit. A more equal education system, they argued, would undermine this legitimacy by exposing contradictions between the distribution of academic achievement and the distribution of economic power. The suggestion that changes towards a more radically egalitarian education system would have little effect on broader inequalities was therefore unwarranted.

Although *Schooling in Capitalist America* suggests that education may in theory have the capacity to transform society, its portrayal of educational systems in practice is somewhat bleaker. Schooling is seen as a central element in social reproduction, not only legitimizing social inequality but, as in Althusser's theorization, reproducing consciousness in order to maintain a broader acceptance of the social relations of production. Bowles and Gintis (1976, p. 143) argue that a *structural correspondence* exists between the social relations of education and those of production: not, as might be understood from liberal theories of industrialism, in terms of the explicit development of relevant cognitive skills, but in a hidden curriculum of socialization into capitalist production relations.

> The structure of social relations in education not only inures the student to the discipline of the work place, but develops the types of personal demeanour, modes of self-presentation, self-image and social-class identifications which are the crucial ingredients of job adequacy.
>
> (Bowles and Gintis 1976, p. 131)

At an aggregate level, relationships within education – between teachers, administrators, students, and the curriculum – 'replicate' the hierarchical division of labour. Features of capitalist production such as lines of command and the fragmentation of work are reflected in educational structures dealing with control, motivation and evaluation. Alienated labour is paralleled by what some authors have called 'alienated learning' (Gereluk 1974; Lave and McDermott 2002), in which a separation between learners and their learning similar to that between wage labourers and their labour process is characterized by lack of control, extrinsic motivation and disengagement. In these terms, the educational disaffection of some students is not to be understood as an individual failing, but as an intrinsic part of the correspondence between schooling and the lower rungs of the capitalist division of labour. Bowles and Gintis (1976, p. 132) argue that the correspondence between production and schooling is differentiated according to the social background of students, influencing the position they are likely to attain within the relations of production. The most disadvantaged students become concentrated in schools with arbitrary and repressive regimes, reflecting the working conditions of inferior employment situations and offering little chance of progression.[8] Other students also receive versions of education broadly aligned with their families' position in society. This proposition received empirical support from the ethnographic work of Jean Anyon, who found that, even within the relatively standardized American elementary school curriculum, social stratification of knowledge was occurring (Anyon 1980, 1981). The nature of schoolwork and the relationships to knowledge inculcated by schools had a strongly reproductive function; that is, these relationships corresponded to modes of thinking that would be required by students entering the same kind of work as their parents. However, the social distribution of knowledge she observed also embodied contradictions which might promote social change: for example, the opportunities for rational social critique offered in the most elite institutions and the reliance on physical rather than ideological control in working-class schools.

The possibility of effecting social change within and through education was one of the points of departure for *Schooling in Capitalist America*. Nevertheless, Bowles and Gintis are often accused of an oversimplified and deterministic approach which neglects human agency and the complexity of the philosophical, economic and political forces shaping educational systems (Swartz 2003; McGrew 2011). To some extent, this is a justified criticism. Although they made clear in the original text that a satisfactory analysis of educational reform must consider processes of class struggle, Bowles and Gintis (1988) later acknowledged that they did not develop an explicit theory of educational contestation, and that the correspondence principle concentrates on the reproductive linkages between education and the economic system whilst passing over a number of *contradictory* linkages. In a reconsideration of their treatment of contradictions in *Schooling in Capitalist America*, Gintis and Bowles (1980) explain the unsatisfactory nature of their original account of educational change in terms of an over-reliance on a strict base-superstructure model. In *Schooling*, educational change occurs because capitalist accumulation drives a constant expansion and restructuring of wage labour (Bowles and Gintis 1976, pp. 235–237). As a result, the correspondence between economic structures and the educational system becomes out of step, rendering existing modes of social control and reproduction inadequate and inviting periodic adjustments – or wholesale transformations – of the education system, particularly when economic panics erupt over the nature of education. Gintis and Bowles (1980, p. 55) describe this relationship between economic and educational change as purely inertial, the educational structure being dragged along by a determining economic base with no possibility of reciprocal action:

> According to this approach, contradictions in the economic system can have reverberations in other spheres of social life, but the latter cannot impart any autonomous contradictory effects to the reproduction process as a whole, save the inertial non-correspondence which then formed the basis of our reasoning.

In place of this rigid model, they develop a more complex account of the contradictory linkages between economy and schooling, in which the correspondence principle is replaced by interaction and conflict between sites of social practice. The term 'site' refers to a cohesive area of social life characterized by distinct rules which regulate the social practices occurring within it: the state, family and capitalist production are all sites in this sense. Education is not an autonomous site, but a system which participates in both the state site and the site of capitalist production. Crucially, these sites are not regarded as constituting society as a harmonious whole, but as a contradictory totality of interacting sites. In a manner reminiscent of Bourdieu's idea of *field*, sites constrain each other's development as they seek to impose their own logics. Thus sites may change in ways that undermine the reproduction of the social practices in other sites, and political practices proven to be effective in one site can be used elsewhere. The first of these mechanisms is anticipated in an example of contradiction provided in *Schooling*:

> It is simply impossible for higher education to conserve its traditional liberal arts structure and to transmit useful high-level skills to students without, at the same time, developing some of the students' critical capacities ... Marx foresaw ... the development of a labour force whose skills and outlook would bring it into conflict with the social relations of production.
>
> (Bowles and Gintis 1976, p. 206)

The difference is that in the theory of sites and practices class struggle and contradiction have become an integral part of a revised correspondence principle, rather than being 'tacked on' as an afterthought. However, this more sophisticated version contains its own difficulties (see Cole 1988) and has received considerably less attention than the original. The turn to culture in the sociology of education, as elsewhere, made accusations of functionalism and determinism even harder to shake off, and Bowles and Gintis quickly became presented as scholars to move past, rather than build on.

Resistance theory and *Learning to Labour*

In his justly famous ethnographic study *Learning to Labour,* Paul Willis (1977) rejects the idea that there is a *direct* correspondence between the requirements of industry and the subjective formation of labour power, whether through the educational system or other kinds of institution. Emphasizing the relative autonomy of education, he proposes that any such correspondence must be mediated by a cultural level 'which is determined by production only partially and in its own specific terms' (Willis 1977, p. 171). Although class relations underlie the working-class cultures of both the large industrial workplace and the school, the relationship between these cultures is complex and underdetermined. Nevertheless, for some pupils induction into a closely-knit, oppositional culture within school is the precursor to a particular kind of workplace culture. Paradoxically, by rejecting education and its values in an act of resistance to middle-class norms, their subordinate position within class relations is reinforced. This inverted outcome of class struggle parallels Althusser's comment on the ideological construction of the subject : 'what thus seems to take place outside ideology ... in reality takes place in ideology ... That is why those who are in ideology believe themselves by definition outside [it]' (Althusser 2001 [1971], p. 118).

The broad themes of *Learning to Labour* are relatively straightforward to state. It deals with a specific cultural milieu: the counter-school culture of a group of 12 White male working-class pupils at a single-sex secondary modern school in the Midlands of England as they enter the final stage of their schooling. This group is not claimed to be representative of all male working-class pupils, and indeed they are explicitly contrasted with, and consciously stand in opposition to, other pupils in the school – the 'ear 'oles' – who largely accept its norms and are determined to 'get on'. The book is based on research conducted between 1972 and 1975, a period overlapping the 1973 oil crisis but preceding the wholesale deindustrialization that affected many regions of the United Kingdom over the next decade. Unlike many later studies, it therefore deals with transitions to work rather than to unemployment or youth training schemes. The central problematic of the book is how its working-class participants end up *without complaint* in manual work of an unrewarding and meaningless nature, not only accepting but in some ways celebrating their destination at the bottom of class society. Willis is concerned, in a manner similar to Althusser, to explore the reproduction of labour power through the formation of consciousness. However, his explanation for this process introduces a radical departure: it is achieved, not through the imprint of an external ideology inculcated by the school, but through a culture of *resistance* to schooling intrinsic to this group of pupils – 'the lads'. In this culture, the social relations of the factory are re-contextualized within the school setting. That is to say, processes of solidarity, self-affirmation and struggles for control which, Willis claims, characterize the response of certain groups of unskilled manual workers to the conditions of their labour are transformed and recreated in the school context.[9] A range of oppositional behaviours express resistance to authority, solidarity and the rejection of the knowledge and values offered by the school: 'having a laff', obscene language and violence are all used to distinguish the 'lads' from teachers and other pupils, and to strengthen the cultural identity of the group. These processes have two complementary effects: they exclude the 'lads' from the academic learning that could help them enter non-manual work, and confirm their belief that unskilled factory work is superior to alternative possibilities. As a result, no coercion is necessary or indeed possible:

> If working-class kids on their way to work did not believe the logic of their actions for themselves, no-one outside, nor outside events, could convince them … The culture provides the principles of individual movement and action.
>
> (Willis 1977, p. 121)

To relate these oppositional cultures to the dynamics of class society, Willis invokes the concept of *penetration*, in which people 'see through' ideology to their objective conditions of existence. However, ideology is not completely transparent, and through processes of *limitation* an accurate perception of class condition is blocked and distorted. Categories of perception which might help working-class pupils to challenge the status quo are thereby transformed into others which effectively maintain it. Class relations become transfigured so that relations between the exploited and their exploiters are misrecognized and replaced by a series of us/them divisions. In the context of the White hyper-masculine school subculture studied by Willis, these divisions emerge most forcefully as lads/'ear 'oles', manual/mental, male/female and White/ Black, representing in different ways the sense of oppression felt by the lads. Thus, although some penetration of class conditions is achieved, this penetration is only *partial*, so that political understanding – which might lead to socially transformative action – is blocked. Accommodation to the status quo, perhaps alongside sporadic acts of resistance, is the natural sequel in later life to the counter-school culture, not organized political activity. This perspective makes it easy to read *Learning to Labour* as a deficit account of working-class culture, in which being working class is in itself an obstacle to educational success or political awakening. However, resistance does not express an inability to conform to middle-class educational norms, but a *refusal* to do so as a particular strategy for contesting class relations. Other strategies are possible – for example through the collective institutions of the adult working class – but for these particular pupils resistance is seen as providing an immediate opportunity for class struggle.

Although its originality has been overstated (see McGrew 2011), *Learning to Labour* was enormously influential in its time, more so than might be expected from a small-scale ethnographic study. On the one hand, by combining meticulous ethnographic description with a neo-Marxist theoretical framework, Willis can be credited as one of the founders of critical ethnography. However, as an account either of social reproduction or of class struggle and resistance it is incomplete, dealing only with the processes involved in reproducing the class positions of a particular subgroup of male working-class youth. The culture of more conformist male pupils within the same school – the 'ear 'oles' – and of pupils elsewhere is treated in a more or less cursory fashion, and mainly as a counterpoint to that of the 'lads'. Unsurprisingly, later studies which paid greater attention to the diversity of cultural productions within the working class revealed a more complex range of processes (for example, Brown 1987). One of the most obvious features of *Learning to Labour* is its marginalization of women and girls, who are largely relegated to the role of adjuncts to its male participants. However, as McRobbie (2000, p. 27) argues, this does not mean that it should be dismissed or replaced with an equally selective focus on girls' culture: rather, it should be 're-read critically so that questions hitherto ignored or waved aside in embarrassment become central ... [and] to see what they say (or fail to say) about working-class [masculinity]'. On one level, the neglect of women and girls was soon remedied by cultural studies of girls' transitions from school to work (for example, Griffin 1985). Resistance to schooling continued to be a central concern, and although girls were sometimes portrayed as adopting alternative, more subtle and covert forms of resistance, other studies have indicated confrontational behaviours – including violence – more akin to the 'lads' (Russell 2011). The questions asked in this kind of research initially paralleled the problems of 'voluntary' social reproduction addressed by Willis, but quickly moved on to more general questions of identity formation within the intersections of class, gender and race (Mirza 1992; Skeggs 1997). These studies highlighted the specific nature of the culture inhabited by the 'lads' by revealing alternative modes of relationship with education and work. Moreover, studies of both male and female pupils have tended to suggest a weaker relationship between resistance and class than Willis observed, and it has become clear that oppositional behaviour does not necessarily imply a complete rejection of schooling (Nolan 2011).

The weakening of links between class and resistance is due in part to economic restructuring and the increased importance of academic credentials; however, it also reflects the complex and sometimes ill-defined nature of the concept of resistance, which has often been romanticized and detached from the neo-Marxist framework provided by Willis.[10] Misleading dichotomies *between* resistance and reproduction have obscured his central thesis that a recognition – albeit partial – of objective class relations leads through subjective processes to self-defeating behaviours and choices. The concept of resistance became diffused as almost any form of behaviour inconvenient to teachers was seen as a stand against authority and labelled accordingly. Hargreaves (1982) argues that this occurred at least partly as a reaction to the perceived determinism of 'direct reproduction' theories such as those of Althusser or Bowles and Gintis. The supposed marginalization of agency in these theories led to a search for contradictions and resistances within schooling that might loosen the confines of reproduction: 'The movement from correspondence to resistance ... has been born less out of scholarly interest ... than out of the academic left's political conscience about the revolutionary (or, rather, non-revolutionary) implications of its own theorizing' (Hargreaves 1982, p. 111). The impact of postmodernism further eroded the concept of resistance as related to the recognition of class relations, and during the 1990s in particular a 'post-subcultural' analysis of lifestyles based on taste, consumption and media culture reflected the marginalization of class occurring elsewhere (Johansson and Lalander 2012). However, in recent years there has been a renewed focus on the structural basis of resistance and youth subcultures (including race and gender as well as class), as the 'cultural turn' in class analysis has opened up new possibilities for exploring the ground between materialist and postmodern accounts of subculture (Hollingworth 2015; Hodkinson 2016).

The decline of Marxist educational theory

The difficulties experienced by Marxist theories of education can be thought of at a structural level in terms of Basil Bernstein's distinction between treating education as a 'relay' for something outside it, and theorizing the constitution of the relay itself (Bernstein 2000, p. 25). Bernstein notes that in the former kind of approach, attention focusses on what is carried or relayed. Marxist approaches represent an advance by recognizing education as partly a carrier for ideology and external power relations, rather than a neutral transmitter of knowledge and skills as claimed by liberal theories. However, their limitation is that the structure of pedagogy itself is left unexamined. As a result, 'despite the focus on ideology and consciousness in neo-Marxism, there is still a very weak ... specification of the relation between the discourses, social relations, division of labour, and transmission systems which create the relation between ideology and consciousness' (Bernstein 1990a, p. 134). For example, Althusser makes no clear distinction between education and schooling, so that institutional forms and functions such as socialization are not differentiated from knowledge construction and transmission. Although Willis provides a convincing account of how some pupils are drawn towards resistance and the recreation of shop floor culture, he offers little insight into how the discourses and practices of the school might reinforce or counterbalance these trends, or what knowledge the 'lads' – even in spite of themselves – acquired and how it was put to use.

Glenn Rikowski (1996, 1997) develops both internal and external reasons for the decline and temporary demise of Marxist educational theory. Externally, the collapse of the Soviet Union and the growth of aggressively capitalist economies in former socialist states were a severe blow to the intellectual and political credibility of a socialist alternative to capitalism. With the rise of New Labour and the adoption of neo-liberal compromises by formerly social democratic parties in other countries, Marxism became increasingly inward-looking and, in Rikowski's term, 'hyper-academic', leading, in turn, to a divorce from practical politics and educational reform. As a result, Marxist theory offered no counterbalance to the depressing vision of education offered by Althusser or Bowles and Gintis, and was unattractive to the practising teachers portrayed as unwitting agents of capital. In fact, Althusser had already acknowledged the bleak implications of his work:

> I ask the pardon of those teachers who, in dreadful conditions, attempt to … 'teach' against the ideology, the system and the practices in which they are trapped … But they are rare and how many (the majority) do not even begin to suspect the 'work' the system … forces them to do….
>
> (Althusser (2001 [1971], p. 106)

Left-inclined teachers and academics moved on to less rigorous but more appealing notions such as critical pedagogy, whilst others moved away from Marxism altogether. Marxist explanations of education became effectively 'squeezed out' between the attractions of postmodernism and identity politics on the one hand, and the increasing dominance of neo-liberal ideas on education. Capitalism itself had moved on, and automation, deindustrialization and globalization had effectively abolished the conditions described by Paul Willis. As Warmington (2015) points out, whilst *Learning to Labour* could have been written in largely similar form during the 1950s, by the mid-1990s this would have been impossible.[11] The problem had changed: from how working-class kids got working-class jobs, to how they could get any jobs at all. In Rikowski's view, such external pressures are supervened by a number of core theoretical problems and weaknesses within Marxist educational theory which are essentially irresolvable. These include a too literal and deterministic understanding of the base/superstructure metaphor which he regards as central to correspondence theory, and a 'facile' functionalism which is descriptive rather than explanatory. Rikowski argues that attempts to resolve these problems only made things worse on a conceptual level, with the application of relative autonomy theory and the possibility of resistances to schooling creating a conceptual 'mess' (Dale 1991). Whatever the merits or demerits of these arguments, it is undeniable that Marxist theories of education have had little traction in recent years, and whilst reports of the 'death' of Marxism may be exaggerated its authority has, to say the least, been limited:

> Today the influence of neo-Marxist structural theory on the sociology of education might best be described as live but intermittent. The reasons for this are myriad but there can be little doubt that our understanding of education *under capitalism* has weakened.
>
> (Warmington 2015, pp. 265–266)

Since the failure of Glenn Rikowski's attempt to found a new Marxist educational theory on a general conception of labour power (Rikowski 1997; Willmott 2001), the influence of Marxist ideas has indeed been intermittent. There have been valuable contributions to the exegesis of Marxist education theory by scholars such as Mike Cole and Dave Hill, who also engage with the challenges posed by post-structuralism and the complex interactions of class, race and gender. Other scholars have explored the educational implications of the adaptation of capitalism to new technologies and new times, focussing on automation, immaterial labour and the commodification of identity and relationship in affective capitalism (Peters 2018). In different ways, these strands of research have attempted to reassert the priority of capitalist social relations in understanding the diverse oppressions and inequalities within contemporary societies. Whilst offering apparently quite different visions of the future of education, they agree that alienated forms of learning will become increasingly important: educational expansion will continue, but in ways that reinforce rather than undermine class relations. For example, Blacker (2013) uses notions of human disposability (Harvey 2014) and eliminationism to forecast a 'falling rate of learning' resulting from increased reliance on fixed capital rather than human labour. This does not imply that education will disappear entirely, but that mass education will become increasingly peripheral to capitalist production, and will tend to concentrate on the needs of consumption and social control. Perhaps more conventionally, authors such as Patrick Ainley (2013) and James Avis (2018) have seen mass education as part of the reconstitution of class, providing capital with a ready pool of labour for service sector work. However, these insights have little new to offer in understanding the structure of education. For all their value, they are essentially restatements of the correspondence principle for modern times, and share in its original deficiencies. This perhaps illustrates a loss of faith in the transformative power of education itself and a renewed focus on the need to achieve a more inclusive society through wider political and economic struggles. Mike Cole (2008, p. 61) writes that 'Marxists look to history to understand both underlying assumptions with respect to social justice *and solutions to social injustice*'.

Calling for a return to Marx, Cole argues that only the working class offers hope of social transformation, not teachers and lecturers (p. 36). According to this viewpoint, true educational change can only be made possible by action outside the educational field.

Notes

1 The relation of Bourdieu to Marx is a controversial subject. Whilst some authors regard him as 'one of the great heirs of the Western Marxist tradition' (Fowler 2011, p. 33), others either deny his connection with Marxism or contend that he used apparently Marxist ideas in ways that diverged significantly from that tradition (Desan 2013).

2 The term 'neo-Marxism' is the subject of some confusion and dispute. It is often used to denote specifically a greater emphasis on culture than is allegedly the case in 'classical' Marxism. More generally, it denotes simply the adaptation of Marxist thought to changing circumstances. However, Cole (2008, p. 145n9) points out that Marxism is a living project, so that the word 'neo' is redundant.

3 For an account of Marx's ideas on education, see Small (2005).

4 From the Preface to his *Contribution to a Critique of Political Economy*, 1859.

5 When Althusser's terminology is used, the term 'State' will be capitalised.

6 Cole (2008, p. 144n6) suggests that recent societal change may have led Althusser to give more weight to culture, in particular the mass media. It is certainly true that with the rise of social media popular culture has some claim to the pervasiveness of education. However, education remains distinctive in a number of ways, not least by its compulsory status throughout the formative years and its close association with the interests of national states.

7 Althusser invokes the notion of interpellation or a 'hailing' of the individual, who in recognizing the call of ideology is constituted as a subject in both of the senses discussed. This account is ridiculed by E.P. Thompson in *The Poverty of Theory* (1978, p. 234).

8 More recently, some researchers in the United States have drawn attention to corre-spondences between 'zero-tolerance' school disciplinary regimes and the criminal justice system (Nolan 2011).

9 Willis (1977, pp. 52–55) describes a 'shopfloor culture' in which masculine chau-vinism, toughness and machismo, informal industrial action and other discourses and behaviours parallel, in expanded form, the counter-school activities of the 'lads'. However, he does not regard this culture as being directly transmitted within families.

10 Willis himself has often been criticized for celebrating and romanticizing the oppo-sitional behaviour he describes. For example, see Walker (1985).

11 This is not to suggest that the conditions and identities discussed in *Learning to La-bour* have been erased. Bright (2018) finds echoes of social violence done in the past and the potential for future action in the experiences of young people in a deindus-trialized former mining community.

6

CULTURAL REPRODUCTION
Habitus, field and capital

Pierre Bourdieu is a dominant figure in the sociology of education, providing a conceptual framework that is almost indispensable to understanding current work in the field. In English-speaking countries, the reaction to Bourdieu's earliest work on schooling was somewhat guarded and even suspicious (see, for example, Nash 1990). However, by the turn of the new century his thought had attained an established position. Indeed, Bourdieu had acquired such currency that Diane Reay (2004) felt it necessary to warn against the use of ideas such as cultural capital and habitus as 'intellectual hair spray', a means of legitimizing otherwise pedestrian research activity. Nevertheless, there are many fine examples of educational research drawing on Bourdieu's ideas. In a review of four recent collections of work in this tradition, Garth Stahl (2016) sees evidence of scholars thinking with and beyond Bourdieu in ways that are 'most vibrant, and perhaps most just, when the analysis had Bourdieu's toolbox in full operation, where it was clear how the tools were used relationally and where one conceptual tool was not used at the expense of another' (p. 1102). Stahl's comment is a reflection of the complexity and density of Bourdieu's framework, in which each idea relies on the others for its full meaning and weight. Moreover, the Bourdieusian tradition is a living one, and scholars have frequently gone beyond Bourdieu to reuse and reinterpret his concepts in ways that diverge to a greater or lesser extent from their original context and meaning. This chapter aims to engage with the complexity of Bourdieu's thought and legacy, beginning with an exposition of the central concepts before moving to an exploration of his theory of class and its relevance to contemporary research on class in education. Although some scholars have claimed that Bourdieu's approach to cultural reproduction is incompatible with observed patterns of educational expansion and inequality, the chapter argues that the relationship between capital, habitus and field is sufficiently flexible to accommodate such patterns.

The relation between habitus and field

Debates over the interaction between social structure and individual agency provide a recurring theme in the sociology of education (Shilling 1992; Farrugia and Woodman 2015). According to some commentators, this has led to an unfortunate divergence between macro-level studies with a deterministic approach to structure, and micro-level research such as case studies of pupil-teacher interactions which appear to take place in a social vacuum. Shilling (1992) describes a *dualism* affecting educational research, in which contradictory views of structure and agency coexist, whilst Willmott (1999) suggests that structure and agency are not absolutely distinct but are irreducible to each other. For Bourdieu, this kind of debate illustrates the inadequacy of any social theory whose ontology is based either on the individual or on external social structures. He acknowledges the scientific value of a 'break' which passes from *phenomenological* knowledge concerning our immediate experience of the social world, to *objectivist* knowledge of the relations structuring social practice. However, Bourdieu argues that it is necessary to go further. Influenced by Wittgenstein's critique of the notion of 'rule', Bourdieu seeks to construct a theory of social practice based on a dialectic between the internalization of structure and the external realization of dispositions. If people from the same social class behave in similar ways, this is not because of a homogeneous class consciousness or some other form of coordination beyond the level of the individual, but because they have been continually exposed to the same class conditions. Bourdieu frequently uses the term *homology* to express this kind of relationship, referring to structural correspondences which arise because they reflect the same underlying principles. The emergence of social regularities such as classed orientations towards education is therefore a matter of homology rather than collective behaviour or consciousness.

In some of Bourdieu's earlier writings, the main focus is on the concept of *habitus*, a term originally used by Aristotle and Thomas Aquinas to refer to an acquired disposition to behave in ways appropriate to a particular situation. However, in other writings, habitus, capital and field are inextricably linked, as expressed in *Distinction* (Bourdieu 1984, p. 95) by the threefold relation:

$$\left[(\text{habitus})\,(\text{capital})\right] + \text{field} = \text{practice}$$

This formula describes specific forms of practice as emerging from a relation between the habitus and the objective conditions within the social environment where this practice is generated. Both habitus and field are historically and culturally situated, bearing the marks of practices and conditions at earlier times. Thus 'The proper object of social science', that is, the relation between habitus and field, is 'the *relation between two realizations of historical action*, in bodies and in things' (Bourdieu and Wacquant 1992, p. 126, original emphasis).

The embodied realization is the habitus, defined broadly as a set of generative principles underlying practices and their representations, and more specifically as a system of dispositions produced by the field:

> The structures constitutive of a particular type of environment (e.g. the material conditions of existence characteristic of a class condition) produce *habitus*, systems of durable, transposable *dispositions*, structured structures predisposed to function as structuring structures, that is, as principles of the generation and structuring of practices and representations....
>
> (Bourdieu 1977a, p. 72, original emphasis)

The realization of historical and social forces in 'things' (that is, in social institutions and processes as well as physical objects) is the *field*, like habitus a complex and multilayered idea. Bourdieu conceives of a field as a relatively autonomous social space of positions relating to some sphere of activity, a space characterized by struggles for domination, structured by relations of power and status but possessing its own internal logic. A field is 'a network, or a configuration, of relations between positions objectively defined, in their existence and in the determinations they impose upon their occupants, agents or institutions' (Bourdieu and Wacquant 1992, p. 97). For example, a university would constitute a field, as would an industrial enterprise (Bourdieu 2005a), although in both cases these individual institutions are themselves located in broader cultural and economic fields. Bourdieu refers to a field of forces, by analogy with force fields in physical science, as well as to a field of conflict. The terms 'game' and 'market' are also used, in a more metaphorical sense but evoking the tensions concerning rule-following that exist in the relation between habitus and field.[1] Not every social space is a field, even if this space is structured in some way and provides an arena for social conflict. To use one of Bourdieu's examples, an arbitrarily selected collection of cultural associations in a geographical region is not necessarily a field, whatever internal politics it may have. What is essential to the concept of field is that the social space it comprises is permeated by objective material and symbolic relations. These relations are the means by which forces external to the field influence what goes on inside; the autonomy of the field is relative, rather than absolute. Although it has a logic and structure that is irreducible to those of other fields, it must be considered in relation to the *field of power*: the space where those agents and institutions who dominate in specific fields struggle to maintain or transform the relations of power within and between fields (Bourdieu 1996, p. 264; see also Schmitz et al. 2017). Whether or not a given social ensemble constitutes a field is a matter for empirical investigation: Bourdieu identifies fields of cultural production, material production and the academic field, as well as subfields of cultural production, such as the media and the political field, but warns that 'It is only by studying each of these universes that you can assess how concretely they are constituted, where they stop, who gets in and who does not, and whether at all they form a field' (Bourdieu and Wacquant 1992, p. 101).

A field provides the objective conditions within which individual agents must act, and unequal power relations limit the strategies available to agents occupying subordinate field positions: 'Those who dominate in a given field are in a position to make it function to their advantage' (Wacquant 1989, p. 40). However, even those in dominant positions cannot easily take a detached view of its constituents and struggles: Bourdieu regards participation in a field as entailing a form of immersion in its values and practices that he calls *illusio*, a term derived from the Latin for 'game' and related to the word 'illusion'. An agent is in a sense a product of the field, singularly adapted to their position and able to function largely intuitively as a result, just as a tennis player will, with little conscious reflection, choose shot, power and direction whilst staying within the rules. This unity of thought, action and value is achieved, according to Bourdieu, by means of the habitus. The relation between habitus and field is partly a conditioning relation, imprinting the habitus with the traces of each field in which the individual participates over their lifetime. It is also a knowledge relation, in which the habitus enables the individual to recognize the field as a meaningful world of sense and value. Consequently, habitus is both a lens through which the social world is perceived and a set of principles governing an agent's responses to it. The resulting behaviours are both regular and regulated – that is, they take place along statistically intelligible lines which are the outcome of principles associated with an individual's positioning within the field. However, the primary mode of operation of the habitus is not obedience to rules or the attempt to attain explicit goals. It derives from the internalization of the structures constituting the field and, conversely, the way in which this environment is perceived: that is, the habitus is *structured by* the field, and at the same time structures an individual's perception *of* the field. Thus, individual actions may not be a result of rational calculation,[2] arising instead from 'the unconscious fit between their habitus and the field they reside in' (p. 24). Echoing Marx in the *Eighteenth Brumaire*,[3] Bourdieu explains: 'We can always say that individuals make choices, as long as we do not forget that they do not choose the principle of these choices' (Wacquant 1989, p. 45).

The relationship between internality and externality inscribed in the habitus underlies the concept of symbolic violence, a typically Bourdieusian 'break' with what he calls 'the scholastic opposition between coercion and consent' (Bourdieu and Wacquant 1992, p. 172). Symbolic violence is essentially a theory of domination in which the legitimation of social order is not (necessarily) the product of deliberate propaganda or imposition, but results from 'the fact that agents apply to the objective structures of the social world structures of perception and appreciation which are issued out of these very structures and which tend to picture the world as evident' (Bourdieu 1989, p. 21). Symbolic violence is therefore the internalization of relations of domination and subordination, entitlement and exclusion as both necessary and right. Archer et al. (2018) use the 'ability grouping' practices discussed in Chapter 4 as an example of symbolic violence, in which setting 'imposes an ideology that legitimates and naturalises relations of inequality between dominant and less-powerful social groups' (p. 123). They describe the confusion and frustration of lower-set students who have 'done well' in these sets but are denied the opportunity to 'move up' in terms of how pedagogy 'can hide the operation of power, making it difficult to question and challenge the "fairness" of particular practices' (p. 134). Although Bourdieu refers to gender domination as 'the paradigmatic form of symbolic violence' (Bourdieu and Wacquant, p. 170), the concept is extensively used in the theory of pedagogy set out in *Reproduction* (Bourdieu and Passeron 1990). In this theory, formal education has a distinctive role in perpetuating class relations because of the State's monopoly over the legitimate use of symbolic violence (see also Bourdieu 2014, p. 4). Under the guise of neutrality, Bourdieu argues, the educational system inculcates a *cultural arbitrary*[4]: cognitive structures which contain tacit evaluations of cultural worth. By privileging the cultural attributes of the dominant classes, education ensures both the class-based differentiation of academic success and its recognition as legitimate. Unsurprisingly, the concept of symbolic violence has provoked amongst teachers and educational researchers similar disquiet to that associated with Althusser's work. Drawing on Foucault's conception of power as potentially enabling, Watkin (2018) suggests that culture contains non-arbitrary elements, so that 'The symbolic violence that pedagogy inflicts is not so much the imposition of a cultural arbitrary by an arbitrary power; rather, it occurs if knowledge and skill are either not, or only minimally, realised' (p. 49). Such arguments may help teachers to feel better about their work; however, they do not really modify the conception of symbolic violence. Bourdieu acknowledges that school knowledge may have intrinsic value. However, he argues that this merely enhances its significance in social reproduction. Indeed, the efficiency of schooling as a carrier for symbolic violence is partially dependent on knowledge having non-arbitrary value, for this helps to conceal the role of power in the social distribution of education (see Bourdieu 1996, pp. 118–119).

Forms of capital

At any given time, an individual's position in a field, their strategies and orientations to strategies – a preference for cautious over risky strategies, for example – and their influence in the field compared to other occupants, depend on the total volume and composition of the *capital* they hold, relative to other occupants. Capital in general may take different forms: economic, cultural and social, together with symbolic capital, a term describing the general recognition of a particular capital as conferring legitimate social esteem on its owner. To a degree depending on its volume and composition, capital confers power in the field, and may facilitate the accumulation of further capital in its different forms. Drawing a parallel between capital as accumulated labour and the social world as accumulated history, Bourdieu (1986, p. 241) describes the structure of capital as representing 'the immanent structure of the social world', expressing its constraints and determining the chances of success for social practices. To use an expression characteristic of Bourdieu, capital is both structuring and structured. For example, in the field constituted by a specific labour market, an educational qualification may at a certain time be sufficiently scarce to place its holders in a strong market position; this form of cultural capital therefore plays an important part in structuring the field. As the qualification becomes more common, its labour-market value falls and people seek out new qualifications to maintain their advantage. The structure of capital itself is thereby changed by field conditions, and different forms of capital become effective at different times in the struggle to appropriate scarce goods such as wealth, education and status.

Economic capital is either already in monetary form or directly convertible into money and is institutionalized by the rights of property and inheritance. Cultural capital may be defined as the ability to appropriate symbolic wealth (Bourdieu 1973, p. 73), that is, to apprehend, appreciate and profit from cultural productions in their varied forms. It can be embodied, expressed in long-lasting dispositions of the mind and body, and objectified, in the form of artworks, books and other cultural goods; it can also exist in institutionalized form as recognized educational qualifications. Finally, social capital consists of an individual's network of social obligations and connections, which give some access to the total volume of capital held by members of such networks. Bourdieu describes these different forms as 'guises' of the general concept of capital, which is essentially synonymous with power, although it is often *dis*guised as a person's intrinsic worth. Indeed, it is the (apparent) legitimacy of the possession of capital that is one of its most powerful aspects, and each guise of capital may be encountered in institutionalized form as a mark of this legitimacy. Although objectively an individual's advantage or disadvantage within a field may be seen in terms of the possession of various quantities and distributions of capital accumulated over several generations, subjectively it may be perceived as deriving from the intrinsic qualities or rights of the individual, as *legitimate* in a social and perhaps legal sense. When this occurs, Bourdieu refers to the relevant accumulations of capital as *symbolic capital*. Although it is 'commonly called prestige, reputation, fame etc.', symbolic capital is 'the form assumed by these different kinds of capital [economic, cultural and social] when they are perceived and recognized as legitimate' (Bourdieu 1991, p. 230). This recognition – or, rather, *mis*recognition – is itself a product of the field in that the categories of perception used to recognize capital as legitimate, such as 'upbringing', 'effort', 'natural ability' or 'thrift', are embodiments of the objective structure of capitals. Thus symbolic capital is capital *naturalized*, simply part of the way things are in society, and through the lens of symbolic capital inequalities in the distribution of goods such as wealth, property or education may not be seen as inherently unjust, even when acquired by inheritance or exploitation.

Cultural capital is not simply a metaphor for symbolic resources: it must be taken more literally as *capital*, resources deployed in order to generate and accumulate further resources – whether symbolic or economic – which themselves can function as capital. Just as wealth only becomes economic capital when it is used to generate profits, generalized cultural competences do not become cultural capital unless they can be made effective in the acquisition, legitimation and reproduction of positions of advantage. Cultural capital includes forms of knowledge and skill, but these forms are incorporated within the person, so that ways of writing, speaking and being knowledgeable add or subtract value to the possession of knowledge or know-how *per se*. Although objectified cultural capital is often neglected in studies of educational settings, it forms part of a hierarchical system of materiality in which the 'powerful symbols' of elite institutions, such as paintings, ancient buildings and comfortable furnishings, are distinguished from the utilitarian facelessness of the common school (Waters 2018). Cultural capital in general is sometimes interpreted as a familiarity and ease with 'highbrow' culture, and some of the illustrations given in Bourdieu's own writings reinforce this impression. However, the concept is actually much broader, and includes any cultural competence that is unequally distributed within society and whose possession affords some advantage (Bourdieu 1986, p. 245). Lareau and Weininger (2003) argue that a 'highbrow' conception of cultural capital is unnecessarily limiting. In an educational context, it should be understood in terms of the 'symbolic products of the educational work of the different social classes' (Bourdieu 1973, p. 82), work which serves to perpetuate even relatively prosaic advantages between generations. Normality and habitude in the manipulation of educational markets, rather than exceptional displays of taste, are what give cultural capital its aggregate force in maintaining inequality:

> One of the most valuable sorts of information constituting inherited cultural capital is practical or theoretical knowledge of the fluctuations of the market in academic qualifications, the sense of investment which enables one to get the best return on inherited cultural capital in the scholastic market or on scholastic capital in the labour market....
>
> (Bourdieu 1984, p. 138)

Bourdieu sees the reproduction of cultural capital as taking place primarily in the family, and requiring significant investments of time, energy and economic capital (see Bourdieu 1977b, p. 654). He places particular emphasis on the early accumulation of cultural capital, an advantage which is most likely in families already richly endowed. This initial advantage is perpetuated in later years, both through further investments within the family and through the greater ease of accumulation made possible by early socialization. Advantages in cultural capital do not therefore simply happen by virtue of a family's location in society: they are the result of sustained application of family resources, economic, social and cultural. For this reason, although the conversion of economic capital into cultural capital is possible, the process of conversion is likely to be prolonged and, for those without already-developed stocks of cultural competence, difficult. Moreover, as Bourdieu points out, 'the transformation of economic capital into cultural capital presupposes an expenditure of time that is made possible by possession of economic capital' (Bourdieu 1986, p. 251). Economic capital, Bourdieu argues, underlies all other forms of capital, which, although they are not reducible to material advantage, cannot be realized without it and function effectively as a cloak, concealing inequalities in economic power beneath differences in taste, cultivation and knowledge.

Bourdieu's theory of class

In April 2013, Mike Savage and his colleagues published the results of their Great British Class Survey (GBCS), a collaborative project between the British Broadcasting Corporation and academics in six universities (Savage et al. 2015). Drawing heavily on Bourdieu, they claimed that class is being fundamentally remade as an individualized hierarchy in which sharp distinctions between top and bottom are complemented by a fuzzy and complex structure in its middle layers. Although the use of Bourdieu's work in studies of class was by then commonplace, the publication of the survey results and their interpretation in terms of seven 'new' classes ignited widespread public comment and a vigorous academic debate. Much of this debate centred on the fidelity and appropriateness of the way in which Bourdieu's approach to class had been deployed. Within minutes of receiving a press release on the classification, Loïc Wacquant – a former colleague of Bourdieu – had emailed a highly critical response (Skeggs 2015). The thrust of Wacquant's critique was that the seven-class scheme employed a one-dimensional status hierarchy rather than the multi-dimensional relational space central to Bourdieu's conceptualization of class. In particular, *time* plays an important role for Bourdieu that is absent in the work of Savage et al., and his notion of class describes a distribution of capitals that evolves both within and between generations. Individuals are thus historically and culturally located in ways not possible in the GBCS scheme, experiencing class as an inertial force rather than a relatively insubstantial function of occupation, age and cultural interests.

Bourdieu draws a distinction between two quite different views of class. On the one hand, debates over the 'reality' of classes oppose the idea of class as existing objectively within the social world to a conception in which class is a convenient scientific construct, introduced by sociologists to explain regularities in observed phenomena. Bourdieu refers to these debates as arising from a substantialist viewpoint which equates reality with direct availability to experience. Instead, reality may be conceived as being about relationships rather than substances. From this *relational* point of view, class does not refer to specific individuals or positions defined by economic and social characteristics: it is a set of relationships located within *social space*, 'a space of differences based on a principle of economic and social differentiation' (Bourdieu 1987, pp. 3–4). Agents, and groups of agents, are then defined by their relative positions within this space. This shift of viewpoint, from class as substance to class as a system of relationships, is one of a series of 'breaks' with Marxist class theory that Bourdieu claims is necessary to construct a theory of social space. These include rejecting the tendency to regard the social field as reducible to relations of economic production, and a recognition of the importance of *symbolic* as well as economic struggles. All social practices, Bourdieu argues, function necessarily as distinctive signs of status which those immersed in a field are able to interpret. Social space is therefore complemented by a symbolic system, a space of life-styles and of status groups characterized by different life-styles.[5] Rather than contrasting the concepts of status group and class, Bourdieu unites the economic and the symbolic so that *Stand* becomes class 'perceived through the categories of perception derived from the structure of [social space]' (Bourdieu 1991, p. 238). His central claim in this respect is the existence of a homology between a three-dimensional social space and the space of lifestyles, a claim set out in *Distinction* (Bourdieu 1984; Brisson and Bianchi 2017) and explored in a number of later studies (Atkinson 2018; Flemmen et al. 2018). This homology arises, Bourdieu argues, because a particular distribution of capitals underlies both position in social space *and* the cultural and economic wherewithal to engage in certain kinds of social practice.

Class condition and constructed class

In a similar distinction to that between 'class in itself' and 'class for itself', Bourdieu differentiates between *objective* class and *mobilized* class. An objective class is not a collective entity, but a set of individuals sharing similar conditions of existence and who possess similar sets of properties, including objectified properties such as material goods and the embodied properties expressed as ways of behaving, thinking and responding. These embodied properties, when arising from the social conditionings imposed by common class conditions of existence, are referred to as the *class habitus* (Bourdieu 1984, p. 95). By contrast, mobilized class implies some form of group identity connected with collective social practices, referring to 'the set of individuals brought together ... for the purpose of the struggle to preserve or modify' the objective class structure (Bourdieu 1984, p. 564). In order to construct objective classes as units of analysis from the multitude of disparate individuals, Bourdieu introduces a social space whose three dimensions are defined by volume of capital, composition of capital and the trajectory of these two properties over time (Bourdieu 1984, p. 108). In this model, the location of an agent in social space indicates both their intrinsic resources and their 'relational properties', or in other words their positioning in relation to other agents (Bourdieu 1991, p. 231). The primary determinant of class – the dimension which fundamentally differentiates conditions of existence – is the total volume of capital, including its economic, cultural and social guises, although Bourdieu mainly emphasizes the first two of these. Individuals may be placed along this dimension according to their occupation, producing a continuous although not uniformly dense distribution from the greatest to the lowest volumes, with the higher professions and senior executives at one end and unskilled manual workers at the other. This distribution enables Bourdieu to distinguish three main classes, which he refers to as the dominant, middle and working classes (Bourdieu 1984, pp. 108–109). However, within classes corresponding to similar volumes of capital, it is possible to distinguish class fractions on the basis of the composition of their capital, that is, the relative importance of economic or cultural capital within the overall total. Although in some cases the structure is symmetrical, for example in the traditional professions where high levels of economic and cultural capital go together, in other cases one kind of capital predominates.

The examples used earlier refer to Bourdieu's data on the class structure of France in the mid-1960s. Since the publication of *Distinction* (Bourdieu 1984), numerous studies have attempted to map the social space of other countries, with varying degrees of sympathy to Bourdieu and with correspondingly varied results. Figure 6.1 shows a recent mapping of the British social space, which closely follows Bourdieu's approach using data from the 2012 sweep of the British Cohort Study (Atkinson 2018). The figure illustrates the positions of several occupational groups within the two-dimensional space defined by volume and composition of capital, and shows a striking similarity to Bourdieu's own mapping (Bourdieu 1984, p. 122). The distribution according to volume of capital, with higher professionals and business executives at one end and unskilled manual workers at the other, is essentially the same. However, some differences are evident in terms of the composition of capital, with business executives and skilled workers showing a greater bias towards economic capital than in Bourdieu's data.[6]

Horizontal alignment of occupational groups corresponds to membership of different class fractions within the same main class. Bourdieu argues that vertical alignment implies a specific kind of homology between members of different classes with similar structures of capital. In Figure 6.1, although professionals, White-collar workers and sales workers have differing amounts of total capital, neither economic nor cultural capital predominates. A similar homology exists between skilled workers, small employers and business executives, for whom economic capital is dominant (see also Bourdieu 1984, p. 109). These homologies distinguish two kinds of class interest, cutting across

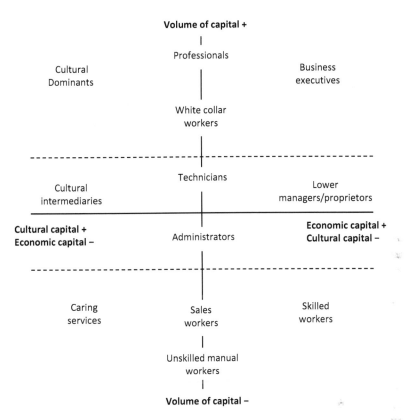

FIGURE 6.1   The British social space. A two-dimensional cross-section showing the positions of occupational groups according to total volume and composition of capital, based on BCS data for 42-year-olds in 2012.

Source: Adapted from Atkinson (2018, p. 487).

differences in total capital: those whose class reproduction depends mainly on the transmission of economic capital, often by inheritance, and those who are more dependent on the transmission of cultural capital, notably formal educational credentials but also including 'softer' expressions of taste and culture. This distinction corresponds to different types of mobility within social space: vertical, in which the total volume of capital changes, but not its composition; or transverse, in which one form of capital is replaced by another as the predominant form. Transverse movements are likely to be more difficult because they require a structural transformation of the capital held by an individual: for example, a shopkeeper who wishes to become a teacher becomes more dependent on cultural capital. Other things being equal, class mobility strategies are therefore likely to centre on vertical movements, which may widen educational inequalities as different classes and class fractions give differing priorities to cultural and economic capital.

This model of class is 'structural' in that it generates positions (and relations between them) which, although occupied by specific individuals at certain times, are independent of those individuals. It is also a continuum of positions rather than a set of categories, so that classes shade into each other rather than being marked by discontinuities in economic or social relations. However, comparisons between Bourdieu's continuum and the one-dimensional gradation contained in a status stratification scheme are of only limited applicability. As Weininger (2005, p. 90) argues, the multidimensional nature of Bourdieu's social space allows the delineation of a complex system of relationships between positions, including an analysis of conflicting interests and forms of mobility. In particular, the third (time) dimension of Bourdieu's social space makes it possible to trace individual class trajectories and to make distinctions even within the relatively homogeneous sets of positions associated with particular class fractions. Social space is also gendered, and, although gender divisions tend to weaken as the volume of capital increases, empirical studies have shown an association between feminized occupations and regions of social space in which cultural capital predominates (Bourdieu 1984, p. 383; Atkinson 2018).

Class boundaries and symbolic struggles

Bourdieu's social space is continuous rather than categorical, and therefore contains no natural boundaries between classes, although the composition of capital held by individuals provides a basis for differentiating between class fractions. Questions about what classes exist and the demarcation between them can therefore be answered only on the basis of empirical determinations of the distribution of capitals and the ways in which they are deployed. Although differences between agents at extreme ends of the class structure may be clearcut, the distribution of economic and cultural capital amongst intermediate positions is complex and more difficult to interpret:

> It is in these intermediate or middle positions of the social space that the indeterminacy and the fuzziness of the relationship between practices and positions are the greatest, and that the room left open for symbolic strategies designed to jam this relationship is the largest.
>
> (Bourdieu 1987, p. 12)

Classes and their boundaries must be understood in terms of social practices, particularly struggles for social and material advantage: 'Boundaries – even the most formal-looking ones ... freeze a particular state of social struggles, i.e. a given state of the distribution of advantages and obligations ...' (Bourdieu 1984, p. 479). What is most distinctive about Bourdieu's position is the importance he gives to struggles over symbolic value, drawing on Weber's conception of status groups as defined by characteristic styles of life: pervasive and habitually maintained practices which function to create and preserve social distance from other groups. In these struggles, objective differences with regard to economic and cultural capital are expressed in a symbolic space of distinctions between practices, a space which has immediate meaning for agents who, through their class habitus, are able to read social positions from their physical manifestations (Bourdieu 1987, p. 11).

Symbolic struggles are not the main determinant of class, but are an important aspect of class formation: they 'contribute to the existence of classes by enhancing the efficiency of the objective mechanisms' (Bourdieu 1984, p. 482). Lifestyles do not merely symbolize class distinctions forged elsewhere; they also *produce* social similarities and social differences: 'Through the minutiae of everyday consumption ... each individual continuously *classifies* him- or herself and, simultaneously, all others as alike or different' (Weininger 2005, p. 99). One's own lifestyle is thereby constructed and distinguished from other styles of life, taking its place in a hierarchy of lifestyles which are valued according to their proximity to what Bourdieu calls the 'legitimate culture'. Boundaries between classes then emerge as frontiers, in attempts to establish marginal practices as part of – or no longer part of – the style of life associated with a class. Educational boundaries, perhaps even more than artistic ones, are a central element in such processes. Divisions between institutions, between state and private education, and between curricula, can all be used to establish distinctions from other groups as well as to gain legitimate cultural capital. For example, Tholen (2017, p. 1074) explores how classification is mobilized within the graduate labour market: 'To be able to define concepts such as "overqualification", "graduate occupation" or "elite schooling" is to dominate the symbolic struggle over labour market value'. In these struggles, Bourdieu regards the dominant classes as having particular advantages, first, in possessing a class habitus aligned with the legitimate culture and, second, in possessing in a high degree the specific forms of capital necessary to appropriate practices as part of this culture. Indeed, the dominant classes are the 'site par excellence of symbolic struggles' whose different fractions – in Bourdieu's France, artists, intellectuals, industrialists – seek to define 'the legitimate principle of domination, between economic, educational or social capital' (Bourdieu 1984, p. 251). These classes therefore act as leaders, as 'taste-makers', constantly recreating and reinterpreting practices, whilst those from less advantaged classes chase the shadow of mobility, attaining 'distinguished' practices only after they have ceased to be a mark of distinction. In this account, the dominated classes – the working class and petty bourgeoisie – are an almost entirely passive force, a foil to the manoeuvring of the dominant classes, 'so strongly are the dominated classes ... imbued with a sense of their cultural unworthiness' (Bourdieu 1984, p. 248). This is explained in part by the lack, in Bourdieu's empirical data, of finer detail on working-class culture, which precluded the identification of distinct fractions and struggles within the working class (see Weininger 2005,

p. 97). However, there is arguably a lack of empathy with the dominated classes in many of Bourdieu's writings. Although later works such as *The Weight of the World* (Bourdieu 1999) contain rich accounts of working-class life, elsewhere Bourdieu provides an almost unrelentingly negative depiction of the working class. In spite of his criticisms of classification processes, this class is presented as lacking any authentic life of its own, and seems to exist as a 'class for others' which can be studied and measured, but from which no cultural value can be derived.

Linguistic capital, unequal selectedness and working-class success

The idea of cultural capital was formulated to explain research findings on the unequal school achievement of children originating from different social classes. This research began as an investigation into pedagogic communication (Bourdieu and Passeron 1990, first French edition published in 1970) which highlighted the importance of *linguistic capital*, a specific form of embodied cultural capital which Bourdieu described as 'one of the best-hidden mediations through which the relationship ... between social origin and scholastic achievement is set up' (p. 116). Linguistic capital in general concerns the deployment of language in such a way that it generates some form of value for its holder (Bourdieu 1991, p. 55). In the context of education, Bourdieu relates linguistic capital to the extent to which a child is literally 'at home' with the language of the school. In a remarkable (although not uncritical) echo of Bernstein, he proposes that the educational value of different linguistic codes depends on the distance separating them from the socially recognized criteria of linguistic 'correctness' (Bourdieu and Passeron 1990, p. 116). However, linguistic capital is more than the degree of alignment between linguistic performance and the conventions of academic study; it also concerns the extent to which it can function as symbolic capital, in being recognized as legitimate and authentic to its holder. A person may be able to generate a certain type of discourse, but their linguistic productions will be seen and evaluated in relation to all the forms of capital with which, to a greater or lesser extent, they are invested. As Bourdieu puts it 'a language is worth what those who speak it are worth' (Bourdieu 1977b, p. 652). Although in later work the concept of linguistic capital often became subsumed within that of cultural capital, the distinction between the two is worth maintaining, and Bourdieu himself continued to refer to linguistic capital as an important aspect of cultural capital in general (see, for example, Bourdieu 1999).

Linguistic capital is about more than the form and structure of discourse: because language provides a system of categories for the recognition and manipulation of meanings, the language acquired within the family sets limits to a student's cognitive facility (Bourdieu and Passeron 1990, p. 73). It may therefore be expected that the distribution of linguistic capital for working-class children in the early stages of schooling will differ substantially from the corresponding distribution for middle-class children. In the French education system, Bourdieu and Passeron (1990) observed precisely this kind of correlation between linguistic capital and social origin within the lower levels of education. However, they show that this does not necessarily remain the case in the later stages of schooling, at least for those young people who remain in education. The propensity of middle-class families to maximize the reproduction of cultural capital through the educational system as well as within the family leads to a lower degree of selectivity in the progression from one level to the next. Put simply, middle-class children with lower levels of linguistic capital are more likely to remain in education, whilst working-class children with similar linguistic capital drop out. The average attainment of working-class children who survive in education therefore becomes progressively closer to that of their middle-class peers. Unequal degrees of selectivity compensate for inequalities in linguistic capital, leading to 'the cancelling out or inversion of the direct relation ... between the possession of cultural capital ... and degree of [educational] success' (Bourdieu and Passeron 1990, p. 73).

Unequal selectedness provides something of a counter-weight to narratives of working-class failure. However, it does not imply that successful students from working-class backgrounds become indistinguishable from middle-class students. Although this may be true in terms of the cultural capital most closely aligned to the educational context, Bourdieu and Passeron (1990, p. 74) note that middle-class advantage reasserts itself when discourse moves away from the standard school curriculum. Working-class students in higher education may therefore be disadvantaged more broadly – particularly in relation to symbolic capital – whilst competing on approximately equal terms in what is explicitly taught and assessed. Moreover, increased participation by working-class students in higher levels of education is likely to decrease the 'selectedness' of these students, thereby reasserting the achievement-origins relationship. The complex relationships between class and educational capitals are illustrated by several recent studies of successful working-class students which adopt a Bourdieusian perspective (Reay et al. 2010; Ingram 2011). These studies tend to invoke notions of a conflicted habitus, drawing on Bourdieu's account of what happens when individuals are confronted with social fields beyond those which shaped their class habitus. In familiar situations, the habitus is self-regulating, and by pre-disposing its bearer towards certain choices 'tends to protect itself from crises and critical challenges by providing itself with a milieu to which it is as pre-adapted as possible' (Bourdieu 1990, p. 61). However, encounters with new fields are more disruptive, and Bourdieu (2005b, pp. 46–47) writes of a 'dialectical confrontation' with objective structures that results in a habitus re-structured, albeit within certain bounds of continuity with its originating conditions. Forms of social capital associated with certain working-class communities may intensify these processes, and have a 'bonding' rather than 'bridging' effect for students considering study at elite universities (Green and White 2008). As a result, contradictory social positions exert 'structural double binds' on their occupants, in which adaptation produces a 'destabilized habitus, torn by contradiction and internal division' (Bourdieu 2000, p. 160). Although these contradictions may initially be concerned with tensions in relationships with family and former friends, Lehmann (2013) suggests that more difficult challenges lie ahead: the symbolic violence that may be encountered in attempting to translate academic success into permanent social mobility. However, even within schools and universities, working-class academic success can mean conflicting loyalties, uncertain and shifting identities, and gendered contradictions between academic and working-class personas (Ingram 2011). It may also be an individualized and isolating experience: Reay et al. (2009) describe their working-class participants as achieving success in spite of a lack of external support and resources, whether at school or at home, and sometimes by self-exclusion from mainstream peer groups.

The challenges facing academically successful working-class students are often related to the concept of *institutional habitus*. McDonough (1997, p. 107) defines the habitus of an educational organization as 'the impact of a cultural group or social class on an individual's behaviour through an intermediate organization'. Reay et al. (2010, p. 111) expand on this broad definition in terms of an organizational ethos 'linked to wider socio-economic and educational cultures through processes in which [institutions] and the different student constituencies they recruit mutually shape and re-shape each other'. More specifically, institutional habitus is held to include aspects of an institution's standing and practices such as academic status, curriculum offer, and expectations of conduct, character and entitlement. Reay et al. (2010, p. 109) describe these latter, regulative, aspects as constituting cultural capital 'embodied in the collectivity of students'. Over the last 20 years, the concept of institutional habitus has been extensively used to understand the exclusions, accommodations and tensions involved in managing social and academic life for working-class students in a range of institutional types. However, whether the term *habitus* can properly be applied to an educational institution is contested. It is difficult to see the definitions discussed earlier as constituting a practice-generating grammar in the way that habitus is meant to underlie an individual's interaction with a field. Although Bourdieu writes of class habitus, this is not the habitus of a class considered as a single entity, but a system of dispositions which is (partially) common to all individuals experiencing similar class conditions. The relationship between the resulting practices is one of homology rather than a communal ethos (Bourdieu 1977a, p. 80), and Bourdieu takes great pains to criticize the substantialist view of class as a collective entity. The concept of institutional habitus does not occur in Bourdieu's own work, and although he refers to 'tendencies immanent in the institutional structures and the dispositions of the agents' in a case study of organizational change (Bourdieu 2005a, p. 219), the context is a discussion of the organization as a *field*. Although Bourdieu writes of the structures of capital within this organization in a similar way to Reay et al. (2010), he does not endow it with any kind of habitus (Bourdieu 2005a, p. 205).

Atkinson (2011) takes up similar points to argue that institutional habitus unhelpfully reifies a system of relations within and between fields, and is in any case a redundant concept, because Bourdieu has already furnished us with tools perfectly adequate for understanding the relevant processes. Moreover, he suggests that institutional habitus may actually *diminish* our understanding, by deflecting attention from processes of differentiation, contestation and subversion within an institution. Responding to these criticisms, Burke et al. (2013) accept that institutional habitus is an immature concept, but defend the utility of a collective understanding of habitus as a socio-analytical tool for highlighting in empirical data 'the way in which we act together and can be held socially and morally responsible for doing so' (p. 179). Their argument is a valuable clarification of how an institution considered as a field – and located within wider fields – interacts with an individual habitus. Whether it demonstrates the conceptual viability of a *collective* habitus is another question. However, for all its flaws, the concept of institutional habitus has opened up an area of research which illuminates the lived experience of institutional stratification and, for successful working-class students, 'the discomforts generated when habitus confronts a starkly unfamiliar field' (Reay et al. 2010).

Educational expansion and transformations of social space

Some critics of Bourdieu use the consequences of educational expansion as evidence against the idea that schools are a conservative force. Halsey et al. (1980) observe that 'schools ... were doing far more than "reproducing" cultural capital; they were creating it too' (p. 77), going on to conclude that 'our evidence does not dispose us to accept any exaggerated claim for the concept of cultural capital as an exclusive means of cultural reproduction of the social classes' (p. 88). More recently, Goldthorpe (2007) has claimed that cultural reproduction implies a widening of class inequalities in education, rather than the observed patterns of stability or gradual reduction. It is therefore of interest to consider how Bourdieu himself dealt with the process of educational expansion, which he discusses in detail in works such as *The Inheritors* (Bourdieu and Passeron 1979; first French edition 1964) and *Distinction* (Bourdieu 1984).[7] Bourdieu argues that class reproduction strategies depend on the structure, at a given time, of the 'instruments of reproduction', which include the education system and its interaction with other fields (Bourdieu 1984, p. 125). Changes in the field – of education or of production – which change the accessibility of cultural capital and its economic convertibility will change the objective conditions of class reproduction. Consequently, educational expansion may arise from factors such as an increased supply of educational opportunities, increased demand for cultural capital as the reproduction of economic capital becomes more difficult for certain class fractions, and a demand for qualifications as opportunities for unqualified labour decline. These kinds of structural change lead to intensified competition and class struggles within the educational field: 'Academic qualifications ... thus become one of the key stakes in an inter-class competition which generates a general and continuous growth in the demand for education and an inflation of academic qualifications' (Bourdieu 1984, p. 127).

The ensuing discussion of struggles for positional advantage in a context of credential inflation, downclassing and upclassing, although located mainly within the expansion of secondary education, foreshadows contemporary debates over the effects of expansion in higher education (for example, Brown et al. 2011).[8] It is hardly consistent with the view that Bourdieu advocated an essentially static model of education; on the contrary, his account of field struggles provides a means to understand patterns of expansion such as MMI and EMI. However, the fact that Bourdieu was aware of processes of educational expansion and provided a theoretical basis for it is not sufficient to refute Goldthorpe's criticisms: it is also possible that Bourdieu's discussion of expansion is not compatible with his broader theoretical framework. The question of habitus *change* is crucial here, and Goldthorpe's charge is that the working-class habitus, as conceptualized by Bourdieu, is so inflexibly alienated by education that expansion should not lead to significant increases in working-class participation. This impression may indeed be given by certain passages in Bourdieu's earlier work, for example in his description of habitus as an 'immanent law ... laid down in each agent by his earliest upbringing' (Bourdieu 1977a, p. 81). Bourdieu also ascribes a hysteresis effect to the habitus, an overreaction in which the habitus clings to earlier practices and is therefore slow to respond to new opportunities (p. 83). However, even in these earlier writings it is clear that the relationship between habitus and field is a dialectical one, so that habitus and practices will change (not necessarily synchronously) as objective conditions change. The restructuring of habitus arising from this 'dialectical confrontation' has already been noted, and in one of his last essays Bourdieu (2005b, p. 47) spells out quite explicitly that 'in rapidly changing societies, habitus changes constantly, continuously, but within the limits inherent in its originary structure'. Rather than being inadequate to understand the realities of educational expansion, Bourdieu's theoretical framework provides considerable insight into the underlying processes.

In addition to individual mobility between structural positions, transformations of the social space itself may occur as educational participation rates increase and occupations are redefined according to changes in the profile of capitals associated with them. In his discussion of these processes, Bourdieu explicitly recognizes that the total 'mass' of cultural capital increases over time, and he provides an extensive empirically based discussion of what he calls the 'displacement' of schooling rates in France, in which participation by all classes increased, and some participation gaps decreased (Bourdieu 1984, p. 155). However, he does not accept that cultural capital becomes of decreasing relevance to social reproduction or that the conception of schooling as a conservative force is incorrect. In the long run, he believes that inequalities are maintained, and that fluctuations in participation gaps are part of the dynamics of adjustment 'at a stage in the evolution of class societies in which one can conserve only by changing' (p. 153). Moreover, Bourdieu regards the key markers of class struggle as lying in the more stable *relational* properties of social space, not in its ever-changing substantial composition:

> Thus, by an apparent paradox, the maintenance of order; that is, of the whole set of gaps, differences, 'differentials', ranks, precedences, priorities, exclusions, distinctions, ordinal properties, and thus of the relations of order which give a social formation its structure, is provided by an unceasing change in substantial (i.e., non-relational) properties.
>
> (Bourdieu 1984, pp. 159–160)

Relational stability is attained through mutually compensating competitive struggles, in which the dominant classes have an inherent advantage. Although the average rate of return on cultural capital may decrease due to credential inflation, this rate depends on the economic and social capital available for its exploitation, so that similar levels of cultural capital may have different rates of return depending on position in social space.[9] Moreover, increasing the total volume of cultural capital contributes to a reconstitution of class, swelling and downgrading the pool of labour qualified to undertake service and knowledge work. Although Halsey et al. (1980) are right to assert that cultural capital is not the *only* factor in social reproduction, there seems little reason to regard educational expansion as evidence against its explanatory power.

Notes

1 'We can indeed, with caution, compare a field to a game although, unlike the latter, a field is not the product of a deliberate act of creation, and it follows rules or, better, regularities, that are not explicit and codified' (Bourdieu and Wacquant 1992, p. 98).

2 Bourdieu (1977a, p. 76) admits the possibility that 'the responses of the habitus may be accompanied by a strategic calculation tending to carry on quasi-consciously the operation the habitus carries on in a quite different way', but asserts the primacy of the habitus in regulating actions and thoughts.

3 'Men make their own history, but they do not make it just as they please; they do not make it under circumstances chosen by themselves, but under circumstances directly encountered, given and transmitted from the past' (Marx and Engels 1979, p. 103).

4 Arbitrary in the sense of a selection of culture not deducible from universal principles.

5 Life-style is used here in the Weberian sense of a 'style of life', a wide-ranging system of cultural practices, rather than the more superficial and consumption-orientated 'lifestyle' of contemporary usage.

6 It should be emphasized that this is not a quantitative model of social space, with axes representing continuous numerical variables. It is rather a representation of a system of differences in relation to specific indicators of economic and cultural capital constructed from survey data.

7 Goldthorpe (2007) does not refer to *Distinction*.

8 Even at the level of the imagery used: Bourdieu describes such processes as 'the cheating of a generation', whilst Brown et al. (2011) have 'the broken promises of education, jobs and incomes'.

9 Current examples of such processes would include the ability of dominant classes to assist their children by supporting higher degrees or unpaid internships, exploiting social connections, and providing cultural capital not commonly obtained through the educational system (see Bourdieu and Passeron 1990, p. 74).

7

PEDAGOGIC CODES

Power and symbolic control

Basil Bernstein was and remains a controversial figure in the sociology of education. For many scholars who have immersed themselves in his work, Bernstein was *the* most interesting and important British sociologist of the late twentieth century (Davies 2001), and his legacy has inspired a thriving tradition of research. To his detractors, however, Bernstein was variously an obscure and unnecessarily difficult writer, a romanticizer of the working class and a theorist of their cultural deprivation (Nash 2006a; Davies 2011). Bernstein himself devoted considerable energy to refuting such criticisms, particularly those which he saw as misunderstanding or misrepresenting his work. He believed that theorization should be led by research, and whether his concepts were difficult or discomforting was secondary to their effectiveness. Rather than simply asserting that education is fundamental to social reproduction, Bernstein aimed to provide an account of precisely *how* pedagogic communication contributes to the maintenance of class relations. This chapter considers some of the main features of Bernstein's approach, beginning with the concept of code and its expression in terms of classification and framing. Its later reformulation in terms of discourse is briefly discussed, as marking a shift from the structure of pedagogy to the structure of knowledge. The focus then falls on Bernstein's understanding of class, including his account of visible and invisible pedagogies as an expression of ideological struggles within the middle class. The chapter concludes with a discussion of recent research which explores radical alternatives to traditional pedagogies.

Pedagogic codes

From the beginning of his career in sociology, Bernstein was interested in the Durkheimian problem of the relation between the inner and outer worlds. He asks: 'How does a given social structure become part of individual experience, what is the main process through which this is achieved, and what are the educational implications?' (Bernstein 1961, p. 288). The idea that the internalization of social structure is mediated by pedagogic communication was already taking shape, although the initial focus was on the acquisition of speech forms rather than the more general concepts which began to emerge in his theory of elaborated and restricted codes. Over time, the conception of code became more general and at the same time richer and more powerful, providing comprehensive theoretical descriptions of pedagogy and its role in cultural reproduction. In a series of retrospectives on his work, Bernstein (1971a, 1975, 1990a, 1999, 2000, pp. 93–100, 207) traces the development of code theory from its origins in his sociolinguistic studies of the late 1950s to the reformulation of code in terms of discourse during the 1990s. What remained constant, Bernstein argues, was the central thesis that class relations regulate the meanings we create, producing cognitive orientations tacitly expressed in 'rules of interpretation, relation, and identity' (Bernstein 1990c, p. 95). From an early stage, this included how class regulates both the structure of communication within the family and the institutionalizing of pedagogic codes in education:

> The class structure distributes power unequally; it distributes access to, control over, and facility to exploit property, whether this property is physical or symbolic. It does this through its penetration into educational arrangements and processes and through its penetration into primary socialization within the family, in such a way that a vicious self-perpetuating circle is often set up between home, school and work.
>
> (Bernstein 1971a, p. 189)

Elaborated codes occupy a privileged position within social institutions such as education, enabling individuals to respond to a particular context in ways that are officially sanctioned and rewarded. They therefore act as *privileging* codes to those who are socialized into them at an early age. This advantage is not confined to cognitive processes: code also regulates dispositions, identities and practices (Bernstein 1990a). One purpose of schooling is to initiate children into the approved ways of organizing experience and making meaning that are associated with educational institutions, constructing educational identity, consciousness and academic skills. However, for middle-class children, school is not the only, or necessarily the primary, site of acquisition: the middle-class home provides a hidden subsidy for its children (Hoadley 2008). Using an Althusserian terminology,[1] Bernstein (1981) explores the relationship between the acquisition of codes and the construction of the subject, a process in which each individual is socialized into recognizing their position in relation to other subjects (and their codes) and acquires internal structures of cognition and feeling. The concept of code therefore bears some relation to habitus: 'code modalities establish and reproduce the practices specific to a field and … in Bourdieu's terms, create the specificity of a habitus' (Bernstein 1981, p. 353). However, Bernstein regarded habitus as a more generalized concept than code, less well adapted to pedagogic contexts and, without further development, unable to provide an adequate language of description for their analysis. Moreover, Bernstein believed that habitus, whilst useful for understanding social reproduction, was inferior to code as a means of conceptualizing how education might bring about social change. By comprehending a range of pedagogic and social arrangements within a unified framework, including as-yet-unrealized possibilities, Bernstein claimed that code provides a basis for understanding the disruption as well as the reproduction of class relations.

Meanings, code and the division of labour

In Bernstein's earliest formulations of code theory, a restricted code was indicated by particularized, context-tied meanings underpinned by homogeneous social relationships, whilst elaborated codes implied universalistic, relatively context-independent meanings based upon differentiated social relationships. Moore (2013, p. 70) characterizes these different orientations in terms of how they give access to meaning. In a restricted code, only people thoroughly familiar with the context can fully understand what is meant by its discourses and practices. Elaborated codes, by contrast, set out to communicate meanings in ways that a non-initiate can comprehend, elaborating[2] on implicit assumptions and conventions so that meaning is liberated from context. Bernstein held that class acted selectively on coding orientations, influencing which code would be adopted in a particular context: middle-class children would tend to give priority to elaborated codes, whilst for working-class children a restricted code would be more likely. An example Bernstein used several times was of a study in which middle-class and working-class children were asked to group – in any way they liked – pictures of different foods. The middle-class children consistently gravitated towards more abstract grouping principles ('They're vegetables', 'they come from the sea'), whilst working-class children used more concrete principles directly related to their own lives ('It's what Mum makes', 'it's what we have for breakfast'). When asked to group the pictures in different ways, the middle-class children often switched to these more concrete principles, whilst working-class children continued with the kind of principles they had used originally (Bernstein 1990c, p. 103). Bernstein's reading of this study is that it demonstrates different coding orientations between working-class and middle-class children, with the latter giving priority to principles having a less direct relation to localized and specific experiences.[3] Because such principles dominate formal education, working-class children are disadvantaged (not deficient) in an educational context. Children from both classes were able to use elaborated *and* restricted codes (by the end of the study around one-third of the working-class children had changed to an indirect principle of classification), but the classes differed in terms of the priority given to them. Bernstein notes that 'The difference between the children is not a difference in cognitive facility/power but a difference in recognition and realization rules used by the children to read the context, select their interactional practice, and create their texts' (Bernstein 1990c, p. 104).

Although Bernstein continued to refine his ideas, he repeatedly emphasized the importance of the formal statement of code theory provided in the paper 'Codes, modalities and the process of cultural reproduction: a model' (Bernstein 1981; revised and reprinted in Bernstein 1990a). This paper asserts the primacy of systems of meaning in the definition of code, which Bernstein expresses formally as 'a regulative principle, tacitly acquired, which selects and integrates: a) relevant meanings b) forms of their realization c) evoking contexts' (Bernstein 1981, p. 328). Acquiring a code involves learning to recognize contexts and how to create, organize and express meanings in ways appropriate to them: this entails the acquisition of 'rules' that enable the acquirer to respond legitimately to meanings and practices encountered in a context. However, the tacit nature of this process conceals its fundamental contribution to maintaining class relations: that the distribution of codes is not class-neutral but depends upon the distribution of power associated with a particular social division of labour. Generalizing the concrete discussions of coding orientations elsewhere in his work, such as the picture-sorting example outlined earlier, Bernstein argues that the form taken by an individual's response to a context – an *orientation to meaning* – is shaped by their position (or their family's position) within the division of labour. This position translates – through inequalities in power and control – into a coding orientation (the priority given to elaborated or restricted codes). Restricted orientations are those in which meanings have a specific and direct relation to the division of labour and its social relations (the 'material base', in Bernstein's terminology). Elaborated orientations are those in which a hierarchy of organizing principles is available, ranging from those close to a material base to more general principles with an indirect and less specific material relation. Bernstein relates the dominance of elaborated codes over restricted codes to increases in the complexity of the division of labour, and particularly to the growth of a service economy. This account of the relation between coding orientation and the social division of labour was particularly important to Bernstein: it implies that these orientations are not intrinsic to people occupying specific class positions, but are socially distributed in ways that reflect class relations and in particular the distribution of power. This results in a *contingent* relationship between class and code but not a necessary one.

Codes, deficit and disadvantage

The terminology of restricted and elaborated codes expresses a qualitative difference in how people from different classes articulate and make sense of their experience. It is therefore not surprising that the idea of code as a mediating factor between class and educational performance has been criticized as a 'deficit theory', in which working-class attributes are seen as inferior to those of the middle classes. Bernstein repeatedly attempted to fend off these criticisms, both by increasingly sophisticated developments of his theory and in discussions of what he saw as the distortion or oversimplification of his work (see, for example, Bernstein 1990c; Bernstein 2000, pp. 126–127). Danzig (1995) argues that code focusses attention on the ways in which performances are judged and evaluated rather than on deficits in children or their families, and Bernstein himself was always careful to make clear that class-based differentiation occurred at the level of performance rather than competence, affecting what children actually did rather than what they were capable of:

> The concept of code presupposes competences that all acquire and share; hence it is not possible to discuss code with reference to cognitive/linguistic deficiencies ... Code refers to a specific cultural regulation of the realization of commonly shared competences.
>
> (Bernstein 1990c, p. 113)

However, these arguments were often ignored or rejected by commentators, and the perception of Bernstein as a theorist of working-class deficits proved difficult to shift. In a discussion based largely on his work before 1971, Bisseret (1979) argues that, although Bernstein aims to remove essentialism from explanations of class differences, he still tends to invoke concepts such as innate ability. At the same time, she continues, Bernstein normalizes elaborated codes from an expression of the interests and modes of thinking of a specific class to a universal and intrinsically more powerful means of representing experience (see also Haavelsrud 2001). These controversies were to some extent neutralized by the shift from code to the broader concept of discourse. Nevertheless, Ivinson (2018) suggests that there is value in reimagining rather than abandoning the idea of restricted codes, which she argues 'enabled Bernstein to genuinely capture phenomena of class difference that remain politically, socially, educationally and theoretically important'. Rather than expressing a deficiency in working-class communities, the linguistic and social practices constituting a restricted code may be seen as an orientation to the values embodied in these communities. Ivinson (2018, p. 541) re-emphasizes restricted codes as a form of knowledge that emphasizes personal relationships, a knowledge 'required for adapting to changing economic conditions in communities where the real, material and financial effects of de-industrialisation are being experienced on a daily basis'. As Bernstein himself wrote,

In a fundamental sense, a restricted code is the basic code. It is the code of intimacy which shapes and changes the very nature of subjective experience, initially in the family and in our close personal relationships. The intensifications and condensations of such communication carry us beyond speech, and new forms of awareness often become possible.

(Bernstein 1971a, p. 196)

Whether Bernstein's subtle and many-layered code theory needs rescuing from accusations of deficit theory is debatable. However, in its earlier forms it left open the critical question of exactly *how* class relations shape coding orientations: if children from different classes use different rules, why is this? How do class interests and the distribution of power influence the adoption of one code rather than another? These were points of which Bernstein became increasingly conscious, and from 1971 onwards he had begun to develop a more sophisticated approach to specifying codes, based on the important concepts of classification and framing. These concepts were held to translate inequalities in power and control into individual consciousness (Bernstein 1971b, 1990c, p. 101) and marked the beginning of a sustained engagement with the processes by which class relations become realized in specific forms of pedagogy. Applying classification and framing to contexts of increasing generality, including the field of production[4] as well as education, Bernstein was able to subsume many of his earlier analyses within a new, more powerful, framework.

Classification and framing

With the publication of his seminal paper on classification and framing in M.F.D. Young's *Knowledge and Control* (Bernstein 1971b), these two concepts occupy an increasingly central role in Bernstein's work. He argues that, within a specific social setting or practice, classification and framing describe the social relationships stemming from external class relations, translating distributions of power and control into ways of experiencing, interpreting and describing the world. The idea of classification is taken from Durkheim, who emphasized the role of symbolic boundaries in constructing categories of thought and maintaining the social order. In *The Elementary Forms of Religious Life*, Durkheim proposes that classification is a fundamental activity in the constitution of society:

Society is possible only if the individuals and things that make it up are divided among different groups, which is to say genera, and if those groups themselves are classified in relation to one another. Thus, society presupposes a conscious organization of itself that is nothing other than a classification.

(Durkheim 1995 [1912], p. 444)

According to Durkheim, social ideas and their associated practices are prior to abstract ideas: logical abstractions, such as space, time and classification itself, are preceded by their concrete instances in specific social circumstances – for example, social space, social time and social categories. In Bernstein's hands, the concept of classification became an expression of power and ideology. Classification 'constructs the nature of social space: stratifications, distributions and locations' (Bernstein 2000, p. 12). In educational institutions, there is an internal classification and distribution of knowledge, in which temporal and social boundaries are established between what is taught to different age groups or to 'low ability' and 'high ability' pupils. At the same time, classification conceals the arbitrary nature of power relations, replacing 'the contingent by the necessary' and constructing 'psychic defences' within the individual, that is internal constraints on the extent to which the individual can question or act against the established social order. Framing is a subsidiary concept to classification, essentially referring to a classification between what is allowed in a given context and what is prohibited. Within educational institutions, this translates into the regulation of the learning process, and particularly into controls over sequencing and pacing: not just those within the remit of individual teachers, but including the curriculum and examination structures established by external agencies (see Moore 2013, p. 129). As Bernstein notes, 'Classification refers to *what*, framing is concerned with *how* meanings are to be put together, the forms by which they are to be made public, and the nature of the social relationships that go with it' (Bernstein 2000, p. 12, original emphasis).

Where classification is strong, boundaries are clearly defined and relatively impermeable, so that categories are well insulated from each other: 'each category has its unique identity, its unique voice, its own specialised rules of internal relations' (Bernstein 2000, p. 7). With weak classification, the distinctions between categories are blurred and identities less specialized; the sense of uniqueness, of difference, is lessened. For example, in the context of the school curriculum, strong classification (C+ or C++, in Bernstein's notation) implies that subjects are sharply distinguished, with curriculum content, teaching staff, facilities and possibly even teaching and assessment methods being specific to the subject (for an exemplary discussion of classification within the mathematics classroom, see Straehler-Pohl and Gellert 2013). Weak classification (C− or C−−) is marked by integrated curricula, topic-based approaches and staff who are generalists or work in mixed-discipline teams. Classification may also operate on other categories, such as gender-segregated as opposed to mixed provision, or in terms of streaming or setting as opposed to mixed-ability teaching; the single-sex, streamed grammar school would represent a strongly classified institutional principle compared to a co-educational comprehensive school with mixed-ability groups. Classifications are also encountered in broader educational contexts. For example, Niemi and Rosvall (2013) discuss the strong classification between theoretical and practical studies embodied in vocational education, relating this to classifications between authentic and inauthentic masculinities in male-dominated vocational areas. More broadly still, Grace (2008) applies the concept of classification to changes in British education policy over five decades, expressing the autonomy of educational systems in terms of the strength of boundaries between education and the 'globally competitive state'.

Strong framing implies that students have little control over a particular dimension of the learning process, whereas weak framing implies more opportunity for the student to regulate their learning. In most pedagogical settings, there will be an explicit content to be acquired: for example a school subject or vocational practice. Dimensions of framing relating to this content, such as controls over the selection and sequencing of knowledge, pacing (the expected rate of acquisition) and assessment criteria, regulate what Bernstein (2000, p. 32) calls the *instructional discourse*. However, there will also be a process of socialization into norms of disposition and behaviour, of learning to understand the forms of hierarchical relationships and to conform to expectations about conduct, character and manner. The rules of this social order constitute the *regulative discourse*, which, Bernstein maintains, dominates and subsumes the instructional discourse. In either discourse, framing refers only to the *apparent* degree of control enjoyed by students (or teachers, for that matter). To weaken framing in a context is a decision only available to those who have power over the context, and is therefore a function of broader classifications in society.

Both classification and framing can have internal and external values, which can in general vary independently of each other. External classification establishes boundaries between categories, whilst internal classification establishes boundaries within the category: for example, specialized spaces within a school or rules concerning types of clothing for certain subjects. Internal framing refers to the controls within a pedagogic context, whilst external framing refers to the extent to which practices outside the pedagogic context can penetrate within (see Bernstein 2000, p. 14). For a given orientation to meaning, particular values of classification and framing across these dimensions define a specific modality of pedagogic discourse:

$$\frac{O}{\pm C^{i \cdot e} / \pm F^{i \cdot e}}$$

In this formula, O refers to orientation to meaning (elaborated or restricted), $i \cdot e$ refers to internal or external relations, and the horizontal line indicates that meanings (above the line) are embedded in power and principles of control, which are realized by specific values of classification and framing (see Bernstein 1990c, p. 108). In more academic forms of education, O will typically imply an elaborated orientation, although this cannot be assumed in all pedagogic settings, including provision for 'less able' students. The formula generates a range of pedagogic modalities differing either by gradations in the strength of classification or framing or, as a more interesting change in modality, a switch from strong to weak C's or F's. The empirical identification of classification and framing values in specific educational contexts is a challenging problem, but observational studies over several decades have established principles of translation between Bernstein's theoretical language and external phenomena. Examples of these analytical frameworks may be found in the work of authors such as Hoadley (2008), Hoadley and Galant (2016), and Morais and Neves (2018).

In their original form (Bernstein 1971b), the concepts of classification and framing were applied to the context of formal education and were developed to describe the underlying structure of three 'message systems': curriculum, pedagogy and evaluation.[5] As Bernstein came to realize the power of these concepts, classification and framing were used in a more general sense and applied to a range of pedagogical and non-pedagogical contexts, including that of material production (Bernstein 1977a). Classification came to refer to categories[6] rather than curriculum contents – whether these categories were discourses, practices, agents or agencies. However, the essential principle remained the same: classification translates power relations, whilst framing translates principles of social control. Bernstein regarded this distinction between power and control as fundamental: in his formulation, power establishes a particular social order, whilst control socializes people into accepting and reproducing that order. More specifically, power is exercised in the creation, legitimization and reproduction of boundaries, whilst control establishes legitimate forms of communication and practice within the categories thus formed. The concepts of power and control operate at different levels of analysis, so that power constructs relations *between* categories, whilst control constructs relations *within* them.

Discourse, knowledge and knowers

By the early 1990s, Bernstein was beginning to reformulate the concept of code in terms of discourse. Whilst code took for granted the form of the discourse transmitted by pedagogic communication, Bernstein had now turned his attention to the structure of knowledge itself. Specific code modalities now came to be seen as realizations of vertical or, alternatively, horizontal discourse.[7] Vertical discourse arises typically in institutions of cultural production such as universities, and is further subdivided into discourses associated with different disciplinary contexts. In vertical knowledge structures such as the physical sciences, the discourse 'takes the form of a coherent, explicit, systematically principled structure, hierarchically organised' (Bernstein and Solomon 1999, p. 273), whilst in horizontal knowledge structures vertical discourse consists of a series of specialized languages as encountered in the humanities or social sciences. Horizontal discourse originates in the world of everyday life: it is tied to specific contexts, face-to-face encounters, and is segmental rather than hierarchically organized, accruing piecemeal from particular areas of experience.

However, the distinction between vertical and horizontal discourse is not between mental and manual; Bernstein describes a craft as a modality of *vertical* discourse, albeit one which is as near to horizontal discourse as it is possible to come whilst remaining a specialized rather than an everyday practice (Bernstein 2000, p. 169; see also Gamble 2004). In making these distinctions, Bernstein is alluding to what he also described as thinkable and unthinkable knowledge: 'two basic classes of knowledge, the esoteric and the mundane; knowledge of the other and the otherness of knowledge' (Bernstein 1990a, p. 181). This is essentially the distinction made by Durkheim (1995 [1912]) between the sacred and the profane, in which ideas, practices and things are classified into two domains characterized by the strength of the boundary dividing them. For Bernstein, these two classes of knowledge and the practices they entail are available in all societies, whether simple or complex, with the precise location of the line between them depending on historical and cultural circumstances. What distinguishes them is their correspondence to two different orders of meaning. Unthinkable knowledge is only indirectly related to a specific social order and is capable of uniting the material and the conceptual worlds, whilst thinkable knowledge is context bound and incapable of providing such a unification. The unthinkable is intrinsically powerful, providing access to a potential *discursive gap,* 'a site for alternative possibilities, for alternative realizations of the relation between the material and the immaterial' (Bernstein 2000, p. 30). For this reason, access to the unthinkable is always regulated in the interests of the most powerful social groups.

A modality of discourse entails more than becoming initiated into specific kinds of knowledge and practice. It is part of the process by which forms of consciousness are distributed, a process in which acquiring knowledge is unavoidably entangled with the question of 'What kind of knower am I?' and ultimately with one's place in the structure of class society. In a similar way to Bourdieu's relation between the worth of a language and the worth of its speakers, Maton (2004) uses the concept of legitimation code to analyse the 'new student' debate which has characterized the expansion of English higher education since the 1960s. The concept of legitimation code is based on the idea that knowledge claims are made by someone and about something, leading to a distinction between the *epistemic relation* between knowledge and its object, and the *social relation* between knowledge and the knower. Where the epistemic relation dominates, 'What matters is what you know', whilst a dominant social relation implies that 'What matters is who you are' (Maton 2004, p. 220). Maton describes how strongly classified social relations were endemic in traditional universities, leading to the problematizing of first-generation higher education students – particularly those from working-class backgrounds – as the 'wrong kind of knower', in conflict with the humanistic ideal of a university, and with only instrumental values in relation to education. These assumptions reinforced the binary divide and, more recently, status distinctions between 'old' and 'new' universities. Whilst all such institutions deal in vertical discourse, the social relations concealed in legitimation codes contribute to status differentiation by adding the social estimation of knowers to the epistemic status of knowledge.

The knowledge embodied in vertical discourse opens up the potential of a discursive gap between meanings and materiality, providing access to the alternative possibilities offered by the unthinkable; horizontal discourse closes down these possibilities, sealing knowledge within the context in which it originated. According to Bernstein, the discursive gap is the site of the *yet to be thought*, the place where true creativity can emerge: 'the discursive gap is where room for manoeuvre occurs, where new concepts and principles can emerge and greater generality be achieved' (Thompson 2009b, p. 46). Above all, vertical discourse is the means of producing and reproducing principled, conceptual knowledge – knowledge that is epistemologically self-aware, expressed in explicit propositional structures and criteria for validity. Although formal education is primarily concerned with the institutionalizing of vertical discourse, Bernstein discusses the insertion of horizontal discourses within school subjects as a strategy to make them more accessible to young people. This process is 'likely to be mediated through the distributive rules of the school [and] is confined to particular social groups, usually the "less able"' (Bernstein 2000, p. 169). Moreover, the appropriation of horizontal discourse is likely to be ineffective as its recontextualization within vertical discourse de-locates it from crucial elements of its original setting, such as space, time and social relation. Elisabeth Bautier (2011, p. 122) suggests that horizontal discourse constitutes a 'trap' for working-class pupils, who are likely to be disadvantaged by the rapid and largely implicit shifts between horizontal and vertical discourse entailed by the inevitably unequal relationship between the two. Although horizontal discourse 'conveys the impression of the potential and equal participation of all pupils', this impression is illusory and replaces socialization into academic norms with a weakening and blurring of messages concerning the nature of knowledge and the criteria for evaluating performance.

Class, economy and education

The concept of class is fundamental to Bernstein's sociology of education, not least in the titles of many of his works. However, the question of what constitutes class is confronted head-on only at a relatively late stage, in the revised and expanded second edition of *Class, Codes and Control*, Volume 3 (Bernstein 1977c). In Bernstein's earlier writings, the meaning of class is either taken for granted or expressed directly in terms of occupational status and education. This led to criticisms that his work lacked any formal definition of class, and an increasing awareness on his part that this was something he needed to rectify. In the first edition of *Class, Codes and Control*, Volume 3 (Bernstein 1975), he had written of the need for a more precise specification of the new middle class, which the second edition provided both in an expanded version of the paper 'Class and pedagogies: visible and invisible' and in a new chapter, 'Aspects of the relation between education and production'. In this chapter, Bernstein writes that class is the *dominant* cultural category in capitalist societies, 'created and maintained by the mode of production' (Bernstein 1977a, p. 175). Class relations had earlier been defined in terms of employment situation, the nature of work tasks and cultural differences rather than as the outcome of inequalities in power and control (Bernstein 1971a, p. 111). Power was now a central part of a new conceptualization of class relations:[8]

> The definition underlying the general discussion is: class relations will be taken to refer to inequalities in the distribution of power between social groups, which are realized in the creation, distribution, legitimation, and reproduction of physical and symbolic values arising out of the social division of labour.
>
> (Bernstein 1977c, p. viii)

Class is therefore understood directly in terms of inequality, within the symbolic economy as well as in the field of physical production. However, the division of labour is not synonymous with class. Rather, class relations are *realized* in its transformation into the inequalities of class society: 'Class acts fundamentally on the division of labour by structuring its moral basis; that is, by creating the underlying relationships of production, distribution and consumption' (Bernstein 1977c, p. 23). Although the principles of distribution associated with the social division of labour are reinforced and legitimated by symbolic control, they originate from material forces. Thus Bernstein (1977a, p. 191) identifies a ruling class characterized by decisive control over the 'means, contexts and possibilities' of production. This class has a fundamental interest in maintaining and reproducing its dominant relation with other classes, but has *direct* control only over relations within the field of production. Its control over education and other ideological agencies must necessarily be indirect. This leaves a crucial role for a 'new' fraction of the middle class, those who are employed in agencies of symbolic control as opposed to the 'old' middle class whose members have roles directly related to production. The forms of control enjoyed by the ruling and middle classes can be expressed by codes – production codes and discursive codes respectively – based on classification and framing values, just as educational codes express the social relations of schooling. The specification of production codes in particular (Bernstein 1977a, pp. 181–185) may be seen as providing a stronger language of description for the material base, introduced in earlier work as a specific social division of labour related to in different ways by elaborated and restricted codes. Nevertheless, the material base remains quite weakly specified. In some of Bernstein's work – for example the early discussions of the picture-sorting exercise outlined earlier and some references to the concept of discursive gap (Bernstein 2000, p. 209) – the material base appears to be synonymous with our direct experience of the world, including experiences and practices unconnected with the social division of labour. Elsewhere, the material base is defined more tightly, as a particular division of labour and its social relations. Whilst this latter interpretation appears to dominate, the resulting ambiguity is unfortunate, particularly in relation to Bernstein's later discussions of scientific knowledge.

Bernstein defines the working class as consisting of those who are dominated by both production and discursive codes, although he allows that this domination may not be accepted passively (Bernstein 1990b, p. 141). The relationship between the working class and agents of symbolic control such as teachers is, Bernstein argues, shaped by the relative importance of education in the formation of their consciousness: for agents of symbolic control, education is the dominant experience in becoming who they are, whilst for the working class, the field of production dominates the formation of consciousness and the role of education is likely to be limited to the regulation of conduct. Relations between working-class pupils and their teachers are therefore shaped by a clash of consciousness, by very different perceptions of the nature of education and its place in their lives. For the majority of the working class, their relationship with education is likely to be characterized by opposition, suspicion and resistance (Bernstein 1990b, p. 143). These are difficult arguments for those who would wish to defend Bernstein against accusations of deficit theory, and seem to suggest that working-class alienation from education is endemic. However, it must be remembered that Bernstein emphasizes the *distribution* of forms of consciousness as part of the essence of symbolic control. Any clash of consciousness between teachers and working-class pupils should be seen, in Bernstein's terms, as a result of exclusion from dominant codes, rather than a lack of propensity for acquiring them.

The distribution of codes is an expression of class relations; ultimately, distributive principles derive from the interests of those who control the means of production. Appearing shortly after the publication of *Schooling in Capitalist America*, 'Aspects of the relation between education and production' shows considerable sympathy with the correspondence principle of Bowles and Gintis (1976). However, Bernstein argues that, whilst education legitimizes values and attitudes relevant to the mode of production, there is only an approximate correspondence between production and education. Education has relative autonomy provided the classification between the category of education and the category of production remains strong, as in most European societies.[9] Bernstein relates the strength of this classification to a *contingent* relationship between economic base and ideological superstructure: the rules expressing class relations 'while having their origin in the social division of labour and its social relations of material production, do *not* necessarily have the conditions of their cultural reproduction located in such a division and relations' (Bernstein 1981, p. 354). There is only an 'attenuated' relationship between the symbolic structures of education and its material base, a parallel, Bernstein (1977a, p. 190) remarks, with the relationships between the Marxist base and superstructure. However, unlike Althusser, he does not regard relative autonomy as a question of the relation between education and the state. Rather, there is an ambiguous relationship between education and production which is repeated in the ambiguities of identity, values and interests of those involved in cultural reproduction (Bernstein 1977a). Categories produced by production and pedagogic codes, the distribution of these categories across the class structure, and the way in which the categories are realized, may correspond more or less closely. Thus categories such as 'academic' and 'non-academic' pupils may relate to professional and manual workers; the distribution of high and low academic attainment may relate to workforce requirements; and the school curriculum may relate more or less closely to the needs of industry. However, class reproduction occurs *irrespective* of the precise nature of these systemic relationships: in this sense, education can be relatively autonomous even though 'the mode of production is anterior to the mode of education' (Bernstein 1977a, p. 186).

Bernstein identifies a number of contradictions between the categories produced by education and those required by the capitalist mode of production: for example contradictions between ideas of education for the self and for the development of human capital. These contradictions provide education with more or less autonomy according to the extent to which the educational system is seen to be meeting the needs of production. Apart from such abstract considerations, Apple (2002) suggests that Bernstein's conception of relative autonomy finds empirical support in studies of particular educational systems: 'There are instances in which education *has* had a powerful, dialectical, and mutually transformative relationship with other fields of power' (p. 615). Referring to conflicts between agents from within the educational field itself and officials from state pedagogic agencies, he notes that contradictions such as those identified by Bernstein can block intended educational change. However, this does not necessarily imply that education can transform class relations. Bernstein, like Bourdieu, regards relative autonomy as apparent rather than real, disguising the class basis of education through 'the appearance of objectivity, of neutrality, and at the same time, of altruistic purpose and dedication' (Bernstein 1977a, p. 190).

Pedagogy and the middle class

Reflecting in 1971 on his research over the previous decade, Bernstein writes that: 'The major starting points are Durkheim and Marx ... Durkheim's work is a truly magnificent insight into the relationships between symbolic orders, social relationships and the structuring of experience' (Bernstein 1971a, pp. 133–134). The influence of Durkheim in particular is reflected in one of

Bernstein's most significant contributions to the class analysis of education: his account of ideological struggles between the old and new middle class over the kind of education their children should receive. Bernstein developed a detailed account of how 'progressive' approaches to education represent a shift from a focus on the social reproduction of property owners and the old professional classes to more fluid and flexible forms of education suited to families from the 'new' middle class. As Power and Whitty (2002) observe, Bernstein recognized clearly the importance of the middle-class relationship to education and the need to explore differences and tensions within the middle class. Bernstein drew particularly upon Durkheim to provide the underpinning conceptual framework, using ideas of social integration and solidarity which had informed his early work on the acquisition of codes.

Organic solidarity and middle-class socialization

Durkheim's theory of social cohesion involves two kinds of solidarity.[10] *Mechanical* solidarity arises within a relatively undifferentiated society with a uniform system of beliefs, in which similarities between people – in their life-styles, values and customs – are much greater than the differences. This type of solidarity, Durkheim remarks, is symbolized by the existence of penal law, in which punishment signifies the outrage of society at the transgression of fundamental norms. However, the term mechanical solidarity is not meant to imply that cohesion is maintained purely by repression or other artificial means; it is produced instead by a pervasive ideology in which the personality is submerged within the collective life:

> We call it [mechanical] only by analogy to the cohesion which unites the elements of an inanimate body, as opposed to that which makes a unity out of the elements of a living body ... In societies where this type of solidarity is highly developed, the individual does not appear ... Individuality is something which the society possesses.
>
> (Durkheim 1933, p. 130)

By contrast, *organic* solidarity arises in societies with a complex division of labour, in which difference is inevitable. In this case, cohesion is produced by the individual's recognition of their dependence on others and the need for co-operation. Whilst mechanical solidarity implies an acceptance of an indivisible social order, organic solidarity must be capable of binding together a society with diverse and conflicting interests. Durkheim suggests that this kind of solidarity is symbolized by restitutive law and the idea of the legally binding contract. Rather than the harmony through uniformity characterizing mechanical solidarity, it involves a permanent tension between individualism and interdependence.

Actual societies are not purely of one type or the other, and features of mechanical solidarity, for example, may be found even in societies with a sophisticated division of labour. Both kinds of solidarity are prone to malfunction, and Durkheim presents a rather interesting discussion of the consequences of a 'forced' division of labour: what would now be called inequality of social opportunity. In such a case, 'only an imperfect and troubled solidarity is possible' (Durkheim 1933, p. 376). Although Durkheim did not see such malfunctions as inevitable, he regarded their amelioration as a necessary condition for organic solidarity. The aim is to create a society in which the division of labour arises 'spontaneously', as a consequence of the fit between individual abilities and social position. However, this can only be achieved if external conditions (for example, inequalities arising from the hereditary transmission of wealth) are equalized as far as possible. This requires that:

> no obstacle, of whatever nature, prevents them from occupying the place in the social framework which is compatible with their faculties. In short, labour is divided spontaneously only if society is constructed in such a way that social inequalities exactly express natural inequalities. But, for that, it is necessary that the latter be neither enhanced nor lowered by some external cause.
>
> (Durkheim 1933, p. 377)

Although Bernstein had used the distinction between mechanical and organic solidarity in other contexts (see Bernstein 1971a, p. 114; 1971b, p. 66), he develops it more fully in the essays 'Open schools – open society?' and 'Class and pedagogies: visible and invisible' (Bernstein 1977c).[11] In the first of these essays, the main focus for discussion is the impact on school structures of the shift from mechanical to organic solidarity. However, 'Class and pedagogies' broadens the discussion to consider the relationship between the social division of labour and the forms of reproduction of the middle class. Bernstein points out that Durkheim considers only one form of organic solidarity, in which the division of labour remains relatively rigid, with strong boundaries between roles and strong regulation of what these roles contain. This form, Bernstein argues, is associated with increasing complexity in the economic division of labour and is particularly appropriate for understanding the socialization and reproduction of the old middle class, which includes members of the 'entrepreneurial' professions, such as lawyers, privately practising doctors and accountants as well as those who own or control the means of production.[12] However, a second form of organic solidarity is possible, characterized by weak role boundaries and more flexibility in role content; Bernstein calls this a *personalized* form of organic solidarity as opposed to the *individualized* organic solidarity discussed by Durkheim. Whilst individualized solidarity is orientated towards distinctive but impersonal roles – for example, managing director or accountant – personalized solidarity is about people, emphasizing uniqueness and legitimizing privileged positions within the division of labour through personal qualities rather than *ex officio* authority.[13] Bernstein also notes that personalized forms of solidarity are associated with a change in the importance of mothers in middle-class social reproduction, from the delegation of caring and education to other women, to active involvement in preparation for later life: 'The mother is transformed into a crucial preparing agent of cultural reproduction who provides access to symbolic forms and shapes the dispositions of her children so that they are better able to exploit the possibilities of public education' (Bernstein 1977b, p. 131). Although this particular passage might be read as a typical positioning of women-as-mothers in (male) sociology of education, Atkinson (1985, p. 161) suggests that Bernstein's interest in gender went deeper than this, being 'underpinned by a sense of the relationship between the gender order and the moral order'. Once again, this aspect of Bernstein's thought can be traced to Durkheim. In her introduction to *The Elementary Forms of Religious Life*, Karen Fields suggests that many of the 'grand oppositions' which Bernstein took from Durkheim – between sacred and profane, social and individual, person and individual – 'are latently an opposition between male and female' (Durkheim 1995 [1912], p. lix). A somewhat Durkheimian note on the cultural specificity of gender markings forms an appendix to Bernstein (1981).

Visible and invisible pedagogies

Bernstein suggests that a shift towards personalized organic solidarity has arisen from greater complexity in the division of labour of 'symbolic control' (Bernstein 1975, p. 121). In his introduction to the second edition of *Class, Codes and Control*, Volume 3, Bernstein (1977c, p. 18) notes the creation of 'a vast range of occupations dedicated to the symbolic shaping and re-shaping of the population' associated with industrialization. Symbolic control refers to the creation and distribution of forms of consciousness, identity and desire, forms which are adapted to and internalize one's place within the system of social relations (Bernstein 2000, p. 201). It is realized through agencies such as health, the media, religion and the law, which specialize in what Bernstein (1990b, p. 134) calls discursive codes, and whose agents dominate discursive resources in a similar way to that in which the ruling class controls material resources related to production (see also Singh 2017).[14] Bernstein claims that these distinct interests should produce ideological differences between different fractions of the middle class:

> Our expectation is that similar occupational functions, whether economic or symbolic, may well produce different interests, different dispositions, different motivations and different ideologies, depending on the field economic, symbolic or cultural in which the function is enacted.
>
> (Bernstein 2001, p. 25)

The development of ideological agencies has provided the conditions for an expansion of middle-class employment in areas such as teaching, the media and social services. Because the social reproduction of this new middle class is less predictable, it depends on keeping open a wide range of options for employment, particularly in newer professions and service industries. These different needs have given rise to an ideological struggle within schooling, as the new middle class have sought to institute practices in education which are more appropriate to the exploitation of changing opportunities in the field of symbolic control. Bernstein characterizes this conflict in terms of two different pedagogic modes: *visible* and *invisible* pedagogies. A visible pedagogy is one in which strong classification between academic categories is maintained through strong framing, in which rules of hierarchy, sequencing and evaluation are made explicit. The focus of attention is upon curriculum content and the student's *performance* in relation to this content, not on the personal development of the student. Visible pedagogies are realizations of a traditional, academic ideology of education whose focus lies in the creation of specialized identities and skills: in the early years, the reader, the writer, the artist; and in later years, the biologist, the mathematician, the classicist.

Invisible pedagogies are those in which regulative and discursive rules (from the perspective of the student) are implicit: the focus is on the student and their uniqueness rather than on curriculum content. Evaluation is less concerned with producing a stratification of the student body against external performance criteria than with facilitating the realization of shared *competences* in ways appropriate to each individual student: 'Differences revealed by an invisible pedagogy are not to be used as a basis for comparison *between* acquirers, for differences reveal *uniqueness*' (Bernstein 1990d, p. 71, original emphasis). Invisible pedagogies correspond to the realization of weak classification between academic categories and weak framing of acquisition. They are associated with particular contradictions and tensions for mothers attempting to reconcile control over cultural reproduction with other aspects of their identity: 'The weak classification and framing of child-rearing firmly anchor her to her child ... For such a mother, interaction and surveillance are totally demanding' (Bernstein 1977b, p. 132). In the early years, play is seen as an essential part of learning: play is work and work is play. Bernstein points out that this theory of learning reveals the class basis of invisible pedagogy, distinguishing between the strong classification between work and play in the condition of the working class and the relative permeability between the two characteristics of the more privileged sections of the middle class. He argues that invisible pedagogies are particularly associated with the new middle class, who prefer educational approaches encouraging uniqueness and the development of abilities related to inter- and intrapersonal control. Bernstein argues that these selections are legitimized by theories of progressive schooling which ostensibly apply to all children but in fact disguise the class interests and ideology underlying them:

> From one point of view this is the origin of the 'spontaneous' child apparently putting it together in his own way. From another point of view, such a form of initial socialization enables parents to screen the child's possibilities so that they ... can take advantage of the diversification of the occupational structure of symbolic control.
>
> (Bernstein 1975, p. 19)

The new middle class is what Bernstein calls an 'interrupter system', engaged in an ideological struggle with existing social arrangements, and in particular against the dominant forms of reproduction of the old middle class. However, their aim is not to change class relations, but to secure the advantages of these relations in relatively precarious conditions. Invisible pedagogies challenge the *form* of social reproduction rather than its substance (Bernstein 1975, p. 121). However romantically it is presented, the struggle for progressive education is not one between the working class and its oppressors: rather, it is between two fractions of the middle class.

A difficulty with these arguments is that whilst more personalized approaches to education have become established within the educational system, this has been most marked in provision for younger children and in low-status education or training for older, low-achieving children. At some point, families from the new middle class must also seek the privileged knowledge embodied in the traditional curricula and teaching methods still prevalent in the higher reaches of education. Bernstein resolves this difficulty by proposing that the new middle class is caught in a contradiction between a progressive ideology and their objective class position. Although initially they need to maintain diverse routes of opportunity for their children, at some point specialization is necessary if a middle-class occupation is to be achieved:

> A deep-rooted ambivalence is the ambience of this group. On the one hand, they stand for variety against inflexibility, expression against repression, the inter-personal against the inter-positional; on the other hand, there is the grim obduracy of the division of labour and of the narrow pathways to its positions of power and prestige.
>
> (Bernstein 1975, p. 123)

It is therefore to be expected that the new middle class will apply contradictory pressures depending on the age of their children: towards invisible pedagogies in the earlier years, and towards visible pedagogies in secondary education. The balance of these pressures will depend on the selection criteria prevalent at specific educational levels: the earlier the shift to visible pedagogy occurs, the more these contradictions will be evident – for example in preparing for the transition to upper-secondary academic tracks or even in selection for private or grammar school education. Indeed, Ivinson (2018, p. 546) suggests that these tensions may work to the detriment of the middle-class child, asking 'What happens if middle-class interactions codify and regulate what can be thought and done, to the extent that spontaneous imaginative flights of fantasy have less opportunity to take off?'

Radical visible pedagogy

A constant theme in Bernstein's work was that his conceptual framework went beyond descriptions or explanations of social reproduction: it opened the way to imagining new forms of pedagogy that could provide routes to high-status knowledge for working-class children. Bernstein emphasized that elaborated codes need not be a middle-class preserve: 'they are not necessarily instruments for the alienation of the working class; neither does it follow that they function as repeaters of a particular class structure' (Bernstein 1971a, p. 187). What matters is the way that elaborated codes are institutionalized in formal education, in the classification and framing values through which they are realized. He later observed that the transmission of social order contains 'tacit principles for the disordering of that order' (Bernstein 1990a, p. 3). The application of this observation to pedagogy is expressed in detail in the paper 'Social class and pedagogic practice' (Bernstein 1990d). Revisiting his distinction between visible and invisible pedagogies, Bernstein notes that in the former, what the student has to do, what they are required to produce and the criteria for evaluating their performance are all clearly visible to both student and teacher. In an invisible pedagogy, the rules are implicit, known only to the teacher. Both types of pedagogy correspond to preferred forms of socialization of middle-class children, in relation to which children from working-class backgrounds are disadvantaged in a number of ways, both materially and discursively.[15] However, Bernstein did not regard the possibilities of visible and invisible pedagogy as being exhausted by these predominantly middle-class realizations: he believed that in place of their emphasis on the competitive development of individuals, the pedagogic focus might be shifted to the development of social groups. By including variation with respect to the focus of change, four modalities of pedagogic practice can be produced, as illustrated in Figure 7.1. The horizontal dimension of this figure corresponds to an emphasis towards visible performance or underlying competence as the focus of evaluation, whilst the vertical dimension refers to an intra-individual or between-group focus of change.

Bernstein notes that pedagogies in which the focus is on the individual are commonly referred to as either 'progressive' or 'conservative' and correspond to existing modes of pedagogic practice. Those which focus on effecting changes between social groups he regards as radical realizations of either conservative

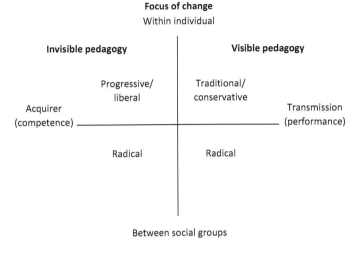

FIGURE 7.1   Modalities of visible and invisible pedagogies.
Source: Adapted from Bernstein (1990d, p. 72).

or liberal-progressive practice, with the lower-left quadrant corresponding to 'critical' pedagogies. However, the lower-right quadrant is an apparently paradoxical, radical realization of a conservative pedagogy – what Bernstein calls a radical visible pedagogy. The paradox is only apparent, as there is no intrinsic reason why a visible pedagogy should disadvantage working-class students:

> It is certainly possible to create a visible pedagogy that would weaken the relation between social class and educational achievement. This may well require a supportive pre-school structure, a relaxing of the framing on pacing and sequencing rules, and a weakening of the framing regulating the flow of communication between the school classroom and the community(ies) the school draws upon.
>
> (Bernstein 1990d, p. 79)

The result is a mixed pedagogy, retaining strong classification and framing in terms of content and evaluation but weakened framing in relation to how learning will occur. These arguments have been developed, both empirically and theoretically, by a number of later authors (see Bourne 2004; Morais and Neves 2018). These authors grapple with the problems of achieving a *local* realization of a radical visible pedagogy, that is, one which can operate within existing capitalist societies and their dominant forms of schooling. For example, Bourne (2004) proposes that the weakening of framing regulating external communication can result in a variety of forms of local, working-class discourse being introduced into the school, in what she terms 'the managed introduction of horizontal discourse' (p. 66). Morais (2002) suggests that weak framing of pacing has generally been unacceptable politically because of its implications for the cost of education. However, she argues that strategies such as interdisciplinary learning and improved teacher training can allow teachers to achieve a more relaxed pacing. Crucially, weak pacing also allows a more thorough explication of evaluation criteria – a cornerstone of the idea of radical visible pedagogy. Morais and Neves (2018, p. 278) emphasize the importance of maintaining the integrity of vertical discourse if a school for all students is to be created, and this implies not only clarity with regard to evaluation but also strong classifications between disciplinary and everyday knowledge: 'To take into account students' social differences does not mean limiting the disadvantaged to knowledge of a lower conceptual level, but using their cultural experiences ... to lead them to acquire the powerful knowledge'. This argument perhaps neglects Bourdieu's distinction between the changing substantial content of education and its relational stability. Nevertheless, a commitment to enriching the education of working-class children is characteristic of much contemporary work in the Bernsteinian tradition.

Notes

1 In relation to the 1981 paper, Bernstein (1990a, p. 4) notes, 'I have always been attracted to Althusser's theory of ideology ... and this was made the basis of the relation between classification, voice and the construction of the subject'.
2 Moore (2013, p. 66) suggests that 'elaborating code', in the sense of unpacking or explicating, is a more helpful term which avoids connotations of verbosity or over-complication.
3 See Nash (2006) for a critique of this reading. Nash suggests that coding orientation is a relatively superficial issue and that socially generated differences in cognitive processing are also important. However, code implies the ability to work within a context as well as to recognize it.
4 Other authors have introduced the concept of class-differentiated gender codes both within and outside education (see Arnot 2002).
5 Bernstein regarded different curriculum and pedagogical structures as corresponding to variations in the strength of classification and framing respectively, whilst evaluation is a function of both classification and framing (Bernstein 1971b, p. 50).
6 Bernstein is here alluding to category in a Durkheimian sense: not just to aspects of education and other institutions as particular spheres of activity, but as fundamental to the organization and ideological construction of society.
7 This does not imply a pairing of vertical discourse with elaborated code. Whilst Bernstein's analysis of discourse is about forms of knowledge, pedagogic codes are concerned with how such knowledge is made available through pedagogic communication.
8 This definition was later slightly modified to include inequalities in the principles of control between social groups. See Bernstein (1981, p. 327).
9 Bernstein cites the case of China during its Cultural Revolution as an example of weak classification between education and production.
10 In his later work, Durkheim moved away from this dualistic conceptualization of solidarity to re-emphasize the importance of collective consciousness and action. See Thijssen (2012).

11 In Bernstein (1977c), the second of these essays appears in a form considerably extended from the original version which appeared in 1973.

12 Moore (2013, pp. 167–168) rightly points out that in his discussions of the old middle class, Bernstein locates their base in the economy and does not mention the traditional 'liberal' professions. However, Bernstein's association of the new middle class with the growth of public sector agencies of symbolic control suggests including *some* traditional professionals in the old middle class.

13 Durkheim writes of 'personal' and 'individual' as follows: 'it is far from true that the more individualized we are, the more personal we are. The two terms are by no means synonymous. In a sense, they oppose more than they imply one another' (Durkheim 1995 [1912], p. 274).

14 As Bernstein (2001) points out, 'new' middle class professions with roles directly related to production also exist (for example, psychologists, personnel officers and market researchers). He also distinguishes between people in similar occupations but located in the fields of cultural production and symbolic control respectively. However, the focus here is on those who are employed in the field of symbolic control.

15 See the sections dealing with the social class assumptions of visible and invisible pedagogies in Bernstein (1990d).

8

RATIONAL ACTION
Modelling educational choice

This chapter discusses the conceptual and empirical basis of rational action theories of educational decision making. The fundamental assumption of these theories is that young people's decisions must be understood in terms of their location within objective social structures. When averaged over large groups of individuals in similar situations, these decisions produce and reproduce structural patterns of inequality without requiring systematic class differences in the *principles* underlying them. Although class-based differences in educational performance are an important part of rational action theories, they are not the most important factor influencing attainment. More significant is the cumulative impact of the decisions made over an educational career, which progressively marginalizes disadvantaged young people or excludes them from education completely. The chapter begins by introducing the important distinction between inequalities in performance and choice, referred to by Raymond Boudon as the primary and secondary effects of social stratification. The main features of rational action theory in education are then outlined, particularly in relation to its formulation by Boudon (1974) and by Breen and Goldthorpe (1997). The chapter then discusses more recent developments, including attempts to test rational action theory empirically, and highlights some of the aspects confirmed – or otherwise – by these analyses. The chapter concludes with a discussion of the role of class in rational action theories of educational decisions.

Primary and secondary effects of social stratification

The distinction between primary and secondary effects originated in studies from the 1950s and 1960s showing that differences in academic performance could not fully explain class inequalities in the transition to secondary education (Jackson 2013). However, Raymond Boudon (1974) was the first to provide a systematic sociological explanation of educational inequality in terms of this distinction.[1] He begins by observing that, after a certain period of schooling, the distribution of academic performance differs according to social background, with those from more advantaged families having – on average – a higher level of performance. These social background differences in the distribution of academic performance are referred to as the *primary effects* of social stratification. Inviting comparison with Pierre Bourdieu's cultural re-production, Boudon (1974, p. 28) regards primary effects as being mediated by 'cultural inequalities', differences in family cultural endowments, attitudes and interests. However, his central argument is that the effects of social background go further than this. Boudon proposes that two children with similar academic performance at a given time, but from different social classes, will have different probabilities of remaining in education thereafter, or of pursuing an academic rather than a vocational route. The *secondary effects* of social background refer to this kind of difference, and represent the effects of social background on educational attainment over and above differences in performance. They may be regarded as the effects of different educational choices made by children with similar educational performance but from different class backgrounds. However, terms such as 'choice' should not be taken as implying unconstrained decisions. Secondary effects stem from a range of influences on educational transitions, deriving not only from individual preferences but also from social position, economic and cultural resources, and local opportunity structures (Thompson and Simmons 2013).

Unlike Bourdieu, for whom inequalities in attainment result from a unitary process which conditions a person's whole experience of education, Boudon regards the processes responsible for primary and secondary effects as being essentially different in nature. The decisions generating secondary effects are not caused by cultural differences between classes: instead, they arise from differences in objective conditions: 'it is assumed (1) that people behave rationally in the economic sense … but that (2) they also behave within decision fields whose parameters are a function of their position in the stratification system' (Boudon 1974, p. 36). The importance of secondary effects is that they accumulate across a series of educational transitions, whilst primary effects become less significant by comparison. At each level, children from less advantaged backgrounds, particularly those with low attainment, are more likely to drop out or be diverted from higher-status routes than more advantaged children with similar academic performance. Conversely, low-attaining students from higher social classes tend to ignore poor grades and simply move on to the next level of education (Bernardi and Triventi 2018). Amongst lower social classes, only higher-attaining children are likely to survive through successive transitions, an effect which tends to equalize the performance distributions in the later years of schooling.[2] It follows that education reform which seeks to address only performance inequalities rather than educational decisions is looking in the wrong place. However, this is not just a question of 'aspiration': the parameters for decisions are provided not only by individuals but also by their interactions with stratified educational systems, the economy and social structures.

Estimating secondary effects

Although it has sometimes been neglected by the sociology of education, the distinction between primary and secondary effects has been extensively investigated and critiqued over many years. Halsey, Heath and Ridge (1980, p. 134) noted its potential for understanding inequality of educational opportunity (IEO), although they concluded that primary effects appeared to have the greatest significance. Since then, a number of methods have been developed to produce quantitative estimates of the relative importance of primary and secondary effects. The most prevalent of these draws on so-called 'counterfactual' reasoning, in which observed data on educational decisions is used to construct class-specific distributions of (a) academic performance and (b) transition probabilities conditional on performance. These distributions are then interchanged to produce artificial transition probabilities combining the performance and choice characteristics of paired social classes. Because secondary effects assume that the relationship between academic performance and educational decisions varies with social background, the difference between the counterfactual and observed proportions is attributed to these effects. The method has been applied by several authors, including Erikson et al. (2005), Jackson et al. (2007) and Jackson (2013), and suggests that in some countries secondary effects are a significant factor in generating IEO at later transitions. Whilst in England secondary effects at the transition to A-level account for less than one-fifth of the log odds ratio between 'salariat' and 'working' class, this proportion rises to nearly two-fifths at the transition to a university degree course; in Italy and the Netherlands, over 90 per cent of the log odds ratio for the latter transition is attributed to secondary effects (Jackson and Jonsson 2013, p. 321). Applying a different decomposition method to transitions to tertiary education in Germany, Schindler and Lörz (2012, p. 657) also find that 'generally secondary effects play a much larger role than primary effects', and that over time secondary effects have increased in importance at this transition.

Combining these findings with the trends discussed in Chapter 3 leads to three conclusions about change in IEO which may appear difficult to reconcile. These are (1) the association between educational attainment and social origins declines between lower and higher transitions; (2) comparing different birth cohorts, equalization has occurred, mainly at lower transitions; and (3) in some countries at least, the importance of secondary effects relative to primary effects increases over successive transitions. Figure 8.1 illustrates how these three

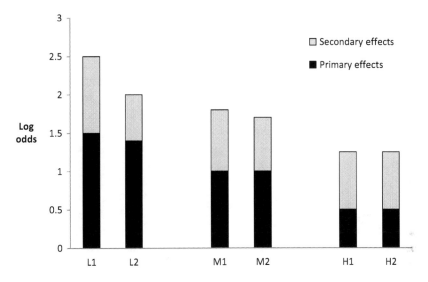

FIGURE 8.1 Contributions of primary and secondary effects over three transitions (*L*, *M*, *H*) for earlier and later cohorts.

conclusions are in fact compatible with one another. For two different (fictitious) cohorts, log odds at three transitions – lower, middle and higher – are shown. For both cohorts, total IEO reduces over the three transitions. At the lower transition, primary effects dominate and IEO is largest; however, IEO declines between the cohorts, mainly because of reduced secondary effects. For the higher transition, secondary effects dominate for both cohorts and there is no change in IEO between cohorts.

Critiques of primary and secondary effects

Although it is generally agreed that the distinction between primary and secondary effects is an important methodological contribution, Boudon's analysis is problematic in a number of ways. Primary effects can be difficult to define precisely: do they refer to attainment at the point when a decision is made, or to some earlier time – perhaps even to performance in the early years of schooling? The counterfactual estimations discussed earlier are based on performance which is contemporaneous with the relevant decision. By contrast, Nash (2006) equates primary effects with cognitive performance at age ten, concluding that these effects provide the dominant contribution to IEO. Although Nash's approach seems tangential to the definition of secondary effects given earlier (Jackson et al. 2007, p. 226), it is certainly the case that different understandings of primary and secondary effects can lead to quite varied conclusions. For example, the work of Jerrim and Vignoles (2015) on university entry in four English-speaking countries can be interpreted as suggesting that, if primary effects are taken to be differences in attainment at age 15, secondary effects are significant, whilst the opposite is true if attainment at age 18 is used. The most reasonable approach is surely to use contemporaneous performance.

The distinction between primary and secondary effects assumes a causal model in which the relationships between class, prior performance and attainment are not compromised by unobserved variables. This model may be represented by the diagram in Figure 8.2 (*a*), in which social class is represented by the node C, prior academic performance by P and educational attainment by A. Social class affects attainment in two ways: indirectly, by influencing performance, which, in turn, affects the level of attainment reached; and directly, through decision-making processes which lead to class-differentiated choices for individuals with the same academic performance. However, unobserved intervening variables may lead to incorrect estimates of secondary effects. Erikson et al. (2005) point out that class differences in *anticipatory decisions*, where students decide some time in advance not to prolong their educational careers and reduce their efforts accordingly, may reduce estimates of secondary effects. This is because lower performance resulting from anticipatory decisions would appear as a primary effect, even though it arose from class differences in educational choices (see Figure 8.2 (*b*)). Taking anticipatory decisions into account may increase estimates of secondary effects significantly (Jackson et al. 2007). More general criticisms have also been made concerning the causal separation of primary and secondary effects (Nash 2005, 2006b). Morgan (2012) argues that complex causal interactions may lead to secondary effects being overestimated, and identifies a particular danger in that exogenous variables such as race could affect class, performance and transition probabilities simultaneously, compromising the assumed causal pathways in Figure 8.2. However, Jackson (2013) distinguishes between the formal separation of primary and secondary effects in the counterfactual approach outlined earlier, and the causal interpretation of these effects in terms of performance and choice. She argues

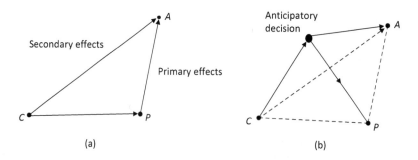

FIGURE 8.2 Causal relationships implicit in models of primary and secondary effects (adapted from Erikson et al. 2005).

that the explanation of primary and secondary effects in these causal terms is then a separate enterprise, which may well involve additional variables but does not invalidate the initial distinction.

Rational action theories and educational decision making

Rational action theories assume that social phenomena are the macro-level result of individual decisions and actions which can be understood as rational. Crucially, rationality needs to be understood from the perspective of the person making a decision:

> Educational sociologists ... often imagine that children from the under-privileged classes have limited educational aspirations as a result of an ('irrational') fidelity to a subculture or a class ethos. But such behaviour is irrational only in terms of the *observer's* situation, when it is obvious that 'rationality' or 'irrationality' can only be determined in relation to the *actor's* behaviour.
>
> (Boudon 1991, p. 50)

People are held to evaluate (explicitly or tacitly) the costs and benefits associated with possible strategies, selecting the one which is most favourable in relation to their goals and preferences (Boudon 2003, pp. 3–4). Boudon's approach is based on methodological individualism, the assumption that social phenomena are 'the statistical imprint of the juxtaposition of a host of individual acts ... [by] individuals who are socially *situated*' (Boudon 1989, p. 6). Subjectively meaningful behaviour is taken to exist only at the level of the individual, ruling out any form of 'class consciousness', whilst statistical regularities are assumed to result from the aggregation of individual behaviour over large numbers of people rather than from collective or coordinated behaviour. The rational action perspective has a long history in sociology, and conditions for its viability were expressed by Max Weber in his discussion of *comprehensibility*. According to Weber (1978 [1922], pp. 12–13), a theory of rational action must combine meaningfulness with objectivity: regularities such as patterns of educational inequality, or demonstrations that certain actions are subjectively meaningful, are not sufficient in themselves. Both aspects must be present if such a theory is to be acceptable.

Rational action theories are often criticized for adopting a purely economic model of human behaviour and failing to acknowledge the diversity of individual motivations. Hatcher (1998, p. 20) argues that 'real-life choices ... cannot be reduced to utilitarian calculations of costs, benefits and probabilities'. However, rationality is interpreted more broadly by some theorists, who relate aims and preferences to factors including identity and social values as well as utilitarian considerations: 'to get a satisfactory theory of rationality, one has to accept the idea that rationality is not exclusively instrumental' (Boudon 2003, p. 17). Nor does rationality imply that actors are perfectly knowledgeable about their situation or always act in accordance with objective circumstances. Goldthorpe (1996) acknowledges that departures from 'perfect' rationality are frequent: people may be unclear about their goals, or the best way of achieving them, and even when they identify a rational course of action they may not pursue it. Nevertheless, rational action theories find it difficult to escape a reductionist view of human behaviour, and as Gambetta (1987) points out, they tend not to conceptualize how preferences are formed, concentrating on choices between alternatives rather than resistance to what is available or the degree of satisfaction with the choices made.

The models proposed by Boudon (1974) and by Breen and Goldthorpe (1997) are attempts to understand IEO within educational systems as a whole, not theories of individual action. They do not claim to represent complex patterns of variation, dealing instead with average effects over a population: 'We ... assume that, *in their central tendencies*, these patterns of educational choice reflect action on the part of children and their parents that can be understood as rational' (Breen and Goldthorpe 1997, p. 277, original emphasis). This assumption is combined with an explanation of educational decisions in which structural location is the main source of classed patterns of behaviour. Social classes are assumed to differ in only two substantive ways: through the primary effects of social stratification, which affect average academic ability and therefore the chances of succeeding at a particular educational level; and through the resources they can draw on to offset the costs and risks of their decisions. Although members of different social classes think in essentially similar ways about educational decisions, the substantive differences in their situation lead to different subjective evaluations of risks, costs and benefits. It is these differences that give rise to secondary effects. Cultural as well as economic resources may be relevant, for example a family's strategic knowledge about the educational system and their ability to help with their children's schooling (Erikson and Jonsson 1996b). The educational system is represented by a sequence of transition points where students choose between alternative pathways. These alternatives include remaining in education or leaving altogether, but more complex models involve a differentiated curriculum, with different risks and rewards (Erikson and Jonsson 1996b; Tutic 2017). The significant factors in making a decision are assumed to be the cost of remaining in education, including opportunity costs such as lost earnings; the potential benefits of the decision, as evaluated by the individual and their family; and the (subjective) chances of success conditional on a particular decision. Whilst Breen and Goldthorpe (1997) include only economic costs in their model, Boudon (1974) argues that social costs must also be included, arising from the effect of educational decisions on family solidarity or peer group relationships.

Breen and Goldthorpe (1997) suggest three possible mechanisms that may generate secondary effects. First, differences in economic resources are likely to place a relatively heavier burden on working-class families whose children remain in education – even when costs are limited to foregone earnings. The social costs proposed by Boudon would reinforce this tendency in systems where higher levels of education are socially selective. Second, objective differences in educational performance arising from primary effects will lead to class differences in the subjective probability of success at higher levels of education. It is also possible that working-class children may require a higher subjective probability of success to continue in education, because of *over-adaptive* responses to objective conditions (Gambetta 1987). Third, and most crucially, in a society which is at least broadly meritocratic, families from higher social classes need more education to maintain their social position. The term *relative risk aversion* (also referred to as *class maintenance*) is used to describe a class-independent desire to avoid downward mobility (Breen and Goldthorpe 1997). This desire directly affects educational decisions: whilst a middle-class child choosing a non-academic route would be likely to experience social demotion, a working-class child has no such imperative to pursue a high-status track. Although the increasing importance of service sector and so-called 'knowledge-based' employment might induce children from working-class backgrounds to obtain more education than previous generations, this would not be to the same extent as those aiming to enter the higher professions. For working-class children, mid-range mobility may be seen as less risky whilst still providing significant, if more modest, rewards.

These assumptions can be expressed in a formal mathematical model which reproduces the patterns observed in conditions of maximally maintained inequality (Breen and Goldthorpe 1997). Expansion is assumed to occur because of shifts in the balance between costs, risks and benefits at a certain level of education. For example, it may happen that lower levels of education become saturated, more places are made available, or costs diminish, perhaps because fees are reduced or opportunity costs decrease due to high levels of youth unemployment. Initially, participation will expand as continuing in education becomes more attractive. However, largely driven by class maintenance, the model predicts greater uptake amongst higher social classes, so that IEO as measured by odds ratios remains unchanged. Once costs have fallen sufficiently to enable all children from higher social classes to continue in education if they so wish – the saturation condition – further reductions will have little impact on these classes, and odds ratios will decrease as participation by lower social classes continues to increase. Unlike the empirical work on MMI discussed earlier, the Breen-Goldthorpe model therefore includes a *theoretical* criterion for saturation. Effectively maintained inequality may also be explained, provided that qualitative differences within an educational level entail different cost burdens, subjective probabilities of success, or probabilities of access to higher social class positions. Moreover, between-country variations may also be explained through differences in the class distribution of resources and the balance between costs and benefits.

The Breen-Goldthorpe model also claims to account for the decline in gender-based differentials which has occurred in virtually all Western nations. Because formerly the returns to education for women were structured differently to men, with flatter gradients in pay and alternative routes to social mobility, the proportion of women remaining in education at each transition point would be expected to be smaller than for men, as would class differentials in educational attainment between women. More recently, the pattern of returns to education for women has changed as labour-market participation rates, especially for married women, have increased and as the financial contribution of a woman's own employment has acquired greater significance to her family. In the Breen-Goldthorpe model, therefore, gender differentials in education should decrease. Class differences amongst women should increase, or at least diminish less, unless other factors intervene. This argument is partly, although not wholly, supported by empirical evidence. Gender differentials in educational attainment have declined, but across countries there appears to be no pattern of higher or lower class differences between men and women, and amongst women class differentials have decreased over time in the same way as men (Breen et al. 2010). Applying the Breen-Goldthorpe explanation of changing gender differentials to the case of Germany, Becker (2014) concludes that the primary effects of gender – in which women now outperform men – cannot entirely explain the long-term emergence of a 'new' gender gap. Like Breen and Goldthorpe (1997), Becker suggests that changing labour-market structures and rewards have driven changes in secondary effects, although horizontal stratification involving feminized and relatively low-paid occupations has been less affected by these changes than access to higher levels of education.

Empirical assessment of the Breen-Goldthorpe model

The motivation for Boudon's model of IEO was the question of why educational inequality had fallen after the Second World War, whilst relative social mobility showed little change. Following the publication of *Persistent Inequality* (Shavit and Blossfeld 1993), the problem shifted to the *stability* of class differentials in education, and it was to confront this issue that the Breen-Goldthorpe model was developed (Goldthorpe 1996). More recently, evidence has again accumulated of a decline in IEO (Breen et al. 2009; Barone and Ruggera 2018). The problematic addressed by rational action theories has therefore been somewhat fluid: it is now best conceptualized in terms of accounting for observed patterns of change in IEO rather than any pre-determined outcome. In this respect, qualified support has emerged from a range of studies, based on two characteristic strategies for assessing the validity of rational action theories (Jaeger

2007; Kroneberg and Kalter 2012). The first involves direct measurement of the subjective preferences motivating individual behaviour. Hypotheses involving these preferences, for example relative risk aversion, are then tested. Because of the practicalities of gathering the relevant data, which has tended to rely on Likert-type statements in survey research (see Tutic 2017 for a summary), this approach has been criticized for abstracting decision-making processes from real-life contexts and their objective conditions (Goldthorpe 1998). The second strategy tests theory indirectly by using it to make behavioural predictions relating to more easily observed data, for example the actual educational choices made by students or observed patterns of inequality in educational attainment (Breen and Yaish 2006). The main difficulty with this approach is theoretical ambiguity – it is difficult to construct hypotheses from rational action theory that rule out competing theories. Although one may be able to conclude that rational action theory is consistent with the data, it is more difficult to assess whether its underlying mechanisms are valid.

Relative risk aversion has generally been presented as the key feature of the Breen-Goldthorpe model (Breen and Goldthorpe 1997, p. 293), and the hypothesis has been tested numerous times across different countries and contexts, although the resulting picture is quite complex. Van de Werfhorst and Hofstede (2007) found near-constancy of class maintenance motivations across social classes, as required by the Breen-Goldthorpe model. Other authors have found that parents from lower social classes attach *greater* importance to avoiding downward mobility than do parents in service class positions (Stocké 2007; Gabay-Egozi 2010; Obermeier and Schneider 2015). Whilst concluding that the great majority of young people act in accordance with relative risk aversion, Jaeger and Holm (2012) find some individual-level heterogeneity in the desire to avoid downward mobility. However, uniformity of class maintenance motivations is not as critical to the Breen-Goldthorpe model as once thought, and Tutic (2017) has shown that it is possible to relax this assumption without seriously affecting the model's predictions. Given the origins of the Breen-Goldthorpe model in methodological individualism, it is perhaps most satisfying to relate relative risk aversion to individual dispositions. Using this approach, Breen et al. (2014) have used data on individual risk aversion to investigate class-based variations in educational decisions. As required by the relative risk aversion hypothesis, they find that an individual preference for avoiding risk did not reduce the probability of choosing the academic route for the most privileged students, whereas such a relationship did exist for students from disadvantaged and middle socio-economic backgrounds.

Other features of the Breen-Goldthorpe model have also been tested. Consistent with its assumptions, class differences in the subjective evaluation of costs and success probabilities are reported by Stocké (2007), Becker and Hecken (2009) and Gabay-Egozi et al. (2010). Hansen (2008) reports a significant impact of parental economic resources on educational attainment, after controlling for parental education and other independent variables. However, studies differ in their evaluation of the Breen-Goldthorpe model as a complete explanation for social class differences in educational attainment (Stocké 2007; Becker and Hecken 2009; Jaeger and Holm 2012). It appears that the model can explain part, but not all, of the social class gradient in educational outcomes, and even at the level of secondary effects rational action does not entirely account for class differences (Stocké 2007). Although an impressive body of evidence has been accumulated in favour of the Breen-Goldthorpe model, it is by no means conclusive.

Class and rational action theory

The explanations of educational inequality discussed earlier in this book are regularly subject to criticisms which focus on their alleged determinism and tendency to essentialize working-class deficiency. Rational action theories, which emphasize that class differences in educational attainment arise from socially situated decisions, offer several advantages over more culturally based approaches. Unlike conceptualizations of young people and their families in terms of relatively permanent systems of disposition, rational action theories understand differences in behaviour as rational responses to differences in economic, cultural and social resources. They also suggest that reformist political action may achieve some reduction in IEO, by changing the parameters of decision fields associated with educational attainment. For example, Neugebauer and Schindler (2012) suggest that in the highly stratified German education system, increased participation rates for working-class students in higher education could be achieved by counteracting secondary effects at the transition to upper-secondary education. However, the theoretical basis of rational action theories is somewhat opaque, and whilst most of its assumptions are plausible some elements, notably relative risk aversion, have an alarmingly *ad hoc* appearance. Nor is it entirely clear what theoretical work is done by class, and to what extent other dimensions of stratification, such as income or parental education, may generate the required patterns of educational inequality. It is therefore of interest to explore these questions in more detail, and in particular to discuss how class contributes to the workings of rational action theory (see Thompson 2018).

In some theorizations of inequality, for example Bourdieu's cultural reproduction, systematic differences are produced in the dispositions of families towards education. Breen et al. (2014) refer to this kind of effect as *socio-economic mediation*: inequalities arise indirectly from class processes which influence consciousness. By contrast, *socio-economic heterogeneity* refers to inequalities that are the direct result of how families are affected by their class position.[3] Such effects might arise in various ways, for example from inequalities in economic resources or from differences in status and treatment within education. Rational action theories employ both kinds of process but give a crucial status to socio-economic heterogeneity. As noted earlier, they conceive the generation of IEO as a two-stage process, in which primary effects arise at least partly from socio-economic mediation, whilst secondary effects are largely due to socio-economic heterogeneity. However, the precise causal links with class processes are less than clear. Boudon claimed that there was 'no satisfactory theory of stratification in industrial society' (Boudon 1974, p. 163) and was deliberately flexible in the way that he conceptualized social background. His model of IEO is largely independent of any specific class theory, and assumes only that class produces a roughly pyramidal stratification. Although Goldthorpe (1996) conceptualizes class explicitly in terms of the Erikson-Goldthorpe schema, in the Breen-Goldthorpe model its use is essentially to generate a hierarchy of status, economic rewards and early academic performance. This is not necessarily a defect of rational action theories, which in this sense demonstrate that an elaborated theory of stratification is not necessary to explain the observed patterns of IEO.

Whatever approach to stratification is used, it needs to explain how primary and secondary effects are produced, and therefore to account for systematic differences in performance and choice between different social strata. For Boudon, performance differences derive from what he calls cultural inequalities, based on the assumption that school achievement is a function of cultural background, which is presumed to be poorer amongst lower social classes. There is an obvious correspondence here with cultural reproduction theories, although Boudon (1974, p. 112) attempts to distinguish his conception of cultural inequalities from the 'critical sociology' represented by Bourdieu.[4] The differences in cultural opportunities which Boudon relies on to produce primary effects cannot be solely the result of inequalities in economic resources; they must also reflect other aspects of class relations. In Bourdieu's account, relational properties such as the distribution and trajectories of cultural capital are of course intrinsic to the concept of class. For Boudon and Goldthorpe, no such *direct* connection between class and cultural inequalities exists. Indeed, Goldthorpe (1996, p. 486) invokes only what he calls a 'minimal' conception of class, eschewing any cultural dimensions and essentially positing the existence of primary effects rather than explaining them in terms of class (see also Breen and Goldthorpe 1997). It is perhaps more appropriate to think of the Breen-Goldthorpe model as an explanation of secondary effects and their contribution to IEO, rather than a comprehensive account of how educational inequality is produced.

The rather cursory treatment of primary effects in the Breen-Goldthorpe model is explained by the contention that patterns of stability and change in IEO are produced largely by the impact of secondary effects. In the production of these effects, class acts structurally, providing a matrix of positions associated with different resources and opportunities. Although Boudon's explanation of primary effects is based on cultural differences, he does not adopt a 'poverty of aspiration' explanation for secondary effects. Rejecting the 'value' theory that working-class families have negative attitudes towards education, Boudon adopted a counterargument proposed by Keller and Zavalloni (1964): the problem is not that working-class families have lower levels of aspiration, but that they must traverse a greater social distance to reach higher educational levels. For a working-class child to reach university may require *greater* aspiration than for a middle-class child. The relative risk aversion hypothesis assumes equality of aspiration, in the sense that all classes strive to avoid downward mobility. This is certainly consistent with the structural explanation of Keller and Zavalloni; however, it offers little further insight into the underlying processes and motivations. Whilst it is certainly plausible that parents should wish their children to be no worse off than they are, it is not self-evident that this should be the limit of their ambitions, particularly if – as Goldthorpe (1996, p. 495) maintains – only the economic rather than the social implications of mobility should be considered. Motivations towards class maintenance rather than upward mobility could arise from social rather than economic factors, and the bonding rather than bridging effects of social capital (Green and White 2008) may be more consistent with the evidence on class variation in relative risk aversion discussed earlier.

Rather than excluding social costs and benefits, Jaeger (2007) suggests that students attempt to maximize *both* the social and economic returns to education. In this respect, the interaction between capital, habitus and field that Bourdieu would invoke seem to offer a more credible (if less parsimonious) explanation of relative risk aversion than the economic arguments deployed by Goldthorpe. Indeed, Bourdieu (1977a, p. 83) writes of the *hysteresis effects* in which the habitus is slow to change when confronted with a changed environment, so that new opportunities are missed rather than grasped. Social costs extend into education itself, and earlier chapters have indicated strategies of social closure and the conflicted habitus produced by educational mobility. Nor should rational choice be assumed to take place against a value-free background. The neo-liberal education reforms in recent decades are part of a dynamic ideological project which individualizes inequality and seeks to locate it in subjectivities rather than institutions. Educational systems reflect class interests, and the framework for decision making is constructed as much from struggles for distinction and control as from the objective consideration of learning and development. These considerations suggest that a deeper approach is needed in rational action theory than merely assuming a hierarchy of classes. Class relations involve struggles over processes of material and cultural production and consumption, and hypotheses such as relative risk aversion should be *derived from* such relations. This would enable rational action theories of education to provide the causal explanations required of class analysis by Breen and Rottmann (1995). The extent to which this may be possible, and the prospects for combining rational action theory and cultural reproduction, will be considered in the final chapter of this book.

Notes

1 The terminology of primary and secondary effects did not appear in the original French edition of *L'inégalité des Chances* (Boudon 1973).
2 Compare the discussion of 'unequal selectedness' in Chapter 6.
3 Gambetta (1987) makes a similar distinction, between cultural and economic causation.
4 Boudon also cites Bernstein's early work on linguistic forms.

9

EDUCATION AND SOCIAL MOBILITY

Social mobility has been a rhetorical centrepiece of government policy in the United Kingdom since the New Labour election victory of 1997. Its importance derived initially from the accommodation between neo-liberalism and social democracy that characterized Tony Blair's 'third way' politics, in which the inequalities associated with market economics were to be legitimized by a more open society. The emphasis on social mobility was therefore about equality of opportunity rather than equality of condition, and substituted a better life for one's children in place of greater equality in the present. Education was positioned as a key factor in achieving this goal, and the assumption that equalizing educational opportunity could help to increase social mobility became entrenched in government circles. This assumption persisted through the recession and into the Coalition and Conservative governments that followed, sustained by debates over whether social mobility had 'stalled' or even gone into reverse (HM Government 2011; Goldthorpe 2013). However, it has been known for many years that educational and social mobility are not automatically linked. As Raymond Boudon (1974, p. xii) notes in the preface to *Education, Opportunity and Social Inequality*, inequality of social opportunity (ISO) and inequality of educational opportunity (IEO) may change in quite different and counter-intuitive ways:

> Most people would probably take for granted that a reduction in IEO should result in a decrease of ISO … However, empirical data show that all Western industrial societies have been characterized since the end of World War II both by a steady decrease in IEO and by an almost complete stability of ISO. Why is that so?

Although liberal-industrial theory predicts that educational attainment will increase in importance as a factor in social achievement, there is still no clear evidence that such a trend exists. On the contrary, some studies have found that the association between individuals' educational attainment and their class destinations has, if anything, tended to weaken (Breen and Luijkx 2004; Bukodi and Goldthorpe 2011). Moreover, the context of social mobility in recent decades has been complicated by factors such as globalization, neo-liberalism and educational expansion. Whilst people with low levels of educational attainment are likely to be disadvantaged in the labour market, other trends are evident, including a growing unpredictability in the transition from education to employment (Bukodi and Goldthorpe 2011). Nevertheless, in modern political discourse Boudon's distinction has often become blurred – or even lost sight of completely – for a number of reasons. First, it is difficult for government policy to affect social mobility directly, and attention is therefore drawn to specific factors with which it is known to be associated – notably education but also family income, employment conditions and welfare policy. Second, there is of necessity a considerable time lag between the implementation of a policy and the emergence of evidence for its effect on social mobility. In the case of policies on preschool education or child poverty, it may be 30 years or more before any confident statements can be made about their impact. By contrast, educational or social policy may produce change on a much shorter timescale in variables which can plausibly be argued as relevant to social mobility.

It is not legitimate simply to equate social mobility with educational mobility: achieving a higher educational standing than one's parents is not in itself evidence that one has 'gone up in the world'. Although factors such as educational attainment are powerful influences on *individual* social mobility, on a societal level it is the interaction between the distribution of educational attainment and the availability of higher social positions that determines whether education can affect rates of *group* mobility. Educational expansion may reduce inequalities in attainment to some extent, but in the relative terms that mainly influence an individual's mobility chances its impact may be negligible (Bukodi and Goldthorpe 2016). Where direct evidence exists of an association between educational expansion and social mobility, it has been shown that social policy more generally is a critical factor, and that expansion acting in isolation may have little effect (Breen 2010; Sturgis and Buscha 2015). In fact, social mobility is affected by a range of variables, including the degree of material inequality within a society, the existing class structure and the way in which the occupational structure is changing. Greater social mobility requires an increase in the number of higher class positions available, or in downward mobility from existing higher class positions. Reducing educational inequality may have a part to play in this, but the interactions involved are complex and difficult to predict. It is well known that the greater class mobility in Britain between the late 1940s and the early 1970s was largely due to the first of these conditions being met (Goldthorpe 1980). The second condition would require a reduction in the effectiveness of class strategies aimed at maintaining the position of more advantaged groups; as we have seen in previous chapters, this would imply a move away from policies such as marketization and diversification which are associated with *greater* inequality – a move unlikely to occur in countries dominated by neo-liberal approaches to managing their economies and educational systems.

Patterns of intergenerational social mobility

Concerns in the United Kingdom over whether social mobility has stalled are echoed in the United States and in many other countries (OECD 2010; Hout 2015). As is often the case, such debates hinge around questions of definition and measurement: what do we mean precisely by social mobility, and how can we measure it? In his pioneering study, Pitirim Sorokin (1927, p. 133) defines social mobility quite generally as the transition of individuals from one social position to another within a society stratified by attributes such as class, status or income. Transitions between positions at similar levels are examples of horizontal mobility, whilst vertical mobility (upwards or downwards) describes transitions between positions on different social levels. As with educational inequality, choices concerning how stratification is measured depend partly on the disciplinary location of researchers: for economists, social position is most often conceptualized in terms of a continuous variable, such as income, whereas for sociologists, categorical variables, such as social class or socio-economic status, are more likely to be of interest. The distinction is of more than academic concern, and one of the most important features of recent debates concerning social mobility in Britain has been the different conclusions reached by researchers using income rather than social class to characterize social position (Blanden and Machin 2007; Erikson and Goldthorpe 2010; Goldthorpe 2013). It is also necessary to distinguish *inter*generational mobility, in which an individual attains a different social position to their parents, from *intra*generational mobility, understood as an individual attaining in later life a different social position to their point of entry in the labour market. In this chapter, the main focus will be on intergenerational class mobility, but other dimensions of stratification will also be considered where appropriate.

Stratification does not imply a static structure of positions between which individuals move: the possibility of structural change must also be considered. Indeed, secular changes in the occupational structure may *force* mobility to occur as certain kinds of work disappear to be replaced by others. Two processes should be distinguished: changes in occupational structure which arise from the shifting balance between industrial sectors, and changes which affect the distribution of jobs with different *kinds* of employment relation (see

Chapter 2). The first type of process does not necessarily entail a change in the class structure, whilst the second does. Comparing two cohorts born in 1946 and 1980–84 respectively, Bukodi et al. (2015, p. 99) note that:

> [W]e would certainly find far fewer miners, iron and steel workers, textile operatives and bus conductors and far more shelf-stackers, care assistants, kitchen staff and security guards. But what is important is that ... the employment relations of the individuals involved, as wage-workers, are essentially comparable.

By contrast, a society restructured in class terms between generations – for example, by a growth in professional and managerial employment at the expense of intermediate or working-class positions – will have fewer opportunities in some classes and more in others for the younger generation, driving mobility through processes of supply and demand. However, inequalities in the chances of attaining more desirable class positions may persist, or even strengthen, if children from more advantaged families take up the newly created higher class positions at a greater rate than those from less advantaged backgrounds. It is therefore important to distinguish between changes in mobility regimes which are structural – that is, arising from changes in the occupational, class or income structure of a society – and those which result from changes in the degree of openness in a society. Before proceeding to discuss the empirical evidence on intergenerational social mobility in the United Kingdom and other countries, it is necessary to review some of the central concepts and measures associated with these two forms of mobility.

Data on class mobility[1] are often summarized in an array known as a *mobility table*, which indicates the numbers or proportions of individuals attaining certain destination class positions according to their class origin. Table 9.1 shows a simplified example of such an array, constructed using data from the British Cohort Study. For men and women separately, the left-hand column shows the class of origin of participants based on their father's occupation, using a three-class version of the National Statistics Socio-economic classification (NS-SEC), whilst the next three columns show the destination class of participants based on their occupation at age 38. In each of the resulting cells, the percentage is shown of participants from a given origin class who had achieved a given class destination. Also shown are the row and column marginal distributions. The row marginal percentages show the proportion of fathers in each origin class, indicating the class distribution in the fathers' generation. In a similar way, the column marginal percentages give the class distribution, for men and women separately, of the children's generation. Inspecting the row and column marginal distribution therefore enables us to see the extent of structural change between generations.

As already seen in Chapter 2, there has been a substantial shift in the availability of class positions from the working class to the salariat, alongside a small

TABLE 9.1 Class mobility table for the British Cohort Study, showing percentages of participants from a given origin class who had achieved a given destination class at age 38

	Destination class (children)				N
	Salariat	Intermediate	Working	% of all fathers	
			Men		
Salariat	61.8	25.7	12.5	28.5	1645
Intermediate	39.9	36.8	23.3	35.9	2069
Working	30.7	34.4	34.9	35.6	2052
% of sons	42.9	32.8	24.4		
			Women		
Salariat	50.5	31.6	17.9	29.3	1739
Intermediate	33.4	36.8	29.8	34.7	2059
Working	26.2	34.5	39.4	36.0	2135
% of daughters	33.1	41.6	25.3		

Source: Calculated from data in Gugushvili et al. (2017, p. 309).

change in the availability of intermediate class positions for men but a notable increase for women. A relatively high level of mobility between classes is therefore to be expected, 'forced' to occur by the change in class structure. Some other broad features are evident from the table: first, there is a substantial inequality between men and women in achieving the highest class position (the 'salariat'), with women from all classes having a lower probability of reaching this class than men from the corresponding class. Second, there are substantial inequalities between classes in reaching the salariat: for men and for women, the chance of being found in the salariat at age 38 for those with a father in that class is approximately double the chance of those whose father was in the working class.

Some care is needed in interpreting mobility tables if it is desired to make comparisons over time or between contexts (for example, comparisons between different countries), and, as noted earlier, it is necessary to distinguish between class mobility arising from structural change and changes in the pattern of underlying associations between social origins and destinations. This distinction is usually expressed in terms of the difference between absolute rates of mobility and social fluidity. Absolute rates may be calculated directly from the mobility table and are defined in simple percentage terms: total absolute mobility is the proportion of individuals found in a different destination class to their class of origin, and is the net result of upward, downward and horizontal components.[2] Absolute mobility is sensitive to structural change, and depends on the relative sizes of the different classes. For example, if growth in the number of professional and managerial positions creates more 'room at the top', it is possible for more people to achieve upward mobility even if those from higher classes retain an advantage in the competition for occupational positions

(Goldthorpe 2013). Trends in absolute mobility will therefore be influenced by changes in the distribution of individuals across the class structure, such as those seen in Table 9.1. Perhaps the most striking finding of mobility studies is that absolute rates are quite high. For example, using a seven-class schema, Goldthorpe and Jackson (2007) find total absolute mobility rates of 74 per cent and 76 per cent for British men born in 1958 and 1970 respectively, together with rates of 80 per cent and 81 per cent for women. The great majority of people in the two birth cohorts therefore found themselves in a different class to their father. As Paterson and Iannelli (2007b, p. 1) put it, 'it is normal for people to occupy a different class to that in which they were brought up'. However, these high levels are not necessarily describing spectacular instances of mobility. Apart from the impact of structural change, they can largely be traced to mobility across relatively small social distances in a fine-grained class schema.[3]

Although absolute mobility is helpful in understanding the extent of social opportunity, its value in assessing inequalities in life chances is limited. It is generally agreed that relative mobility rates defined by odds ratios are more suitable for understanding change over time. These rates are unaffected by changes in the marginal distributions of mobility tables, so that social mobility can be seen net of changes in the class structure. The resulting pattern of associations between origin and destination classes is referred to as social fluidity (Goldthorpe 1980; Breen and Jonsson 2005). The array of possible odds ratios can be conceptualized as a series of contests in which individuals from one of two origin classes are allocated to one of two destination classes. For each contest, the odds ratio represents the relative chances of the competing individuals being found in one of the destination classes as opposed to the other.

In Table 9.2, odds ratios calculated from the percentages in Table 9.1 are shown for each combination of origin pair and destination pair.[4] In such a

TABLE 9.2 Social fluidity table for the British Cohort Study, showing odds ratios corresponding to the percentage data in Table 9.1

Origin pair	Destination pair		
	S, I	S, W	I, W
	Men		
S, I	2.2	2.9	1.3
S, W	2.7	5.6	2.1
I, W	1.2	2.0	1.6
	Women		
S, I	1.8	2.5	1.4
S, W	2.1	4.2	2.0
I, W	1.2	1.7	1.4

table, an odds ratio of unity corresponds to no association between origins and destinations (perfect mobility); the further the odds ratio rises above unity, the stronger is the (positive) association between origin and destination. Although it is a simplified example, Table 9.2 shows some typical features of more detailed social fluidity tables, including substantially lower relative chances of 'long-range' mobility (movement between the working class and salariat) and greater fluidity (lower odds ratios) amongst women. Because it aggregates finer categories, the three-class version of the NS-SEC used in Table 9.2 leads to smaller odds ratios than would be found with a more detailed classification. The large sample sizes made possible by drawing on linked census data enable Buscha and Sturgis (2018) to use a seven-class NS-SEC, providing a picture of the scale of inequality across the entire class structure. In their analysis, for people born between 1975 and 1981, the odds of an individual born into NS-SEC Class 1 being in that class by age 30 were 20 times those for an individual born into NS-SEC Class 7. The relatively small changes in social fluidity discussed later need to be seen in this context.

Social mobility in comparative perspective

The methods outlined earlier have been applied in a number of international comparative studies of social mobility, in parallel to the studies of educational inequality discussed in Chapter 3. Two questions have dominated these studies: to what extent do countries differ in their patterns of mobility, either in absolute rates or social fluidity; and how do these patterns of difference change over time? An early answer to the first question was that, because of an increasing convergence of occupational structures amongst industrialized societies, differences between countries would be small (Lipset and Zetterburg 1959). However, Erikson et al. (1979) found that certain countries had distinctive absolute mobility profiles arising from historically determined differences in their class structures. Using data from the CASMIN[5] project, which included mobility tables covering the late 1960s and 1970s in 12 European countries and the United States, Australia and Japan, these authors concluded that the relatively small differences between the countries in their study were better explained by specific features of the societies involved rather than by macrosocial trends such as industrialization.

More recently, the Lipset–Zetterburg thesis has been described as premature rather than mistaken, and by the 1990s absolute mobility rates in countries at similar stages of development had indeed converged, so that variations in class structure and in upward and downward mobility were much less than in the 1970s (Breen and Jonsson 2005). Nevertheless, absolute mobility rates continue to fluctuate both within and between societies (Yaish and Andersen 2012; Curtis 2016). An alternative version of the Lipset–Zetterburg thesis, that similarity between countries should be found at the level of social fluidity rather than in absolute rates of mobility, was initially more consistent with empirical studies (Erikson et al. 1982, 1983). However, the hypothesis of 'common social fluidity' is not fully supported by the available data, and although between-country differences in fluidity are not large they are nevertheless significant. In particular, the social democracies of Norway and Sweden are generally held to be associated with greater social fluidity than countries such as Britain, France and Germany (Breen and Luijkx 2004; Blanden 2013). Evidence on the United States is uncertain: some studies have found that social fluidity there is comparable to that in Britain, whilst others find greater openness and fluidity, more comparable to the situation in Sweden (Breen and Jonsson 2005). This contrasts with studies of income mobility, in which the United States appears to be much less open than the Nordic countries and more similar to Britain (Breen and Jonsson 2005; Gregg et al. 2017).

On the question of change over time in social mobility, the central hypothesis has been that 'constant social fluidity' prevails. This hypothesis asserts that, even though systematic shifts in absolute mobility may occur over time, social fluidity will remain largely unaltered, or if change occurs it will be 'trendless' in the sense of fluctuating without a permanent shift in any direction.[6] Evidence for constant social fluidity was found by Erikson et al. (1983) and in the CASMIN project (Erikson and Goldthorpe 1992). However, a study of 11 European countries (Breen and Luijkx 2004) which used data from the period 1970 to 2000 found a general tendency towards greater social fluidity, albeit limited and with significant cross-national variations, including stable social fluidity in Britain and Germany.[7] In many European countries, *absolute* mobility for men has shown little change over the past 40 years, with rates of upward mobility remaining approximately twice those for downward mobility throughout the period (Breen and Luijkx 2004; Erikson et al. 2010). For women, there has been on average some increase in upward mobility at the expense of downward mobility. Overall, the evidence from international social mobility studies suggests that, although there has been some increase in the degree of openness within many societies, changes in class mobility regimes since the Second World War have been driven more by structural factors within and between countries than by major changes in social fluidity. Substantial inequality remains, particularly in mobility/immobility between the highest and lowest class positions. The impact of educational expansion must of necessity have been small, and *prima facie* it appears likely that any increase in educational opportunity has been driven by, rather than being responsible for, structural mobility. Social mobility appears to be more strongly influenced by economic inequality than by educational expansion, at least at the level of income mobility. There is a strong positive association between a country's income inequality and the extent to which levels of income persist across generations (the 'Great Gatsby' curve; see Jerrim and Macmillan (2015). However, this does not mean that education is not important for social mobility, for the 'Great Gatsby' association is mainly driven by the association between income inequality and educational inequality.

Social mobility in Britain

The case of Britain has received considerable attention in recent years, largely because of the political capital invested in the issue of social mobility by successive governments. Nevertheless, the extent of change is debatable. Following the pioneering studies by David Glass in 1949 (Glass 1954), John Goldthorpe and his colleagues in the Social Mobility Group at Oxford University highlighted the strength and persistence of associations between social origins and destinations. Goldthorpe (1980, p. 252) found 'inequalities that are of a quite striking kind' in the patterns of social fluidity for cohorts born in the first half of the twentieth century, patterns which 'reflect inequalities of opportunity that are rooted in the class structure'. These inequalities were softened in the two decades following the Second World War by structural trends in which the demand for professional, managerial and technical labour far outstripped supply from the children of the pre-war middle class. For some time afterwards, studies of class mobility showed little evidence of any significant change in absolute rates for men, although for women marked changes in both upward and downward mobility underlay a largely constant net rate (Goldthorpe and Jackson 2007; Goldthorpe and Mills 2008). However, amongst men and women aged 23–62 in 1999, Paterson and Iannelli (2007b) found a substantial reduction in upward mobility between the oldest and youngest cohorts, with a corresponding increase in downward mobility. A different analysis by Bukodi et al. (2015), covering four cohorts born between 1946 and 1984, also suggests a decline in upward mobility and an increase in downward mobility for both men and women. However, there appears to have been little change in social fluidity (Paterson and Iannelli 2007; Goldthorpe and Mills 2008). Trends in absolute mobility should therefore be seen as structurally determined rather than arising from greater openness in the opportunities for people of different classes. This conclusion is broadly supported by Goldthorpe and Jackson (2007), and by Li and Devine (2011), although in the latter case a small increase in social fluidity was evident alongside declining (absolute) upward mobility for men. Buscha and Sturgis (2018), using census data covering the period 1971–2011, also find a small but significant increase in social fluidity between cohorts born in the late 1950s and those born a decade later.

The evidence on social mobility in Britain, understood as intergenerational movements between classes, therefore supports the view that any changes in mobility patterns have been limited, and have been largely confined to absolute mobility rates rather than social fluidity. Nevertheless, there is a widespread perception that social mobility in Britain has ground to a halt. Although scholars have warned against political confusion over the interpretation of mobility research (Erikson and Goldthorpe 2010; Goldthorpe 2013), this perception is not unreasonable. First, it is clear that the rapid occupational upgrading which occurred after the Second World War has slowed markedly. As a result, the children of an expanded middle class find further upward mobility, or even class maintenance, a difficult proposition. The larger pool of well-educated labour arising from greater opportunity for the working class and for women of all classes adds to the 'social congestion' (Brown 2013) caused by these factors. The declining upward mobility and increasing downward mobility noted by Paterson and Iannelli (2007) and Bukodi et al. (2015) are consistent with these points. Moreover, it is absolute mobility which represents the direct individual experience of men and women, so that although social fluidity – which as noted earlier has remained largely unchanged – may be a better objective measure of a society's openness, *subjectively* social mobility has indeed 'stalled', even if findings on income mobility are set aside. However, this is not to say that the policy solutions adopted by successive UK governments since 1997 are likely to have any significant impact. These policies, which have centred on education and the raising of aspirations, are essentially individualizing responses to a structural problem. In the absence of any renewal of occupational upgrading, educational expansion will simply add to social congestion. This point, and the wider relationship between education and social mobility, will be explored in the next two sections.

Education and labour-market outcomes

Human capital theory remains the dominant *political* account of the relationship between education and labour-market outcomes. It regards education as largely an absolute good, so that people achieving a given level of education will always be considered more productive than those who do not, irrespective of how many people reach that level. Individuals with similar skills should therefore be rewarded equally, and can expect their education to generate an absolute return in terms of wage earnings (Bol 2015). Although educational expansion will intensify competition for jobs at a particular level of skill, human capital theory expects a balancing of supply and demand, so that declining returns will slow expansion in areas where an oversupply of skills exists. A development of the human capital approach is the so-called 'neo-liberal opportunity bargain', which claims that market forces will in fact deliver greater prosperity and opportunity for all. It is argued that returns on education need not decline, because educational expansion is not a zero-sum game. Increasing the pool of human capital in a society both stimulates innovation and attracts inward investment, resulting in more jobs corresponding to higher levels of education rather than increased competition over a fixed number of jobs. However, these arguments must be evaluated in light of the evidence on social mobility, particularly the recent decline in upward mobility and the lack of a substantial increase in social fluidity. Brown (2013, p. 683) suggests that, in the United Kingdom and many other countries, the economy has not delivered the kind of structural change required to fulfil the opportunity bargain. In consequence, 'the experiences of many working-class and middle-class families are not defined by intergenerational social mobility but by the realities of social congestion'. Although these experiences have become more acute since the 2008 financial crisis, their underpinning trends have been evident for many years. The growth of knowledge work and other aspects of the shift to higher skills discussed in Chapter 1 have not led to a continued upgrading in the social structure. Educational expansion, together with the codification and digitization of more routine forms of White-collar work, has created downward pressure on certain forms of professional and managerial employment (Brown et al. 2011). In fact, both graduates and less-educated workers in the United Kingdom have seen a downgrading in their expectations in the last few decades as average levels of education have increased (Salvatori 2015). Human capital theory cannot be regarded as a satisfactory explanation of the education-labour market relationship.

Di Stasio et al. (2016) identify two further groups of theories about the relationship between education and labour-market outcomes: signalling theory and social closure theory. Signalling theorists reject the idea that education directly influences productivity but retain the market aspects of human capital theory. They regard any job-specific skills resulting from education as of secondary importance. What really counts is the correlation of educational attainment with unobservable aspects of productivity potential, such as effort, motivation, perseverance, and capacity to acquire new knowledge and skills. Education is therefore a signalling device, helping employers to rank candidates in terms of their standing relative to other potential employees (Van de Werfhorst 2009). In this process, education is a *positional* good: the absolute level of educational attainment is less important in the competition for employment than a person's attainment relative to that of other candidates.[8] Educational expansion therefore implies a need for individuals to run in order to stand still: whilst education can continue to be enjoyed as an absolute good in a consumption sense, there is a need to make strategic investments in education which maintain or improve one's standing in the labour market: 'Education enjoyed in its own right is capable of indefinite extension; as an instrument for entree into top jobs, it is not...' (Hirsch 1976, p. 59).

Social closure theory rejects functionalist explanations such as human capital or signalling theory in favour of a conflict model: education is not primarily concerned with developing individual productivity but with reinforcing advantage and reproducing class relations. Education is regarded as mainly a gateway to credentials: educational qualifications which operate as formal entry requirements regulating access to certain occupations. In particular, social closure theory regards the higher professions as interest groups that aim to establish and maintain social and legal boundaries to the advantage of their members, reinforcing higher class immobility and restricting opportunities for outsiders (Ruggera and Barone 2017). In some ways, this might suggest a counter-tendency to increasing positionality in education: either one has a relevant qualification for entry to an occupation, or one does not. However, whilst signalling theory implies that education will become increasingly positional because of competition between people with relevant skills, social closure suggests a positionality based on the desire to control advantageous occupations and exclude interlopers. For example, opportunities to train for high-status professions may be restricted, shifting positionality to selection for entry routes rather than professional qualifications themselves; entry to medical courses in the United Kingdom is an obvious example. Moreover, the boundaries protecting higher professions may be social as well as academic. As Weber (1978 [1922], p. 45) points out, closure can operate within a formally qualified group, with internal differentiation taking various forms. Although not explicitly formulated in educational terms, these may include indications of whether certain social criteria are satisfied, such as whether the 'right' school or university has been attended. Social closure in the Weberian sense may be seen as an inherent, rather than accidental, feature of the relationship between education and the labour market as privileged groups struggle to maintain their advantage.

The OED triangle and the direct effect of social origins

Although education cannot guarantee social mobility, it is well established that educational attainment is the single most important factor in determining an individual's destination class (see Marshall et al. 1997). For British men born between 1925 and 1954, Breen and Karlson (2014) show that the proportion of the total association between origin and destination classes which is mediated by education ranges between around 40 and 60 per cent depending on the specific origin-destination pairs under consideration. However, educational attainment is not the *only* factor in social fluidity, and there is clear evidence that social origins in themselves are an important factor in an individual's class destination, over and above their impact on educational attainment (Bukodi and Goldthorpe 2016; Gregg et al. 2017; Gugushvili et al. 2017). It has become conventional to express educational and non-educational components of social destination in terms of an origin-education-destination (OED) triangle, in which the association between origin and destination class is made up of a component mediated by education and a *direct* component which remains after controlling for educational attainment (Bukodi and Goldthorpe 2019; see also Figure 9.1).

The overall association between origins and destinations depends on the level of educational inequality (O-E association), the labour-market advantages

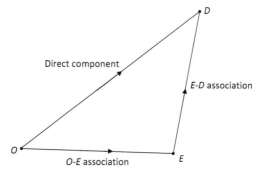

FIGURE 9.1 The OED triangle, showing two components of the association between social origins (*O*) and social destinations (*D*): the component mediated by education (*E*) and the direct component.

afforded by education (E-D association), and the direct effect itself (unmediated O-D association). There is some evidence that a weakening of the direct effects of social origins has occurred in countries such as Sweden and the Netherlands (Ballarino and Bernardi 2016). However, in a range of other countries including the United Kingdom, a direct effect of social origins makes a persistent or even increasing contribution to social destinations. Moreover, this direct effect is stronger when measured later in working life than at labour-market entry, suggesting that it cannot be explained as a phenomenon of youth or of transitions from school to work. The resulting impact on social mobility is described by Gugushvili et al. (2017) in terms of 'glass floors', which protect individuals from more advantaged backgrounds against downward mobility, as well as 'glass ceilings', which prevent long-range upward mobility.

Various explanations have been proposed to account for the direct effect of social origins. Inequalities of wealth and income are perhaps the most obvious of these, in addition to their impact on educational outcomes. Pfeffer and Hällsten (2012) propose that parental wealth can act as a form of privatized insurance against social risks, making possible more ambitious occupational choices conditional on educational attainment as well as improving the chances of educational success. Other possible factors include social class differences in (non-financial) parental assistance in the labour market and the effect of parental education over and above its impact on educational attainment. Surprisingly, Gugushvili et al. (2017) find that, whilst there is a significant effect of parental education, parental assistance in finding work has little effect except in the case of children who become employed by their parents. Much of the direct effect of social origins remains unaccounted for by these variables. It is therefore possible that other factors, such as a range of practices associated with social closure, are important as part of an overall strategy of 'opportunity hoarding' (Tilly 1998; McKnight 2015).

Relative measures of education

Studies of the contribution made by education to social mobility have traditionally measured education in absolute terms, for example using years of schooling completed or highest qualification achieved. However, because education functions in the labour market more in positional than in absolute terms, it may be preferable to use a relative measure of education. These measures take into account the significance of certain levels of education in terms of their signalling function to employers. In his model of the relationship between IEO and ISO, Boudon (1974, p. 148) shows that the structure of expectations associated with particular levels of education can persist until the process of expansion results in a discontinuous change in the destination classes to which it provides access. Using a similar idea, Bukodi and Goldthorpe (2016) construct a relative measure based on groups of qualification levels that change over time. For a cohort born in Britain in 1946, the 'top level' of education comprises the attainment of two A-levels or above; however, for the BCS cohort born in 1970, this top level comprises only first degree level or above. The pattern of associations within the OED triangle shows distinct differences according to whether absolute and relative measures of education are used. With an absolute measure, there is a clear decline in both the O–E association and the E–D association; however, when the relative measure is used there is no definite change over time in either relationship, or indeed in the direct effect of social origin. Overall, the contribution of relative educational level to social destination remained stable over the period covered by the study.

Compositional effects

The degree of social fluidity, and the relative strength of education-mediated and direct effects of social origin, depends on the precise nature of the associations between the three corners of the OED triangle. For example, if educational attainment comes to depend less on class origins (O–E association weakens), the link between origins and class destinations will also weaken. Equalization in educational opportunity is therefore one way in which education might cause an increase in social fluidity, and has of course received the most attention in political discourse. However, the overall relationship between origins and destinations may also be affected by a *compositional effect* (Breen and Jonsson 2007) arising from a gradient in the O–D association according to level of education. This effect operates if the direct association between origins and destinations is weaker for individuals with higher levels of educational attainment, as would be expected if greater universalism applies in relation to employment at these levels (Breen 2010). The compositional effect requires both educational expansion and a particular kind of three-way interaction between origins, education and destinations (O–E–D association).

If educational expansion leads to an increasing proportion of each cohort attaining higher levels of education, there would be an overall reduction in the association between origins and destinations. Such an effect has been reported in a number of countries, including Sweden (Breen and Jonsson 2007; Breen 2010), Germany and Britain (Breen 2010; see also Iannelli and Paterson 2007b for Scotland), and the United States (Hout 1988). Some scholars have seen the compositional effect as the main potential driver of an increase in social fluidity. Commenting on a decrease of around 30 per cent in the association between origins and destinations in the United States, Hout (1988, p. 1384) states that: 'I am tempted to ascribe all the change in inequality of occupational opportunity to the increase in college graduates in the labour force'. Indeed, in Britain and the US, the compositional effect has been the only factor tending to produce any increase in social fluidity in recent decades (Breen 2010; Pfeffer and Hertel 2015). However, there is now evidence in the United States for a 'U-shaped' distribution of the direct effects of social origins, in which these effects decline for holders of first degrees but reassert themselves for those with postgraduate qualifications (Torche 2011). This is partly because of horizontal stratification in postgraduate education, with institutional selectivity, field of study and type of programme all being important factors. These complex effects suggest that, although the weakening of the O-D association predicted by liberal-industrial theory has been observed, it is not uniformly distributed across levels of education. Whilst occupational selection may have become more meritocratic in certain sectors of the labour market, the effects of social origins are still influential for those with lower attainment and possibly also for those with advanced qualifications.

Social mobility and the curriculum

There is some evidence that the mediating effect of education takes place partly through the nature of the curriculum studied. It appears that more academic curricula provide a significant advantage over vocational study in terms of social mobility, both on career entry and later in life. Iannelli (2013) finds that after controlling for ability, around one-quarter of the overall association between class origins and destinations is accounted for by a combination of curriculum and school type, with the great majority of this effect arising from curriculum. In the less stratified Scottish system of education, Iannelli and Duta (2018) found that, for leavers at age 16, social background differences in labour-market prospects were significant but explained more by attainment than by subject choices. For leavers at age 17 or 18, a substantial direct effect of social origin was observed. In the E-D association, attainment and subject choice were equally important, suggesting that by this level of study certain subjects confer a concrete labour-market advantage. However, it was unclear whether explanations based on human capital or on signalling effects are more appropriate.

Although school type has some effect on mobility chances, its total impact in England is small, limited to a few per cent of the overall association between origin and destination class (Iannelli 2013). This small total effect hides a more complex picture, particularly in terms of the distinction between grammar and comprehensive schools (Boliver and Swift 2011). Working-class children with similar characteristics appear to have a greater chance of long-range mobility if they attend grammar schools, but are just as likely to be immobile whether they attend a grammar or a comprehensive school. Moreover, grammar schools confer just as much advantage on service-class children as those from working-class backgrounds, protecting them from downward mobility whilst helping working-class children move up. Taking into account the negative impact on mobility of attending a secondary modern school, school type effects almost entirely cancel out.

Notes

1 A significant factor in social mobility research is the nature and quality of the available data. These include repeated cross-sectional samples from a population, census data and cohort studies. For a general discussion of data sources and the issues associated with them, see Goldthorpe and Mills (2008) and, for intergenerational income mobility, Gregg et al. (2017).

2 Because a class schema may not be fully hierarchical, between-class movements are possible which cannot be characterized as upward or downward mobility. See Goldthorpe and Jackson (2007).

3 In the more coarse-grained class schema used in Table 9.1, the total mobility rates are lower: 57 per cent for men and 58 per cent for women.

4 The method of calculation is illustrated by the following expression for the combination salariat/working class origin and salariat/working class destination:

$$O_{S,W \rightarrow S,W} = \frac{P(S|S)/P(W|S)}{P(S|W)/P(W|W)}$$

In this expression, each of the right-hand terms is the probability of an individual being found in a specific destination class, conditional on being from a given origin class.

5 Comparative Analysis of Social Mobility in Industrial Nations.

6 The idea of 'trendless' change is proposed in Sorokin's celebrated early study of social mobility (see Sorokin 1927, p. 152).

7 As a result, over the last quarter of the twentieth century Britain moved from being one of the more open countries to one of the less open (Breen and Jonsson 2005).

8 A positional good is one which is 'either (1) scarce in some absolute or socially imposed sense or (2) subject to congestion or crowding through more extensive use' (Hirsch 1976, p. 27). The second sense of the term is used here.

10
CONCLUSION

This book began by discussing conceptions of social justice in relation to educational inequality. Whilst quite radical standpoints on redistribution and equality of outcome are possible, a political consensus has emerged around the idea of equality of opportunity. This standpoint is reinforced theoretically by two related discourses, of liberal–industrial theory and meritocracy. The first asserts that social achievement *will*, and the second asserts that it *should*, move towards greater universalism, in which allocation to social positions occurs on the basis of rationality and economic efficiency. For some commentators, these discourses envision a society open to talents, in which social background is increasingly irrelevant to life chances and where effort and ability are justly rewarded. The contrary viewpoint, that meritocracy is simply a 'myth', a rather flimsy attempt to disguise and legitimate persistent material and cultural inequalities, is powerfully expressed by many of the scholars cited in previous chapters. Observed patterns of educational and social opportunity, however, show that a more complex analysis is required than to simply assert or deny progress towards universalism. Commenting on their investigation into the relationships between social background, education and social mobility in mid-twentieth-century Britain, Marshall et al. (1997, p. 188) write that

> we find the claim that Britain is meritocratic in the sense that people get jobs on the basis of their ability to do them well ... rather more plausible than the claim that this ability is justly rewarded in class terms.

The essence of this comment is that meritocracy, along with the liberal–industrial theory that underpins and claims to explain it, is not indivisible: it contains a number of separate claims that, whilst structurally related, are substantially independent. This concluding chapter begins by identifying the structural components of meritocracy and evaluating their claims in relation to the quantitative evidence discussed in earlier chapters. It then considers two aspects of the theoretical perspectives that form the other major strand of the book: their substantive contribution to the evaluation of meritocratic claims and other attempts to reconcile social inequality with social justice; and their respective contributions *as theory* to understanding how educational inequality is produced. In the course of this discussion, the possibilities offered by theory development are considered, particularly developments arising from the traditions of Bernstein and Bourdieu and the potential for combining relational and rational action perspectives. The chapter concludes by briefly reviewing some implications of the intersectional view of class, race and gender and asserting the continued relevance of a class-based analysis.

Meritocracy, inequality and education

The central assumption of meritocracy is that inequalities in condition may be *just* if they reflect differences in ability. In most discussions of the concept, meritocracy refers to relations between people arising from their participation in the labour market and other public spheres, rather than to more general aspects of social interaction. For example, few people would advocate applying meritocratic principles within the family, where a conception of social justice based on need is more appropriate (see Chapter 1). In a labour-market context, meritocracy can be broken down into more specific claims concerning access to desirable employment opportunities. The first claim is that occupational competence, gained through a combination of factors such as education and work experience, is the chief arbiter of employment situation and its material rewards. The second is that occupational competence is a reflection of meritorious qualities such as ability, effort and perseverance; and a third claim is that extraneous factors, such as race, gender and class origins, have no influence over opportunities to develop occupational competence. In Chapter 1, these claims were subjected to *logical* scrutiny in relation to social justice; it is now possible to compare them with empirical findings.

As Marshall et al. (1997) suggest, the first meritocratic claim has some plausibility. In the previous chapter, it was shown that education is the main factor in social mobility, accounting for up to 60 per cent of the association between class origins and destinations. Although this leaves considerable room for direct effects of social origin, it can also plausibly be argued that some of these direct effects arise from non-cognitive aspects of job performance rather than – for example – strategies associated with social closure or 'opportunity hoarding'. The second claim has two difficulties. First, as we saw in Chapter 1, the claim that certain qualities are meritorious is inherently problematic: why these qualities and not others, and why should qualities whose possession is involuntary be regarded as conferring merit on their holder? Moreover, whilst it is again plausible that educational success and, ultimately, occupational competence should be at least partly determined by effort and cognitive ability, it is also clear that other factors are involved. In particular, educational success largely depends on economic, cultural and social resources, and is both competitive and positional. Achieving the most prestigious qualifications involves strategic behaviours in competitive education markets, and the labour-market significance of a given level of attainment changes over time, so that structural factors, not just individual merit, make an important contribution to the development of occupational competence.[1]

The third meritocratic claim is the one confronted most directly by the evidence in this book. Essentially, it asserts that equal opportunity exists in relation to educational attainment, or in a weaker version of the claim, that society is progressively moving towards equality of opportunity. Both empirically and theoretically, the first of these assertions is systematically undermined by the evidence presented in earlier chapters. *Inequality* of educational opportunity is the characteristic experience of young people in the United Kingdom and other countries, with structures of disadvantage and privilege maintaining wide disparities in educational experience and attainment. Relational theories of education, in which class interests and distributions of power and advantage are embedded in and concealed by discourses of education as a transformative process, appear to provide a more accurate picture of educational attainment. Nevertheless, some care is needed in summarizing the findings discussed in earlier chapters: evaluating patterns of change in educational stratification highlights specific aspects where limited progress can be claimed. The first point to make is that, in Western liberal democracies, expansion has transformed the educational experiences and achievements of young people from working-class and lower middle-class backgrounds. These young people stay far longer in school than was the case a century ago, and their chances of attending a university are many times greater. Shavit et al. (2007) argue that, whilst it is true that *relative* inequalities in chances of access to higher education remained largely stable in the last decades of the twentieth century, it is nevertheless legitimate to say that education systems became more inclusive. That is, if education is conceived as an absolute good, the process of expansion has extended this opportunity to people from all backgrounds. From the functional perspective on social justice, the persistence of relative inequalities is simply the price of greater inclusiveness: we are all better off than if expansion had not occurred. Although this argument neglects the positional significance of education, in which value and inclusiveness are to some extent opposed to each other, it illustrates the importance of relating quantitative studies of educational attainment to a more complex normative framework than is captured by participation rates or odds ratios in isolation.

A second important point is that even relative inequalities have declined to some extent, with greater reductions occurring when social background is measured by occupational class rather than parental education or status. This weakening in class effects may be caused partly by lower economic rewards associated with intermediate class positions, but also by greater heterogeneity within social classes in terms of educational attainment and cultural preferences, a manifestation of the individualizing trends discussed in Chapter 2. That is, whilst parental education retains a strong influence over educational attainment, a compositional effect has occurred in which the average attainment of people in lower occupational classes has increased. Although it is seldom expressed in this way, the working class is now an educated class, with greater experience of the education system than in earlier generations. Whilst educational failure and exclusion are more likely to affect people from working-class backgrounds, schooling histories may be positive even when attainment is relatively modest. In England, around one-third of pupils eligible for FSM achieve five or more A*-C grades at GCSE (see Figure 3.4), and by no means all of these pupils will attain middle-class positions. However, whether these trends towards equalization are evidence in support of liberal-industrial theory or a decline in the importance of class is debatable. Country-specific factors appear to have more influence than macrosocial trends such as industrialism. Germany and Britain have shown a relatively small decline in IEO, whilst larger reductions, and greater equality overall, appear to be associated with social democratic regimes in the Nordic countries. Changes in the relative importance of occupational class and parental education demonstrate the power of a broader, more culturally based conception of class, not a reduction in class effects *per se*. Substantial inequality remains, and the most significant declines have affected earlier transitions, whilst inequalities in higher education access have been remarkably persistent. What Barone and Ruggera (2018) call the 'golden age' of equalization was associated with far-reaching educational reform in the middle decades of the twentieth century, alongside declining wealth inequality overall. There is no guarantee that reductions in IEO will continue, and in several recent comparative studies there is at least a suggestion that the 'golden age' is now concluded.

Although much of the focus in this book has been on educational *disadvantage*, it must not be forgotten that the reproduction of elites parallels, and in some ways reinforces, the reproduction of class structures further down the social scale. As Waters (2018, p. 413) suggests, social mobility is largely incompatible with elite social reproduction: 'true social mobility cannot be achieved whilst a narrow segment of society is able to hold on to resources, power and prestige across generations'. This draws attention to the relationship between inequality of educational opportunity and broader inequalities in society. The 'illusory' nature of equal opportunity in a grossly unequal society is highlighted by R.H. Tawney, and we have seen that, in *The Division of Labour in Society*, Durkheim regarded equal opportunity as indispensable to organic solidarity. Contemporary political discourse contains numerous examples of essentially the same idea. However, there has been little – if any – increase in social mobility for many years, and after a significant decline over much of the twentieth century, wealth inequality is again on the rise. The so-called 'Great Gatsby' curve implies that the increasing wealth and income inequality of recent decades is likely to reduce social mobility, although the different patterns of intergenerational association according to income or social class suggest that this will happen in complex ways, and with different kinds of impact on educational inequality. What is abundantly clear, however, is the weight of contradictions between the political promises of neo-liberalism and current educational systems, particularly those with high levels of stratification and selectivity. Marketized, differentiated and stratified systems create spaces within which the material and cultural advantages of higher social classes can be realized in strategic and exclusionary behaviours and discourses. The 'social imaginaries' describing many schools are *middle-class* imaginaries, demonizing schools in working-class areas and constructing others as safe spaces, legitimate sites for middle-class engagement with publicly funded education. Where middle-class parents make 'counter-intuitive' school choices, opting for comprehensive state education, this is not necessarily the result of a political commitment to inclusive schooling, but yet another strategic investment, aimed this time at maximizing children's non-cognitive skills within a multicultural and multiclass environment (James et al. 2010).

Whilst empirical research uncovers relationships between inequality and structural features of educational systems, theories of class in education highlight the dynamics underlying the creation and exploitation of these features. What the theoretical accounts discussed in this book have in common is that they locate educational inequality not at the level of the individual but within the relations of society as a whole, including cultural as well as economic relations. This is not to dismiss the importance of agency, but to emphasize that agency is socially situated in ways that advantage some and disadvantage others. Although rational action theories focus mainly on the positional and economic consequences of class location, Marxist perspectives or the cultural reproduction theories of Pierre Bourdieu and Basil Bernstein provide broader accounts of the formation and distribution of subjectivities. Underpinned by material inequalities, the theories of Althusser, Bourdieu and Bernstein address in different ways what Bourdieu (1977a, p. 72) describes as 'the dialectic of the internalization of externality and the externalization of internality'. These are theories not only of class interest and struggle but also of ideological processes which seek to conceal and neutralize the *consciousness* of struggle within 'mythological discourses' of horizontal solidarity (Bernstein 2000, p. xxiii). By normalizing middle-class identity and aspirations, these discourses provide one section of society with cultural advantages disproportionate to their means, realized in academically and socially selective schools and elite universities. At the same time, they render invisible a global elite, the true ruling class in which the top 0.1 per cent control a share of global wealth that has increased by more than half since 1980 (WIL 2018, p. 203). In the United Kingdom, Stephen Ball (2018) writes of 'the tragedy of state education in England', and argues that a system characterized by reluctance, meddlesomeness and muddle has failed seriously to address educational inequality, reflecting instead the interests of middle-class parents. This perhaps reverses the direction of causality, underestimating the extent to which reluctance and muddle – for example, over the status of private education, academic and social selection, and post-16 educational reform – have been the direct consequences of middle-class interests. Nevertheless, Ball's comments raise further questions of social justice, concerning legal and moral rights. If private investment in education through fee-paying schools, private tuition or house purchase is considered as just, the legitimate disposal of wealth to benefit one's own children, it follows that inequality of educational opportunity is also just. If, from a needs-based conception of social justice, society wishes to redress the results of parental choice, considerable public expenditure must be undertaken, redistributing the costs of self-interest beyond those whom it benefits. Moreover, in countries such as the United Kingdom, the institutional arrangements that enable material advantage to be translated into educational advantage must be regarded as democratically established. If justice is equated with equality of opportunity, must democracy then be regarded as unjust? Although David Miller's contextual model of social justice might offer a way through these conundrums, the causal and moral relationships involved seem almost intractable. Conversely, a simpler normative approach – such as equal opportunity at all costs – seems to entail widespread dissent and social conflict.

Theory and languages of description

The empirical chapters of this book should not be considered simply as a set of 'facts' by which 'theory' is confirmed or refuted. Post-empiricist epistemologies rightly consider observations, facts and data to be 'theory-laden', in the sense of being embedded in specific conceptual and theoretical frameworks. Even when observational statements are expressed in apparently innocuous and everyday language, 'in every empirical assertion that can be used as a starting point of scientific investigation and theory, we employ concepts that interpret the data in some general view of the world' (Hesse 1972, p. 280). However, the assertion that observation statements are theory-laden does not imply a descent into relativism, only that research findings must be seen as part of a wider epistemological and normative complex incorporating values, theories and research practices in addition to observation statements. Questions of what and how to measure in studies of educational inequality – for example, whether to use absolute or relative measures of attainment – are more than just technical problems; they also express wider theoretical debates with fundamentally different positions. This is particularly evident in relation to the measurement of social background, in which empirical data on class and status are linked to the specific theoretical accounts discussed in Chapter 2. To take just one example, in traditional Weberian or Marxist class analysis the distribution of attributes such as wealth, educational credentials, and cultural possessions is a phenomenon to be causally accounted for by deeper relations grounded in the economic sphere. By contrast, Bourdieu claims to transcend this distinction, in a post-substantialist theory of class where distributions of cultural as well as economic capital are both *part of* the conception of class and a dynamic configuration whose trajectory is accounted for *by* class relations. Although scholars such as Rosemary Crompton (2006) advocate a 'positive pluralism', these different accounts are often taken to be competing paradigms rather than complementary perspectives (Moore and Maton 2001). The measurement of class in quantitative research, and more broadly controversies over the project of class analysis itself, may therefore be seen as part of struggles for control and legitimacy within intellectual fields.

Gabriel Abend (2008) identifies no fewer than seven uses or meanings of theory in social science. These range from broadly empiricist meanings closely related to the use of theory in the more quantitative chapters of this book, to theory in normative or constructivist senses. Hypotheses such as maximally maintained inequality are 'theory$_2$', attempts to explain a particular social phenomenon: in this case patterns of change in IEO during periods of educational expansion, which, in turn, relate to theory$_1$, systems of general propositions establishing relationships between variables. By contrast, theory$_5$ is more pertinent to the theoretical positions discussed in other chapters:

> A theory$_5$ is a *Weltanschauung*, that is, an overall perspective from which one sees and interprets the world ... theories$_5$ are not about the social world itself, but about how to look at, grasp, and represent it. That is, theories$_5$ focus on our conceptual and linguistic equipment ... the nature of our conceptual scheme, the categories into which we group things, and the logical relations that there can be between concepts.
>
> (Abend 2008, p. 179)

This implies that such theories, if they are to have originality and value, are incommensurable with other theories, providing accounts of the social world from distinct discursive locations. As Bernstein (2000) puts it, sociological theories of this kind are specialized languages, with characteristic modes of inquiry and ways of expressing their claims. Disciplines in the humanities and social sciences consist of a series of such languages, a form of vertical discourse Bernstein calls a *horizontal knowledge structure* and which can be expressed in the form $L_1, L_2, L_3 \ldots L_n$. In the present context, these specialized languages include functionalist explanations of education such as liberal-industrial theory, and relational theories such as Marxism, Bourdieu's cultural reproduction, and Bernstein's own theory of pedagogic discourse.

Bernstein suggests that the languages within a horizontal knowledge structure are not translatable, and therefore cannot be integrated at a higher level as might be possible in hierarchical, 'vertical' knowledge structures such as physics. This incommensurability is also seen at the level of a theoretical community: 'the speakers of each language become as specialized and excluding as the language. Their capital is bound up with the language and therefore defence of and challenge of other languages is intrinsic to a horizontal knowledge structure' (Bernstein 2000, p. 162). But if struggles over the hegemony and legitimacy of particular specialized languages are fundamental to sociology, how then to evaluate these languages in anything other than their own terms? Bernstein suggests that they may be distinguished in terms of their relationship with the social world, using the terms strong and weak grammar to describe the degree to which a language is able to provide relatively precise empirical descriptions. Within vertical knowledge structures, the language internal to the theory already contains principles for the description of external phenomena (Young and Muller 2013), whilst horizontal knowledge structures require an explicit syntax by which the 'invisible' conceptual interior of a specialized language is made visible. In general, Bernstein regards sociology as having a weak grammar, but set himself the task of creating within his own theory a stronger external relation. Other theories of cultural reproduction, he argues, suffer from their focus on 'relations to' rather than 'relations within'. That is to say, they focus on the relations between education and class society at the expense of analyzing the structural features within education that make social reproduction possible. Bernstein writes, 'Any theory of cultural reproduction must be able to generate principles of description of its own objects'. He claims that the conceptual framework presented in Willis (1977) and Bourdieu and Passeron (1990) is too limited to support this requirement: 'There is no way, on the basis of such concepts, that one can generate an empirical description of any specific agency of cultural reproduction' (Bernstein 1990a, p. 171). The concept of habitus receives particular criticism for lacking a precise description of its internal structure and how a particular habitus is formed; this weakens the theory because there are no criteria for establishing legitimate pathways between habitus formation and habitus effects. Diane Reay (2004) writes of the 'conceptual looseness' of habitus arising from Bourdieu's attempts to avoid determinism. This looseness leaves room for agency; however, it also results in a conception of habitus having *hermeneutic* rather than predictive power: in applying habitus to empirical situations the challenge, 'You said habitus would do this and it didn't' never precludes the response, 'No, actually in this situation habitus does something completely different'.

Bernstein's criticisms of cultural reproduction may also be applied to Marxist theories such as the correspondence principle. By explaining everything in a single totalizing idea of external relations, they explain nothing. If educational inequality is caused by capitalism's requirement for a workforce socialized into the capitalist mode of production, then reductions in inequality are also a product of capitalism. Whether such criticisms are entirely justified is another matter. Marxist accounts have often been stronger on a macrosocial scale than in studies of educational processes in their immediate historical and cultural context. However, even the correspondence principle contained an internal conceptual structure capable of producing definite descriptions of its phenomena, and although later formulations of resistance theory may be considered as having very weak grammars indeed, in Willis (1977) resistance is a quite precise concept. In Bourdieusian research, it is probably fair to say that delicate explorations of pedagogical structures in a narrow sense are lacking compared with the Bernsteinian position. However, Bourdieu's point is surely that whatever specific pedagogical approaches are used, education is so thoroughly suffused by symbolic violence that cultural reproduction, like water flowing downhill, will always find a way. Many Bourdieusian studies are highly precise explorations of how class penetrates educational settings, as the individual habitus is confronted with field conditions in different kinds of institution. Indeed, Bourdieu's conception of class in terms of particular distributions of economic and cultural capital, together with their trajectory over time, offers distinct advantages in these contexts. Factors affecting educational attainment such as parental education and status become directly *part of* the class concept in a similar way to the multidimensional approach to class contained in recent quantitative studies (for example, Bukodi et al. 2018). However, to gain the maximum advantage from this approach it is necessary to construct quite detailed accounts of how capital is structured in specific settings, rather than employing broad notions of cultural deficit and advantage.

When Bourdieu's conception of class is used in a thorough and committed way, it does indeed provide researchers with a means to reach out from the internal language to the external world. By contrast, the success of Bernstein's project in creating a strong external language of description in relation to pedagogy has led to difficulties in describing class. Numerous studies of educational settings have used his concepts to describe pedagogic practices and interactions within schools. The work of Ana Morais and Isabel Neves, for example, has provided both detailed analyses of pedagogic modalities and ways of imagining new, potentially more inclusive practices (Morais 2002; Morais and Neves 2018). However, in these and many other studies class is either implicitly absorbed into pedagogic modalities or is described in terms contrasting markedly with the grammatical strength of their analysis of pedagogy. Nor is there a developed sense of resistance or class struggle: where new pedagogic practices are introduced (for example, Bourne 2004; Morais and Neves 2018), these tend to appear as interventions, introduced by teachers or researchers rather than arising – as in Bernstein's own discussions of visible and invisible pedagogies – from specific class interests. This is not to say that Bernsteinian approaches are inherently unsatisfactory in this respect. Where more detailed attention is paid to class and its interaction with pedagogy, as in Arnot and Reay (2004) and in Ivinson (2018), the greater clarity and power of the analysis are palpable compared with studies in which the structure of pedagogy alone is the focus.

Theory development: synthesizing rational action and cultural reproduction?

Progress and development within horizontal knowledge structures take place through the creation of new specialized languages as well as the refinement of existing ones. Bernstein (2000, p. 162) writes that 'A new language offers the possibility of a fresh perspective, a new set of questions, a new set of connections, and an apparently new problematic'. This suggests that theory can be judged in terms of its productivity, its ability to generate new sublanguages or provoke entirely new departures. Richard Swedberg (2016) proposes that before theory comes *theorizing*, the process of developing new insights and understandings in relation to a social phenomenon. Whilst theory belongs to the context of justification, theorizing spans both justification and the context of discovery, describing conceptual structures that are provisional and immature but capable of a more rigorous formulation. However, Swedberg perhaps underemphasizes the role of existing theory within these processes. Theorizing does not occur outside previous conceptions, but within them, and should be viewed historically in terms of the resources and problematics provided by a specialized language. Marxist educational theory, for example, was highly productive during the 1970s, a period when it seemed eminently possible to change the world as well as understand it.[2] As circumstances altered, and the conceptual problems described by Rikowski (1997) became increasingly apparent, Marxist understandings of education were afflicted by theoretical exhaustion and other languages competed to fill the space it left. By contrast, the work of Bourdieu and Bernstein is still immensely fertile, being developed in new ways as well as providing a lens through which to view traditional problems. The provisional nature of theorizing is perhaps illustrated by debates over institutional habitus, but a common feature of such developments is their use of the conceptual world view inherent in an understanding of their parent theories as 'theory$_5$'. The explorations of gender codes by Arnot (2002), and of the epistemic device by Moore and Maton (2001), are distinctive developments of Bernstein's work but formulate new ideas in terms of his conceptual legacy: classification and framing are as important to these authors as they were to Bernstein. In a similar way, Bourdieu's concepts have been taken in new directions within and outside education, encompassing feminist theory (Adkins and

Skeggs 2004) and new understandings of class (Savage et al. 2015). If these departures have sometimes been controversial, this simply attests to their position in the activity of theorizing rather than as completed and frozen theories.

The conception of sociological theory development as a series of struggles between specialized languages suggests that an attempt to achieve a synthesis of any two of these languages would be futile. Nevertheless, there have been some attempts to combine rational action approaches with Bourdieu's cultural reproduction theory. At a somewhat minimal level, it has been accepted that distinguishing between primary and secondary effects is useful methodologically, in highlighting the persistence of class differences in educational attainment after controlling for performance (Nash 2005, 2006b). However, Nash disputes the proposition that primary and secondary effects arise from distinct processes, regarding the distinction as a purely formal one achieved by mathematical decompositions such as Jackson (2013) and her colleagues use. More fundamentally, Glaesser and Cooper (2013) argue that habitus and relative risk aversion can be complementary, with habitus providing boundaries for an essentially 'subjective' rationality. Their approach is made easier by the theoretical bifurcation of rational action models noted in Chapter 8, in which primary and secondary effects are conceptualized in different ways. However, both Bourdieu and Boudon would have been unsympathetic to this project. Boudon (1974, p. 112) describes cultural reproduction as based on 'a tautological postulate, of questionable value', whilst although Bourdieu acknowledges that strategic deliberations may override the habitus in certain circumstances (see Chapter 6), he rejects rational action as a fundamental explanation of practice. Where rational action posits goals, economic constraints and methodological individualism, Bourdieu sees the alignment between habitus and field, and the effects of homology. Nevertheless, Glaesser and Cooper (2013) consider that subjective rationality is a useful explanatory notion, and see no contradiction with Bourdieu's conceptual framework. Indeed, Bourdieu himself writes that habitus 'is the product of a particular economic condition, defined by the possession of the minimum economic and cultural capital necessary actually to perceive and seize the "potential opportunities" formally offered to all' (Bourdieu and Wacquant 1992, p. 124). Whilst habitus has of course a wider significance in the theory$_5$ sense, at the level of modelling secondary effects there would seem to be little conflict between a Bourdieusian approach and a rational action model.

Afterword

There can be few sociological fields as exciting, challenging and significant as the study of educational inequality. Empirical data, almost overwhelming in its scope and complexity, continues to accumulate, with increasingly sophisticated quantitative studies complementing equally rich and theoretically informed qualitative research. Theoretical developments, whilst perhaps centring more in recent years on the exploration of established perspectives, have been equally rewarding, and the struggles between competing languages provide a fascination in themselves. Class, as noted in the introduction to this book, remains at the heart of patterns of inequality, and the class processes described here remain as relevant to twenty-first-century capitalism as in any previous generation. At the same time, certain limitations to a class-based approach abstracted from other power relations must be acknowledged. As Yuval-Davies (2006) argues, an additive model of advantage and disadvantage in which race, gender and class are stacked on top of each other is untenable. These aspects of power and identity cannot be taken apart, analysed separately, and then put together again without losing something. A full understanding of class effects in education must therefore involve the different ways in which class permeates, and is permeated by, gender and race. This book has touched only briefly on such issues; it assumes that, at the level of the large-scale trends affecting education in many post-industrial societies, a relatively exclusive focus on class remains of value. By contributing to an understanding of how class acts as a central social formation, the book has aimed to illuminate the shaping of educational inequality. In particular, it shows that working-class (relative) failure and middle-class (relative) success cannot be reduced to essences, or to mediating factors such as class differences in aspiration, parenting behaviours and attitudes to learning. Competitive struggles for scarce educational and social goods run far deeper than this, and are radically skewed by differences in cultural and economic resources rooted in the large-scale organization of society. If *all* classes are to have a fair chance in education, fundamental social – not educational – change is required.

Notes

1 As discussed in Chapter 9, although the relevance of educational credentials to occupational competence may be absolute, opportunities to enter training programmes for prestigious occupations is likely to be positional.

2 In the eleventh thesis on Feuerbach, Marx [1845] wrote that 'The philosophers have only *interpreted* the world in various ways; the point is to *change* it' (Marx and Engels 1976b, p. 5). Abend (2008) refers to theory understood in a normative as well as an epistemological sense as 'theory$_6$'.

APPENDIX

RECENT TRENDS IN EDUCATIONAL ATTAINMENT

TABLE A.1 International trends in educational attainment of 25- to 34-year-olds by ISCED level 2000–2016. Percentages of age group

	Below upper secondary (ISCED 0–2)			Upper secondary or post-secondary non-tertiary (ISCED 3–4)			Tertiary (ISCED 5–8)		
	2000	2010	2016	2000	2010	2016	2000	2010	2016
Australia	32	15	11	37	40	39	31	44	49
France	24	16	13	45	41	43	31	43	44
Germany	15	14	13	63	60	56	22	26	31
Italy	44	29	26	46	50	48	10	21	26
Netherlands	26	17	14	48	42	41	27	41	45
Spain	44	35	35	22	25	24	34	40	41
Sweden	13	9	17	54	49	36	34	42	47
UK	33	17	13	38	37	36	29	46	52
USA	12	12	9	50	46	44	38	42	48
OECD Average	25	19	16	50	45	42	26	37	43

Source: OECD (2017b).

TABLE A.2 International Standard Classification of Education (ISCED), with UK equivalents

ISCED code	Programme name	UK (England) programmes and qualifications
0	Less than primary education	Early years education; Reception year
1	Primary education	Primary school: Key Stage 1; Key Stage 2
2	Lower secondary education	Lower secondary school: Key Stage 3
3	Upper secondary education	Upper secondary school: Key Stage 4 (GCSE)
		Vocational upper secondary: Level 1 and 2 Upper secondary school: Key Stage 5 (AS/A level)
		Vocational upper secondary: BTEC Level 3
4	Post-secondary non-tertiary education	
5	Short-cycle tertiary education	Higher education: Foundation degrees, vocational qualifications at Level 4/5
6	Bachelor's or equivalent level	Higher education: BA/BSc etc.
7	Master's or equivalent level	Higher education: postgraduate certificates, diplomas, Master's degrees
8	Doctoral or equivalent level	Doctoral degree (PhD)
9	Not elsewhere classified	

Sources: UNESCO (2012); OECD (2016).

BIBLIOGRAPHY

Abend, G. (2008) The meaning of 'theory'. *Sociological Theory*, 26(2), 173–199.

Adams, M. & Bell, L. (Eds.) (2016) *Teaching for Diversity and Social Justice*. 3rd Edition. Abingdon: Routledge.

Adkins, L. & Skeggs, B. (2004) *Feminism after Bourdieu*. Oxford: Blackwell.

Ainley, P. (2013) Education and the reconstitution of social class in England. *Research in Post-Compulsory Education*, 18(1–2), 46–60.

Allen, R. & Vignoles, A. (2006) *What Should an Index of School Segregation Measure?* London: Centre for Economics of Education.

Allmendiger, J. (1989) Educational systems and labor market outcomes. *European Sociological Review*, 5(3), 231–250.

Althusser, L. (1969) *For Marx*. London: Allen Lane, The Penguin Press.

Althusser, L. (2001) Ideology and ideological State apparatuses (notes towards an investigation). In L. Althusser (Ed.) *Lenin and Philosophy and Other Essays*. New York: Monthly Review Press.

Anderson, P. (2009) Intermediate occupations and the conceptual and empirical limitations of the hourglass economy thesis. *Work, Employment and Society*, 23(1), 169–180.

Andrews, J., Hutchinson, J. & Johnes, R. (2016) *Grammar Schools and Social Mobility*. Research Report. London: Education Policy Institute.

Anyon, J. (1980) Social class and the hidden curriculum of work. *Journal of Education*, 162(1), 67–92.

Anyon, J. (1981) Social class and school knowledge. *Curriculum Inquiry*, 11(1), 3–41.

Apple, M. (2002) Does education have independent power? Bernstein and the question of relative autonomy. *British Journal of Sociology of Education*, 23(4), 607–616.

Archer, P. & Orr, R. (2011) Class identification in review: past perspectives and future directions. *Sociology Compass*, 5(1), 104–115.

Archer, L., Francis, B., Miller, S., Taylor, B., Tereshchenko, A., David Pepper, A.M. & Travers, M⊠C. (2018) The symbolic violence of setting: a Bourdieusian analysis of mixed-methods data on secondary students' views about setting. *British Educational Research Journal*, 44(1), 119–140.

Arnot, M. (2002) *Reproducing Gender? Critical Essays on Educational Theory and Feminist Politics.* London: Routledge Falmer.

Arnot, M. & Reay, D. (2004) The framing of pedagogic encounters: regulating the social order in classroom learning. In J. Muller, B. Davies & A. Morais (Eds.) *Reading Bernstein, Researching Bernstein.* London: Routledge Falmer, 138–150.

Atkinson, A.B. (2015) *Inequality: What Can be Done?* Cambridge, MA: Harvard University Press.

Atkinson, P. (1985) *Language, Structure and Reproduction.* London: Methuen.

Atkinson, W. (2011) From sociological fictions to social fictions: some Bourdieusian reflections on the concepts of 'institutional habitus' and 'family habitus'. *British Journal of Sociology of Education,* 32(3), 331–347.

Atkinson, W. (2018) The social space, the symbolic space and masculine domination: the gendered correspondence between class and lifestyles in the UK. *European Societies,* 20(3), 478–502.

Atkinson, A., Gregg, P. & McConnell, B. (2006) *The Result of 11-Plus Selection: An Investigation into Opportunities and Outcomes for Pupils in Selective LEAs.* Working Paper No. 06/150. Bristol: University of Bristol Centre for Market and Public Organisation.

Avis, J. (2018) The re-composition of class relations: neoliberalism, precariousness, youth and education. In R. Simmons & J. Smyth (Eds.) *Education and Working-Class Youth: Reshaping the Politics of Inclusion.* Basingstoke: Palgrave Macmillan, 131–154.

Ball, S. (2003) *Class Strategies and the Education Market: The Middle Classes and Social Advantage.* Abingdon: Routledge Falmer.

Ball, S. (2018) The tragedy of state education in England: reluctance, compromise and muddle – a system in disarray. *Journal of the British Academy,* 6, 207–238.

Ball, S. & Nikita, D. (2014) The global middle class and school choice: a cosmopolitan sociology. *Zeitschrift für Erziehungswissenschaft,* 17(Supplement), 81–93.

Ballarino, G. & Bernardi, F. (2016) The intergenerational transmission of inequality and education in fourteen countries: a comparison. In F. Bernardi & G. Ballarino (Eds.) *Education, Occupation and Social Origin: A Comparative Analysis of the Transmission of Socio-Economic Inequalities.* Cheltenham: Elgar, 255–279.

Barone, C. & Ruggera, L. (2018) Educational equalization stalled? Trends in inequality of educational opportunity between 1930 and 1980 across 26 European nations. *European Societies,* 20(1), 1–25.

Bathmaker, A-M. (2017) Post-secondary education and training, new vocational and hybrid pathways and questions of equity, inequality and social mobility: introduction to the special issue. *Journal of Vocational Education & Training,* 69(1), 1–9.

Bautier, E. (2011) The analysis of pedagogic discourse as a means of understanding social inequalities in schools. In D. Frandji & P. Vitale (Eds.) *Knowledge, Pedagogy and Society: International Perspectives on Basil Bernstein's Sociology of Education.* London: Routledge, 34–46.

Beck, U. (1992) *Risk Society: Towards a New Modernity.* London: Sage.

Beck, U. & Willms, J. (2004) *Conversations with Ulrich Beck.* Cambridge: Polity Press.

Becker, G.S. (1993) *Human Capital: A Theoretical and Empirical Analysis with Special Reference to Education.* 3rd Edition. Chicago, IL: University of Chicago Press.

Becker, R. (2014) Reversal of gender differences in educational attainment: an historical analysis of the West German case. *Educational Research,* 56(2), 184–201.

Becker, R. & Hecken, A. (2009) Higher education or vocational training? An empirical test of the rational action model of educational choices suggested by Breen and Goldthorpe and Esser. *Acta Sociologica,* 52(1), 25–45.

Bell, D. (1976) *The Coming of Post-Industrial Society.* Harmondsworth: Penguin.

Bell, L. (2016) Theoretical foundations for social justice education. In M. Adams & L. Bell (Eds.) *Teaching for Diversity and Social Justice.* Abingdon: Routledge.

Beller, E. (2009) Bringing intergenerational social mobility research into the twenty-first century: why mothers matter. *American Sociological Review,* 74, 507–528.

Bernardi, F. & Triventi, M. (2018) Compensatory advantage in educational transitions: trivial or substantial? *Acta Sociologica.* doi:10.1177/0001699318780950

Bernstein, B. (1961) Social class and linguistic development: a theory of social learning. In A.H. Halsey, J. Floud & C.A. Anderson (Eds.) *Education, Economy and Society: A Reader in the Sociology of Education.* New York: The Free Press.

Bernstein, B. (1970) Education cannot compensate for society. *New Society,* 15, 387, 344–347.

Bernstein, B. (1971a) *Theoretical Studies towards a Sociology of Language. Class, Codes and Control Vol. I.* London: Routledge & Kegan Paul.

Bernstein, B. (1971b) On the classification and framing of educational knowledge. In M.F.D. Young (Ed.) *Knowledge and Control: New Directions for the Sociology of Education.* London: Collier-Macmillan.

Bernstein, B. (1975) *Towards a Theory of Educational Transmissions. Class, Codes and Control Vol. III.* London: Routledge & Kegan Paul.

Bernstein, B. (1977a) Aspects of the relations between education and production. In B. Bernstein (Ed.) *Towards a Theory of Educational Transmissions. Class, Codes and Control Vol. III.* 2nd Edition. London: Routledge & Kegan Paul, 174–200.

Bernstein, B. (1977b) Class and pedagogies: visible and invisible. In B. Bernstein (Ed.) *Towards a Theory of Educational Transmissions. Class, Codes and Control Vol. III.* 2nd Edition. London: Routledge & Kegan Paul, 116–156.

Bernstein, B. (1977c) *Towards a Theory of Educational Transmissions. Class, Codes and Control Vol. III.* 2nd Edition. London: Routledge & Kegan Paul.

Bernstein, B. (1981) Codes, modalities, and the process of cultural reproduction: a model. *Language in Society,* 10, 327–363.

Bernstein, B. (1990a) Education, symbolic control, and social practices. In B. Bernstein (Ed.) *The Structuring of Pedagogic Discourse. Class, Codes and Control Vol. IV.* London: Routledge, 133–164.

Bernstein, B. (1990b) Elaborated and restricted codes: overview and criticisms. In B. Bernstein (Ed.) *The Structuring of Pedagogic Discourse. Class, Codes and Control Vol. IV.* London: Routledge, 94–130.

Bernstein, B. (1990c) Social class and pedagogic practice. In B. Bernstein (Ed.) *The Structuring of Pedagogic Discourse. Class, Codes and Control Vol. IV.* London: Routledge, 63–93.

Bernstein, B. (1990d) *The Structuring of Pedagogic Discourse. Class, Codes and Control Vol. IV.* London: Routledge.

Bernstein, B. (2000) *Pedagogy, Symbolic Control and Identity: Theory, Research, Critique.* Revised Edition. Oxford: Rowman and Littlefield.

Bernstein, B. (2001) Symbolic control: issues of empirical description of agencies and agents. *International Journal of Social Research Methodology,* 4(1), 21–33.

Bernstein, B. & Solomon, J. (1999) 'Pedagogy, identity and the construction of a theory of symbolic control': Basil Bernstein questioned by Joseph Solomon. *British Journal of Sociology of Education,* 20(2), 265–279.

Berrington, A., Roberts, S. & Tammes, P. (2016) Educational aspirations among UK young teenagers: exploring the role of gender, class and ethnicity. *British Educational Research Journal,* 42(5), 729–755.

Bhopal, K. & Preston, J. (2012) *Intersectionality and 'Race' in Education*. Abingdon: Routledge.

BIS (2010) *Full-time Young Participation by Socio-economic Class: 2010 Update*. London: Department for Business, Innovation and Skills.

BIS (2016) *Post-16 Skills Plan*. Cm 9280. London: Department for Business, Innovation and Skills.

Bisseret, N. (1979) *Education, Class Language, and Ideology*. London: Routledge & Kegan Paul.

Blacker, D. (2013) *The Falling Rate of Learning and the Neoliberal Endgame*. Alresford: Zero Books.

Blanden, J. (2013) Cross-country rankings in intergenerational mobility: a comparison of approaches from economics and sociology. *Journal of Economic Surveys*, 27(1), 38–73.

Blanden, J. & Machin, S. (2007) *Recent Changes in Intergenerational Mobility in Britain*. London: Sutton Trust.

Blanden, J. & Macmillan, L. (2016) Educational inequality, educational expansion and intergenerational mobility. *Journal of Social Policy*, 45(4), 589–614.

Blau, P.M. & Duncan, O.D. (1967) *The American Occupational Structure*. New York: Wiley.

Blossfeld, P., Blossfeld, G. & Blossfeld, H-P. (2015) Educational expansion and inequalities in educational opportunity: long-term changes for East and West Germany. *European Sociological Review*, 31(2), 144–160.

Boaler, J. (1997) Setting, social class and survival of the quickest. *British Educational Research Journal*, 23(5), 575–595.

Board of Education (1938) *Report of the Consultative Committee on Secondary Education with Special Reference to Grammar Schools and Technical High Schools*. The Spens Report. London: HM Stationery Office.

Bogliacino, F. & Maestri, V. (2016) Wealth inequality and the great recession. *Intereconomics: Review of European Economic Policy*, 2, 61–66.

Bol, T. (2015) Has education become more positional? Educational expansion and labour market outcomes, 1985–2007. *Acta Sociologica*, 58(2), 105–120.

Boliver, V. (2011) Expansion, differentiation and the persistence of social class inequalities in British higher education. *Higher Education*, 61, 229–242.

Boliver, V. (2015) Are there distinctive clusters of higher and lower status universities in the UK? *Oxford Review of Education*, 41(5), 608–627.

Boliver, V. & Swift, A. (2011) Do comprehensive schools reduce social mobility? *British Journal of Sociology*, 62(1), 89–110.

Bolton, P. (2017) *Grammar School Statistics*. House of Commons Library Briefing Paper No. 1398. London: House of Commons Library.

Booth, C. (1887) The inhabitants of Tower Hamlets (School Board Division), their condition and occupations. *Journal of the Royal Statistical Society*, 50(2), 326–401.

Bottero, W. (2004) Class identities and the identity of class. *Sociology*, 38(5), 985–1003.

Boudon, R. (1973) *L'inégalité des Chances*. Paris: Librairie Armand Colin.

Boudon, R. (1974) *Education, Opportunity and Social Inequality: Changing Prospects in Western Society*. London: John Wiley.

Boudon, R. (1989) *The Analysis of Ideology*. Cambridge: Polity Press.

Boudon, R. (1991) *Theories of Social Change*. Cambridge: Polity Press.

Boudon, R. (2003) Beyond rational choice theory. *Annual Reviews of Sociology*, 29, 1–21.

Bourdieu, P. (1973) Cultural reproduction and social reproduction. In R. Brown (Ed.) *Knowledge, Education and Cultural Change*. London: Tavistock, 71–112.

Bourdieu, P. (1974) The school as a conservative force: scholastic and cultural inequalities. In J. Eggleston, (Ed.) *Contemporary Research in the Sociology of Education.* London: Methuen, 32–46.

Bourdieu, P. (1977a) *Outline of a Theory of Practice.* Cambridge: Cambridge University Press.

Bourdieu, P. (1977b) The economics of linguistic exchanges. *Social Science Information,* 16(6), 645–668.

Bourdieu, P. (1984) *Distinction: A Social Critique of the Judgement of Taste.* London: Routledge, Kegan & Paul.

Bourdieu, P. (1986) The forms of capital. In J. Richardson (Ed.) *Handbook of Theory and Research for the Sociology of Education.* New York: Greenwood, 241–258.

Bourdieu, P. (1987) What makes a social class? On the theoretical and practical existence of groups. *Berkeley Journal of Sociology,* 32, 1–17.

Bourdieu, P. (1989) Social space and symbolic power. *Sociological Theory,* 7(1), 18–25.

Bourdieu, P. (1990) *The Logic of Practice.* Cambridge: Polity Press.

Bourdieu, P. (1991) *Language and Symbolic Power.* Cambridge: Polity Press.

Bourdieu, P. (1996) *The State Nobility.* Cambridge: Polity Press.

Bourdieu, P. (1999) *The Weight of the World: Social Suffering in Contemporary Society.* Stanford, CA: Stanford University Press.

Bourdieu, P. (2000) *Pascalian Meditations.* Stanford, CA: Stanford University Press.

Bourdieu, P. (2005a) *The Social Structures of the Economy.* Cambridge: Polity Press.

Bourdieu, P. (2005b) Habitus. In J. Hillier & E. Rooksby (Eds.) *Habitus: A Sense of Place.* 2nd Edition. Aldershot: Ashgate.

Bourdieu, P. (2014) *On the State: Lectures at the Collège de France, 1989–1992.* Cambridge: Polity Press.

Bourdieu, P. & Passeron, J-C. (1979) *The Inheritors: French Students and their Relation to Culture.* Chicago, IL: University of Chicago Press.

Bourdieu, P. & Passeron, J.-C. (1990) *Reproduction in Education, Society and Culture.* London: Sage.

Bourdieu, P. & Wacquant, L. (1992) *An Invitation to Reflexive Sociology.* Cambridge: Polity Press.

Bourne, J. (2004) Framing talk: towards a 'radical visible pedagogy'. In J. Muller, B. Davies & A. Morais (Eds.) *Reading Bernstein, Researching Bernstein.* London: Routledge Falmer, 61–74.

Bowles, S. & Gintis, H. (1976) *Schooling in Capitalist America: Educational Reform and the Contradictions of Economic Life.* New York: Basic Books.

Bowles, S. & Gintis, H. (1988) Schooling in capitalist America: reply to our critics. In M. Cole (Ed.) *Bowles and Gintis Revisited: Correspondence and Contradiction in Educational Theory.* London: Routledge, 235–246.

Bowles, S. & Gintis, H. (2002) Schooling in capitalist America revisited. *Sociology of Education,* 75(1), 1–18.

Bowles, S. & Levin, H. (1968) The determinants of scholastic achievement: an appraisal of some recent evidence. *Journal of Human Resources,* 3(1), 3–24.

Breen, R. (2010) Educational expansion and social mobility in the 20th century. *Social Forces,* 89(2), 365–388.

Breen, R. & Goldthorpe, J. (1997) Explaining educational differentials: towards a formal rational action theory. *Rationality and Society,* 9(3), 275–305.

Breen, R. & Jonsson, J. (2005) Inequality of opportunity in comparative perspective: recent research on educational attainment and mobility. *Annual Reviews of Sociology,* 31, 223–243.

Breen, R. & Jonsson, J. (2007) Explaining change in social fluidity: educational equal-
ization and educational expansion in twentieth⊠century Sweden. *American Journal of
Sociology*, 112(6), 1775–1810.
Breen, R. & Karlson, K. (2014) Education and social mobility: new analytical ap-
proaches. *European Sociological Review*, 30(1), 107–118.
Breen, R. & Luijkx, R. (2004) Social mobility in Europe between 1970 and 2000. In
R. Breen (Ed.) *Social Mobility in Europe*. Oxford: Oxford University Press, 37–75.
Breen, R. & Rottman, D. (1995) Class analysis and class theory. *Sociology*, 29(3),
453–473.
Breen, R. & Yaish, M. (2006) Testing the Breen-Goldthorpe model of educational
decision making. *Mobility and Inequality*, 232–258.
Breen, R., van de Werfhorst, H. & Jaeger, M. (2014) Deciding under doubt: a theory
of risk aversion, time discounting preferences, and educational decision-making.
European Sociological Review, 30(2), 258–270.
Breen, R., Luijkx, R., Müller, W. & Pollak, R. (2009) Nonpersistent inequality in
educational attainment: evidence from eight European countries. *American Journal of
Sociology*, 114(5), 1475–1521.
Breen, R., Luijkx, R., Müller, W. & Pollak, R. (2010) Long-term trends in educational
inequality in Europe: class inequalities and gender differences. *European Sociological
Review*, 26(1), 31–48.
Bright, G. (2018) 'A chance to talk like this': gender, education and social haunting in a
UK coalfield. In R. Simmons & J. Smyth (Eds.) *Education and Working-Class Youth:
Reshaping the Politics of Inclusion*. Basingstoke: Palgrave Macmillan, 105–130.
Brisson, R. & Bianchi, R. (2017) Distinction at the class-fraction level? A re-
examination of Bourdieu's dataset. *Cultural Sociology*, 11(4), 489–535.
Brown, P. (1987) *Schooling Ordinary Kids: Inequality, Unemployment and the New Vocation-
alism*. London: Tavistock.
Brown, P. (2013) Education, opportunity and the prospects for social mobility. *British
Journal of Sociology of Education*, 34(5–6), 678–700.
Brown, P., Lauder, H. & Ashton, D. (2011) *The Global Auction: The Broken Promises of
Education, Jobs, and Incomes*. Oxford: Oxford University Press.
Bruckauf, Z. & Chzhen, Y. (2016) *Education for All? Measuring Inequality of Educational
Outcomes among 15-year-olds across 39 Industrialized Nations*. Innocenti Working Paper
No. 2016–8. Florence: UNICEF Office of Research.
Brunello, G. & Checchi, D. (2007) Does school tracking affect equality of opportunity?
New international evidence. *Economic Policy*, 22(52), 783–861.
Buchmann, C. & Park, H. (2009) Stratification and the formation of expectations in
highly differentiated educational systems. *Research in Social Stratification and Mobility*,
27(4), 245–267.
Buchmann, C., DiPrete, T. & McDaniel, A. (2008) Gender inequalities in education.
Annual Review of Sociology, 34, 319–337.
Bukodi, E. & Goldthorpe, J. (2011) Class origins, education and occupational attainment
in Britain: secular trends or cohort-specific effects? *European Societies*, 13(3), 347–375.
Bukodi, E. & Goldthorpe, J. (2013) Decomposing 'social origins': the effects of parents'
class, status, and education on the educational attainment of their children. *European
Sociological Review*, 29(5), 1024–1039.
Bukodi, E. & Goldthorpe, J. (2016) Educational attainment – relative or absolute – as a
mediator of intergenerational class mobility in Britain. *Research in Social Stratification
and Mobility*, 43, 5–15.

Bukodi, E. & Goldthorpe, J. (2019) *Social Mobility and Education in Britain: Research, Politics and Policy.* Cambridge: Cambridge University Press.

Bukodi, E., Erikson, R. & Goldthorpe, J. (2014) The effects of social origins and cognitive ability on educational attainment: evidence from Britain and Sweden. *Acta Sociologica,* 43, 293–310.

Bukodi, E., Goldthorpe, J., Waller, L. & Kuha, J. (2015) The mobility problem in Britain: new findings from the analysis of birth cohort data. *British Journal of Sociology,* 57(4), 93–117.

Bukodi, E., Eibl, F., Buchholz, S., Marzadro, S., Minello, A., Wahler, S., Blossfeld, H-P., Erikson, R. & Schizzerotto, A. (2018) Linking the macro to the micro: a multidimensional approach to educational inequalities in four European countries. *European Societies,* 20(1), 26–64.

Burger, K. (2016) Intergenerational transmission of education in Europe: do more comprehensive education systems reduce social gradients in student achievement? *Research in Social Stratification and Mobility,* 44, 54–67.

Burgess, S., Crawford, C. & Macmillan, L. (2017) *Assessing the Role of Grammar Schools in Promoting Social Mobility.* Working Paper 17–09. London: UCL Institute of Education.

Burke, C., Emmerich, N. & Ingram, N. (2013) Well-founded social fictions: a defence of the concepts of institutional and familial habitus. *British Journal of Sociology of Education,* 34(2), 165–182.

Burston, W.H. (1969) *James Mill on Education.* Cambridge: Cambridge University Press.

Buscha, F. & Sturgis, P. (2018) Declining social mobility? Evidence from five linked censuses in England and Wales 1971–2011. *British Journal of Sociology,* 69(1), 154–182.

Bynner, J. & Joshi, H. (2002) Equality and opportunity in education: evidence from the 1958 and 1970 birth cohort studies. *Oxford Review of Education,* 28(4), 405–425.

CACE (Central Advisory Council for Education (England)) (1963) *Half Our Future.* The Newsom Report. London: Her Majesty's Stationery Office.

Carchedi, G. (1977) *On the Economic Identification of Social Classes.* London: Routledge & Kegan Paul.

Chan, T. & Goldthorpe, J. (2007) Class and status: the conceptual distinction and its empirical relevance. *American Sociological Review,* 72(4), 512–532.

Chien, C-L., Montjouridès, P. & van der Pol, H. (2016) Global trends of access to and equity in postsecondary education. In A. Mountford-Zimdars & N. Harrison (Eds.) *Access to Higher Education: Theoretical Perspectives and Contemporary Challenges.* London: Routledge.

Chowdry, H., Crawford, C., Dearden, L., Goodman, A. & Vignoles, A. (2012) Widening participation in higher education: analysis using linked administrative data. *Journal of the Royal Statistical Society: Series A (Statistics in Society),* 176, 431–457.

Coe, R., Jones, K., Searle, J., Kokotsaki, D., Kosnin, A. & Skinner, P. (2008) *Evidence on the Effects of Selective Educational Systems.* A Report for the Sutton Trust. Durham: University of Durham Centre for Educational Management.

Coldron, J., Cripps, C. & Shipton, L. (2010) Why are English secondary schools socially segregated? *Journal of Education Policy,* 25(1), 19–35.

Cole, M. (2008) *Marxism and Educational Theory: Origins and issues.* London: Routledge.

Coleman, J.S. (1966) *Equality of Educational Opportunity.* The Coleman Report. Washington: National Center for Educational Statistics.

Collins, R. (1971) Functional and conflict theories of educational stratification. *American Sociological Review,* 36, 1002–1019.

Costa, R. & Machin, S. (2017) *Real Wages and Living Standards in the UK*. Paper EA036. London: Centre for Economic Performance.

Coyle, D. (2017) Precarious and productive work in the digital economy. *National Institute Economic Review*, 240, R5–R14.

Craft, M. & Craft, A. (1983) The participation of ethnic minority pupils in further and higher education. *Educational Research*, 25(1), 10–19.

Crawford, C. & Greaves, E. (2015) *Socio-Economic, Ethnic and Gender Differences in HE Participation*. BIS Research Paper No. 186. London: Department for Business, Innovation and Skills.

Crawford, C., Macmillan, L. & Vignoles, A. (2017a) When and why do initially high-achieving poor children fall behind? *Oxford Review of Education*, 43(1), 88–108.

Crawford, C., Dearden, L., Micklewright, J. & Vignoles, A. (2017b) *Family Background and University Success: Differences in Higher Education Access and Outcomes in England*. Oxford: Oxford University Press.

Cribb, J., Sibieta, L. & Vignoles, A. (2013) Entry into Grammar Schools in England. In J. Cribb, D. Jesson, L. Sibieta, A. Skipp & A. Vignoles (Eds.) *Poor Grammar: Entry into Grammar Schools for Disadvantaged Pupils in England*. London: Sutton Trust.

Crompton, R. (2006) Class and family. *The Sociological Review*, 54(4), 658–677.

Crompton, R. (2008) *Class and Stratification*. 3rd Edition. Cambridge: Polity Press.

Croxford, L. & Raffe, D. (2013) Differentiation and social segregation of UK higher education, 1996–2010. *Oxford Review of Education*, 39(2), 172–192.

Croxford, L. & Raffe, D. (2015) The iron law of hierarchy? Institutional differentiation in UK higher education. *Studies in Higher Education*, 40(9), 1625–1640.

Curtis, S.J. (1952) *Education in Britain since 1900*. London: Andrew Dakers.

Curtis, J. (2016) Social mobility and class identity: the role of economic conditions in 33 societies, 1999–2009. *European Sociological Review*, 32(1), 108–121.

Dale, M. (1991) Social science knowledge and explanations in educational studies. *Educational Theory*, 41, 135–152.

Danzig, A. (1995) Applications and distortions of Basil Bernstein's code theory. In A. Sadovnik (Ed.) *Knowledge and Pedagogy: The sociology of Basil Bernstein*. Norwood, NJ: Ablex Publishing Corporation.

Davies, B. (2001) Introduction. In A. Morais, I. Neves, B. Davies & H. Daniels (Eds.) *Towards a Sociology of Pedagogy: The Contribution of Basil Bernstein to Research*. New York: Peter Lang, 1–14.

Davies, B. (2011) Why Bernstein? In D. Frandji & P. Vitale (Eds.) *Knowledge, Pedagogy and Society: International perspectives on Basil Bernstein's Sociology of Education*. London: Routledge, 34–46.

DCSF (2008) *Youth Cohort Study & Longitudinal Study of Young People in England: The Activities and Experiences of 16 Year Olds*. Statistical Bulletin B01/2008. London: Department for Children, Schools and Families.

Demack, S., Drew, D. & Grimsley, M. (2000) Minding the gap: ethnic, gender and social class differences in attainment at 16, 1988–95. *Race, Ethnicity and Education*, 3(2), 117–143.

Desan, M. (2013) Bourdieu, Marx and capital: a critique of the extension model. *Sociological Theory*, 31(4), 318–342.

Devine, F. & M. Savage (2000) Conclusion: renewing class analysis. In R. Crompton, F. Devine, M. Savage & J. Scott (Eds.) *Renewing Class Analysis*. Oxford: Blackwell, 184–199.

Dewey, J. (1930) *Democracy and Education: An Introduction to the Philosophy of Education.* New York: Macmillan.

DfE (2014) *GCSE and Equivalent Attainment by Pupil Characteristics in England, 2012/13.* Statistical First Release SFR 05/2014. London: Department for Education.

DfE (2015) *GCSE and Equivalent Attainment by Pupil Characteristics, 2013 to 2014 (Revised).* Statistical First Release SFR 06/2015. London: Department for Education.

DfE (2016) *Revised GCSE and Equivalent Results in England, 2014 to 2015.* Statistical First Release SFR 01/2016. London: Department for Education.

DfE (2017a) *Participation in Education, Training and Employment by 16–18 Year Olds in England: End 2016.* Statistical First Release SFR 29/2017. London: Department for Education.

DfE (2017b) *Participation Rates in Higher Education: Academic Years 2006/07–2015/16 (Provisional).* Statistical First Release SFR 47/2017. London: Department for Education.

DfE (2017c) *Widening Participation in Higher Education, England: 2014/15 Age Cohort.* Statistical First Release SFR 39/2017. London: Department for Education.

Di Stasio, V. (2017) 'Diversion or safety net'? Institutions and public opinion on vocational education and training. *Journal of European Social Policy*, 27(4), 360–372.

Di Stasio, V., Bol, T. & Van de Werfhorst, H. (2016) What makes education positional? Institutions, overeducation and the competition for jobs. *Research in Social Stratification and Mobility*, 43, 53–63.

Dollmann, J. (2016) Less choice, less inequality? A natural experiment on social and ethnic differences in educational decision-making. *European Sociological Review*, 32(2), 203–215.

Dumay, X. & Dupriez, V. (2008) Does the school composition effect matter? Evidence from Belgian data. *British Journal of Educational Studies*, 56(4), 440–477.

Durkheim, E. (1933) *The Division of Labour in Society.* Glencoe, IL: The Free Press.

Durkheim, E. (1977) *The Evolution of Educational Thought.* London: Routledge & Kegan Paul.

Durkheim, E. (1995) *The Elementary Forms of Religious Life.* Translated by Karen E. Fields. New York: The Free Press.

Durkheim, E. & Mauss, M. (1969) *Primitive Classification.* 2nd Edition. London: Cohen & West.

Erben, M. & Gleeson, D. (1975) Reproduction and social structure: comments on Louis Althusser's sociology of education. *Educational Studies*, 1(2), 121–127.

Erikson, R. & Goldthorpe, J. (1992) *The Constant Flux: A Study of Class Mobility in Industrial Societies.* Oxford: Clarendon Press.

Erikson, R. & Goldthorpe, J. (2010) Has social mobility in Britain decreased? Reconciling divergent findings on income and class mobility. *British Journal of Sociology*, 61(2), 211–230.

Erikson, R. & Jonsson, J. (Eds.) (1996a) *Can Education be Equalised? The Swedish Case in Comparative Perspective.* Boulder, CO: Westview Press.

Erikson, R. & Jonsson, J. (1996b) Explaining class inequality in education: the Swedish test case. In R. Erikson & J. Jonsson (Eds.) *Can Education be Equalised? The Swedish Case in Comparative Perspective.* Boulder, CO: Westview Press, 1–64.

Erikson, R., Goldthorpe, J. & Portocarero, L. (1979) Intergenerational class mobility in three Western European societies: England, France and Sweden. *British Journal of Sociology*, 30(4), 415–441.

Erikson, R., Goldthorpe, J. & Portocarero, L. (1982) Social fluidity in industrial nations: England, France and Sweden. *British Journal of Sociology*, 33(1), 1–34.

Erikson, R., Goldthorpe, J. & Portocarero, L. (1983) Intergenerational class mobility and the convergence thesis: England, France and Sweden. *British Journal of Sociology*, 34(3), 303–343.

Erikson, R., Goldthorpe, J., Jackson, M., Yaish, M. & Cox, D. (2005) On class differentials in educational attainment. *Proceedings of the National Academy of Sciences of the United States of America*, 102(27), 9730–9733.

ETF (2017) *College-based Higher Education*. London: Education and Training Foundation.

European Commission (2016) *A New Skills Agenda for Europe: Working together to Strengthen Human Capital, Employability and Competitiveness*. Brussels: European Commission.

Evans, G. & Tilley, J. (2017) *The New Politics of Class: The Political Exclusion of the British Working Class*. Oxford: Oxford University Press.

Farrugia, D. & Woodman, D. (2015) Ultimate concerns in late modernity: Archer, Bourdieu and reflexivity. *British Journal of Sociology*, 66(4), 626–644.

Feinstein, L. (2003) Inequality in the early cognitive development of British children in the 1970 cohort. *Economica*, 70, 73–97.

Feinstein, L., Jerrim, J. & Vignoles, A., Goldstein, H. & French, R., Washbrook, E. & Lee, R. & Lupton, R. (2015) Social class differences in early cognitive development debate. *Longitudinal and Life Course Studies*, 6(3), 331–376.

Ferreira, F. & Gignoux, J. (2011) *The Measurement of Educational Inequality: Achievement and Opportunity*. IZA Discussion Paper No. 6161. Bonn: Institute for the Study of Labour.

Flemmen, M. (2013) Putting Bourdieu to work for class analysis: reflections on some recent contributions. *British Journal of Sociology*, 64(2), 325–343.

Flemmen, M., Jarness, V. & Rosenlund, L. (2018) Social space and cultural class divisions: the forms of capital and contemporary lifestyle differentiation. *British Journal of Sociology*, 69(1), 124–153.

Floud, J.E., Halsey, A.H. & Martin, F.M. (1956) *Social Class and Educational Opportunity*. London: Heinemann.

Foucault, M. (1978) *The History of Sexuality. Volume 1: An introduction*. New York: Pantheon Books.

Foucault, M. (1983) The subject and power. In H. Dreyfus & P. Rabinow (Eds.) *Michel Foucault: Beyond Structuralism and Hermeneutics*. 2nd Edition. Chicago, IL: University of Chicago Press, 208–226.

Fowler, B. (2011) Pierre Bourdieu: unorthodox Marxist? In S. Susen & B. Turner (Eds.) *The Legacy of Pierre Bourdieu: Critical essays*. London: Anthem Press, 33–58.

Francis, B., Archer, L., Hodgen, J. & Pepper, D. (2017) Exploring the relative lack of impact of research on 'ability grouping' in England: a discourse analytic account. *Cambridge Journal of Education*, 47(1), 1–17.

Fritzell, C. (1987) On the concept of relative autonomy in educational theory. *British Journal of Sociology of Education*, 8(1), 23–35.

Fuchs, C. (2016) *Reading Marx in the Information Age*. Abingdon: Routledge.

Gabay-Egozi, L., Shavit, S. & Yaish, M. (2010) Curricular choice: a test of a rational choice model of education. *European Sociological Review*, 26(4), 447–463.

Gambetta, D. (1987) *Were they Pushed or did they Jump? Individual Decision Mechanisms in Education*. Cambridge: Cambridge University Press.

Gamble, A. (2009) *The Spectre at the Feast: Capitalist Crisis and the Politics of Recession*. Basingstoke: Palgrave Macmillan.

Gamble, J. (2004) Retrieving the general from the particular: the structure of craft knowledge. In J. Muller, B. Davies & A. Morais (Eds.) *Reading Bernstein, Researching Bernstein*. London: Routledge Falmer, 189–203.

Gamoran, A. (2010) Tracking and inequality: new directions for research and practice. In M. Apple, S. Ball & L. Gandin (Eds.) *Routledge International Handbook of the Sociology of Education*. Abingdon: Routledge.

Garrouste, C. (2010) *100 Years of Educational Reforms in Europe: A Contextual Database*. Luxembourg: Publications Office of the European Union.

Gereluk, W. (1974) Alienation in education: a Marxian re-definition. *McGill Journal of Education*, 9(1), 34–50.

Giddens, A. (1973) *The Class Structure of the Advanced Societies*. London: Hutchinson.

Giddens, A. (1991) *Modernity and Self-Identity: Self and Society in the Late Modern Age*. Cambridge: Polity Press.

Giddens, A. (1998) *The Third Way: The Renewal of Social Democracy*. Cambridge: Polity Press.

Gillborn, D., Warmington, P. & Demack, S. (2018) QuantCrit: education, policy, 'Big Data' and principles for a critical race theory of statistics. *Race, Ethnicity and Education*, 21(2), 158–179.

Gintis, H. & Bowles, S. (1980) Contradiction and reproduction in educational theory. In L. Barton, R. Meighan & S. Walker (Eds.) *Schooling, Ideology and the Curriculum*. Barcombe: Falmer Press, 51–65.

Glaesser, J. & Cooper, B. (2013) Using rational action theory and Bourdieu's habitus theory together to account for educational decision-making in England and Germany. *Sociology*, 48(3), 463–481.

Glass, D.V. (Ed.) (1954) *Social Mobility in Britain*. London: Routledge & Kegan Paul.

Goldthorpe, J.H. (with C. Llewellyn) (1980) *Social Mobility and Class Structure in Modern Britain*. Oxford: Clarendon.

Goldthorpe, J. (1996) Class analysis and the reorientation of class theory: the case of persisting differentials in educational attainment. *British Journal of Sociology*, 47(3), 481–505.

Goldthorpe, J. (1998) Rational action theory for sociology. *British Journal of Sociology*, 49(2), 167–192.

Goldthorpe, J. (2007) *'Cultural Capital': Some Critical Observations*. Sociology Working Papers, No. 2007–07. Oxford: University of Oxford Department of Sociology.

Goldthorpe, J. (2013) Understanding – and misunderstanding – social mobility in Britain: the entry of the economists, the confusion of politicians and the limits of educational policy. *Journal of Social Policy*, 42(3), 431–450.

Goldthorpe, J. (2016) Social class mobility in modern Britain: changing structure, constant process. *Journal of the British Academy*, 4, 89–111.

Goldthorpe, J. & Jackson, M. (2007) Intergenerational class mobility in contemporary Britain: political concerns and empirical findings. *British Journal of Sociology*, 58(4), 525–546.

Goldthorpe, J. & Marshall, G. (1992) The promising future of class analysis: a response to recent critiques. *Sociology*, 26(3), 381–400.

Goldthorpe, J. & Mills, C. (2008) Trends in intergenerational class mobility in modern Britain: evidence from national surveys, 1972–2005. *National Institute Economic Review*, 205, 83–100.

Goos, M. & Manning, M. (2007) Lousy and lovely jobs: the rising polarisation of work in Britain. *The Review of Economics and Statistics*, 89(1), 118–133.

Gorard, S. (2008) Who is missing from higher education? *Cambridge Journal of Education*, 38(3), 421–437.

Gorard, S. (2009) Does the index of segregation matter? The composition of secondary schools in England since 1996. *British Educational Research Journal*, 35(4), 639–652.

Gorard, S. (2012) Who is eligible for free school meals? Characterising free school meals as a measure of disadvantage in England. *British Educational Research Journal*, 38(6), 1003–1017.

Gorard, S. (2015) The uncertain future of comprehensive schooling in England. *European Educational Research Journal*, 14(3–4), 257–268.

Gorard, S. (2016) The complex determinants of school intake characteristics and segregation, England 1989 to 2014. *Cambridge Journal of Education*, 46(1), 131–146.

Gorard, S. & Siddiqui, N. (2018) Grammar schools in England: a new analysis of social segregation and academic outcomes. *British Journal of Sociology of Education*, 39(7), 909–924.

Gorard, S., Rees, G. & Salisbury, J. (2001) Investigating the patterns of differential attainment of boys and girls at school. *British Educational Research Journal*, 27(2), 125–139.

Gordon, L. (1989) Beyond relative autonomy theories of the State in education. *British Journal of Sociology of Education*, 10(4), 435–447.

Gospel, H. (1995) The decline in apprenticeship training in Britain. *Industrial Relations Journal*, 26(1), 32–45.

Gottesman, I. (2016) *The Critical Turn in Education: From Marxist Critique to Post-Structuralist Feminism to Critical Theories of Race*. New York: Routledge.

Grace (2008) Changes in the classification and framing of education in Britain, 1950s to 2000s: an interpretive essay after Bernstein. *Journal of Educational Administration and History*, 40(3), 209–220.

Gray, J. & Moshinsky, P. (1935) Ability and educational opportunity in relation to parental occupation. *The Sociological Review*, 27(3), 281–327.

Green, A. (2013) *Education and State Formation: Europe, East Asia and the USA*. 2nd Edition. Basingstoke: Palgrave Macmillan.

Green, A. & Pensiero, N. (2016) The effects of upper-secondary education and training systems on skills inequality. A quasi-cohort analysis using PISA 2000 and the OECD survey of adult skills. *British Educational Research Journal*, 42(5), 756–779.

Green, A. & White, R. (2008) Shaped by place: young people's decisions about education, training and work. *Benefits*, 16, 213–224.

Gregg, P., Jonsson, J., Macmillan, L. & Mood, C. (2017) The role of education for intergenerational income mobility: a comparison of the United States, Great Britain, and Sweden. *Social Forces*, 96(1), 121–152.

Griffin, C. (1985) *Typical Girls? Young Women from School to the Job Market*. London: Routledge.

Gugushvili, A., Bukodi, E. & Goldthorpe, J. (2017) The direct effect of social origins on social mobility chances: 'glass floors' and 'glass ceilings' in Britain. *European Sociological Review*, 33(2), 305–316.

Haavelsrud, M. (2001) Classification strength and power relations. In A. Morais, I. Neves, B. Davies & H. Daniels (Eds.) *Towards a Sociology of Pedagogy: The Contribution of Basil Bernstein to Research*. New York: Peter Lang, 319–338.

Habermas, J. (1976) *Legitimation Crisis*. London: Heinemann.

Haim, E. & Shavit, Y. (2013) Expansion and inequality of educational opportunity: a comparative study. *Research in Social Stratification and Mobility*, 31, 22–31.

Halsey, A.H., Heath, A.F. & Ridge, J.M. (1980) *Origins and Destinations: Family, Class and Education in Modern Britain*. Oxford: Clarendon Press.

Hansen, M. (2008) Rational action theory and educational attainment: changes in the impact of economic resources. *European Sociological Review*, 24(1), 1–17.

Hargreaves, A. (1982) Resistance and relative autonomy theories: problems of distortion and incoherence in recent Marxist analyses of education. *British Journal of Sociology of Education*, 3(2), 107–126.

Harris, R. & Rose, S. (2013) Who benefits from grammar schools? A case study of Buckinghamshire, England. *Oxford Review of Education*, 39(2), 151–171.

Hart, R., Moro, M. & Roberts, J.E. (2012) *Date of Birth, Family Background, and the 11-plus Exam: Short- and long-term Consequences of the 1944 Secondary Education Reforms in England and Wales*. Stirling Economics Discussion Paper 2012–10. Stirling: University of Stirling Management School.

Harvey, D. (2005) *A Brief History of Neoliberalism*. Oxford: Oxford University Press.

Harvey, D. (2014) *Seventeen Contradictions and the End of Capitalism*. London: Profile Books.

Hatcher, R. (1998) Class differentiation in education: rational choices? *British Journal of Sociology of Education*, 19(1), 5–24.

Heath, A. (2000) The political arithmetic tradition in the sociology of education. *Oxford Review of Education*, 26(3–4), 313–331.

Heath, A., Mills, C. & Roberts, J. (1992) Towards meritocracy? Recent evidence on an old problem. In C. Crouch & A. Heath (Eds.) *Social Research and Social Reform: Essays in Honour of A.H. Halsey*. Oxford: Oxford University Press.

Heckman, J. (2007) The economics, technology, and neuroscience of human capability formation. *Proceedings of the National Academy of Sciences*, 104(33), 13250–13255.

Hesse, M. (1972) In defence of objectivity. *Proceedings of the British Academy*, 58, 275–292.

Hick, R. & Lanau, A. (2017) *In-Work Poverty in the UK*. London: Nuffield Foundation.

Hillmert, S. & Jacob, M. (2003) Social inequality in higher education: is vocational training a pathway leading to or away from university? *European Sociological Review*, 19(3), 319–334.

Hirsch, F. (1976) *Social Limits to Growth*. Cambridge, MA: Harvard University Press.

HM Government (2011) *Opening Doors, Breaking Barriers: A Strategy for Social Mobility*. London: Cabinet Office.

Hoadley, U. (2008) Social class and pedagogy: a model for the investigation of pedagogic variation. *British Journal of Sociology of Education*, 29(1), 63–78.

Hoadley, U. & Galant, J. (2016) Specialization and school organization: investigating pedagogic culture. *British Journal of Sociology of Education*, 37(8), 1187–1210.

Hobbs, G. & Vignoles, A. (2010) Is children's free school meal 'eligibility' a good proxy for family income? *British Educational Research Journal*, 36(4), 673–690.

Hodgson, A. & Spours, K. (2014) Middle attainers and 14–19 progression in England: half-served by New Labour and now overlooked by the Coalition? *British Educational Research Journal*, 40(3), 467–482.

Hodkinson, P. (2016) Youth cultures and the rest of life: subcultures, post-subcultures and beyond. *Journal of Youth Studies*, 19(5), 629–645.

Hollingworth, S. (2015) Performances of social class, race and gender through youth subculture: putting structure back in to youth subcultural studies. *Journal of Youth Studies*, 18(10), 1237–1256.

Hollingworth, S. & Williams, K. (2010) Multicultural mixing or middle-class reproduction? The white middle classes in London comprehensive schools. *Space and Polity*, 14(1), 47–64.

Holmes, C. & Mayhew, K. (2012) *The Changing Shape of the UK Job Market and its Implications for the Bottom Half of Earners*. London: Resolution Foundation.

Hout, M. (1988) More universalism, less structural mobility: the American occupational structure in the 1980s. *American Journal of Sociology*, 93(6), 1358–1400.

Hout, M. (2015) A summary of what we know about social mobility. *Annals of the American Academy of Political and Social Science*, 657(1), 27–36.

Hupkau, C., McNally, S., Ruiz-Valenzuela, J. & Ventura, G. (2017) Post-compulsory education in England: choices and implications. *National Institute Economic Review*, 240, R42–R57.

Iannelli, C. (2007) Inequalities in entry to higher education: a comparison over time between Scotland and England and Wales. *Higher Education Quarterly*, 61(3), 306–333.

Iannelli, C. (2013) The role of the school curriculum in social mobility. *British Journal of Sociology of Education*, 34(5–6), 907–928.

Iannelli, C. & Duta, A. (2018) Inequalities in school leavers' labour market outcomes: do school subject choices matter? *Oxford Review of Education*, 44(1), 56–74.

Iannelli, C. & Paterson, L. (2007) Education and social mobility in Scotland. *Research in Social Stratification and Mobility*, 25, 219–232.

Iannelli, C., Smyth, E. & Klein, M. (2016) Curriculum differentiation and social inequality in higher education entry in Scotland and Ireland. *British Educational Research Journal*, 42(4), 561–581.

Ilie, S., Sutherland, A. & Vignoles, A. (2017) Revisiting free school meal eligibility as a proxy for pupil socio-economic deprivation. *British Educational Research Journal*, 43(2), 253–274.

Ingram, N. (2011) Within school and beyond the gate: the complexities of being educationally successful and working class. *Sociology*, 45(2), 287–302.

Irwin, S. (2015) Class and comparison: subjective social location and lay experiences of constraint and mobility. *British Journal of Sociology*, 66(2), 259–281.

Irwin, S. (2018) Lay perceptions of inequality and social structure. *Sociology*, 52(2), 211–227.

Ivinson, G. (2018) Re-imagining Bernstein's restricted codes. *European Educational Research Journal*, 17(4), 539–554.

Jackson, M. (Ed.) (2013) *Determined to Succeed? Performance versus Choice in Educational Attainment*. Stanford, CA: Stanford University Press.

Jackson, M. & Jonsson, J. (2013) Why does inequality of educational opportunity vary across countries? Primary and secondary effects in comparative perspective. In M. Jackson (Ed.) *Determined to Succeed? Performance versus Choice in Educational Attainment*. Stanford, CA: Stanford University Press, 306–337.

Jackson, B. & Marsden, D. (1962) *Education and the Working Class*. London: Routledge & Kegan Paul.

Jackson, M., Goldthorpe, J. & Mills, C. (2005) Education, employers and class mobility. *Research in Social Stratification and Mobility*, 23, 3–33.

Jackson, M., Erikson, R., Goldthorpe, J. & Yaish, M. (2007) Primary and secondary effects in class differentials in educational attainment: the transition to A-level courses in England and Wales. *Acta Sociologica*, 50(3), 211–229.

Jaeger, M. (2007) Economic and social returns to educational choices: extending the utility function. *Rationality and Society*, 19(4), 451–483.

Jaeger, M. & Holm, A. (2012) Conformists or rebels? Relative risk aversion, educational decisions and social class reproduction. *Rationality and Society*, 24(2), 221–253.

James, D., Reay, D., Crozier, G., Beedell, P., Hollingworth, S., Jamieson, F. & Williams, K. (2010) Neoliberal policy and the meaning of counterintuitive middle-class school choices. *Current Sociology*, 58(4), 623–641.

Jencks, C., Smith, M., Acland, H., Bane, M., Cohen, D., Gintis, H., Heyns, B. & Michelson, S. (1972) *Inequality: A Reassessment of the Effect of Family and Schooling in America.* New York: Basic Books.

Jenkins, S., Micklewright, J. & Schnepf, S. (2008) Social segregation in secondary schools: how does England compare with other countries? *Oxford Review of Education*, 34(1), 21–37.

Jerrim, J. & Macmillan, L. (2015) Income inequality, intergenerational mobility and the Great Gatsby Curve: is education the key? *Social Forces*, 94(2), 505–533.

Jerrim, J. & Vignoles, A. (2011) *The Use (and misuse) of Statistics in Understanding Social Mobility: Regression to the Mean and the Cognitive Development of High Ability Children from Disadvantaged Homes.* DoQSS Working Paper No. 11–01. London: Institute of Education.

Jerrim, J. & Vignoles, A. (2015) University access for disadvantaged children: a comparison across countries. *Higher Education*, 70, 903–921.

Johansson, T. & Lalander, P. (2012) Doing resistance – youth and changing theories of resistance. *Journal of Youth Studies*, 15(8), 1078–1088.

Karabel, J. (2005) *The Chosen: The Hidden History of Admission and Exclusion at Harvard, Yale and Princeton.* Boston, MA: Houghton Mifflin.

Karabel, J. & Halsey, A. (1977) *Power and Ideology in Education.* New York: Oxford University Press.

Keep, E. & Mayhew, K. (2010) Moving beyond skills as a social and economic panacea. *Work, Employment and Society*, 24(3), 565–577.

Keller, S. & Zavalloni, M. (1964) Ambition and social class: a respecification. *Social Forces*, 43(1), 58–70.

Kerckhoff, A. (2001) Education and social stratification processes in comparative perspective. *Sociology of Education*, 74(Extra Issue), 3–18.

Kerckhoff, A., Fogelman, K. & Manlove, J. (1997) Staying ahead: the middle class and school reform in England and Wales. *Sociology of Education*, 70(1), 19–35.

Khattab, N. & Modood, T. (2018) Accounting for British Muslim's educational attainment: gender differences and the impact of expectations. *British Journal of Sociology of Education*, 39(2), 242–259.

Kingdon, G. & Cassen, R. (2010) Ethnicity and low achievement in English schools. *British Educational Research Journal*, 36(3), 403–431.

Kirk, N. (2017) *Social Class and Marxism: Defences and challenges.* Abingdon: Routledge.

Koo, H. (2016) The global middle class: how is it made, what does it represent? *Globalizations*, 13(4), 440–453.

Kroneberg, C. & Kalter, F. (2012) Rational choice theory and empirical research: methodological and theoretical contributions from Europe. *Annual Reviews of Sociology*, 38, 73–92.

Lareau, A. & Weininger, E. (2003) Cultural capital in educational research: a critical assessment. *Theory and Society*, 32, 567–606.

Lash, S. (1992) *Modernity and Identity.* Oxford: Blackwell.

Lave, J. & McDermott, R. (2002) Estranged learning. *Outlines*, 1, 19–48.

Lazzarato, M. (1996) Immaterial labour. In P. Vimo & M. Hardt (Eds.) *Radical Thought in Italy: A Potential Politics.* Minneapolis: University of Minnesota Press, 133–150.

Lehmann, W. (2013) Habitus transformation and hidden injuries: successful working-class university students. *Sociology of Education,* 87(1), 1–15.

Lenin, V.I. (1965) Speech at the First All-Russia Congress on Education, August 28, 1918. In J. Riordan (Ed.) *Lenin: Collected Works,* Vol. 28. Moscow: Progress Publishers, 85–88.

Levacic, R. & Marsh, A. (2007) Secondary modern schools: are their pupils disadvantaged? *British Educational Research Journal,* 33, 155–178.

Li, Y. & Devine, F. (2011) Is social mobility really declining? Intergenerational class mobility in Britain in the 1990s and the 2000s. *Sociological Research Online,* 16(3), 4.

Lipset, S. & Zetterburg, H. (1959) Social mobility in industrial societies. In S.M. Lispset, H.L. Zetterburg & R. Bendix (Eds.) *Social Mobility in Industrial Society.* Berkeley: University of California Press.

Littler, J. (2018) *Against Meritocracy: Culture, Power and Myths of Mobility.* Abingdon: Routledge.

Liu, Y., Green, A. & Pensiero, N. (2016) Expansion of higher education and inequality of opportunities: a cross-national analysis. *Journal of Higher Education Policy and Management,* 38(3), 242–263.

Lucas, S. (2001) Effectively maintained inequality: education transitions, track mobility, and social background effects. *American Journal of Sociology,* 106(6), 1642–1690.

Lucas, S. (2009) Stratification theory, socioeconomic background, and educational attainment: a formal analysis. *Rationality and Society,* 21(4), 459–511.

Mare, R. (1981) Change and stability in educational stratification. *American Sociological Review,* 46, 72–97.

Marks, G. (2014) *Education, Social Background and Cognitive Ability: The Decline of the Social.* Abingdon: Routledge.

Marks, G. (2015) Are school-SES effects statistical artefacts? Evidence from longitudinal population data. *Oxford Review of Education,* 41(1), 122–144.

Marshall, G., Swift, A. & Roberts, S. (1997) *Against the Odds? Social Class and Social Justice in Industrial Societies.* Oxford: Clarendon Press.

Marx, K. & Engels, F. (1976a) *Karl Marx and Frederick Engels Collected Works, Vol. 5: Marx and Engels 1845–47.* London: Lawrence & Wishart.

Marx, K. & Engels, F. (1976b) *Karl Marx and Frederick Engels Collected Works, Vol. 6: Marx and Engels 1845–48.* London: Lawrence & Wishart.

Marx, K. & Engels, F. (1979) *Karl Marx and Frederick Engels Collected Works, Vol. 11: Marx and Engels 1851–53.* London: Lawrence & Wishart.

Marx, K. & Engels, F. (1985) *Karl Marx and Frederick Engels Collected Works, Vol. 21: Marx and Engels 1867–70.* London: Lawrence & Wishart.

Marx, K. & Engels, F. (1987) *Karl Marx and Frederick Engels Collected Works, Vol. 29: Marx 1857–61.* London: Lawrence & Wishart.

Marx, K. & Engels, F. (1996) *Karl Marx and Frederick Engels Collected Works, Vol. 35: Capital Volume 1.* London: Lawrence & Wishart.

Marx, K. & Engels, F. (1998) *Karl Marx and Frederick Engels Collected Works, Vol. 37: Capital Volume 3.* London: Lawrence & Wishart.

Maton, K. (2004) The wrong kind of knower: education, expansion and the epistemic device. In J. Muller, B. Davies & A. Morais (Eds.) *Reading Bernstein, Researching Bernstein.* London: Routledge Falmer, 218–231.

McCulloch, G. (1998) *Failing the Ordinary Child? The Theory and Practice of Working-Class Secondary Education*. Buckingham: Open University Press.

McDonough, P. (1997) *Choosing Colleges: How Social Class and Schools Structure Opportunity*. Albany: State University of New York Press.

McDowell, L. (2003) *Redundant Masculinities: Employment Change and White Working Class Youth*. Oxford: Blackwell.

McGrew, K. (2011) A review of class-based theories of student resistance in education: mapping the origins and influence of *Learning to Labour* by Paul Willis. *Review of Educational Research*, 81(2), 234–266.

McKenzie, L. (2015) *Getting By: Estates, Class and Culture in Austerity Britain*. Bristol: Policy Press.

McKnight, A. (2015) *Downward Mobility: Opportunity Hoarding and the 'Glass Floor'*. Research Report. London: Social Mobility and Child Poverty Commission.

McRobbie, A. (2000) *Feminism and Youth Culture*. 2nd Edition. New York: Routledge.

Mijs, J. (2016) The unfulfillable promise of meritocracy: three lessons and their implications for justice in education. *Social Justice Research*, 29, 14–34.

Milios, J. & Economakis, G. (2011) The middle classes, class places, and class positions: a critical approach to Nicos Poulantzas's theory. *Rethinking Marxism*, 23(2), 226–245.

Miller, D. (1999) *Principles of Social Justice*. Cambridge, MA: Harvard University Press.

Mirza, H. (1992) *Young, Female and Black*. London: Routledge.

Moore, R. (2013) *Basil Bernstein: The Thinker and the Field*. Abingdon: Routledge.

Moore, R. & Maton, K. (2001) Founding the sociology of knowledge: Basil Bernstein, intellectual fields, and the epistemic device. In A. Morais, I. Neves, B. Davies & H. Daniels (Eds.) *Towards a Sociology of Pedagogy: The Contribution of Basil Bernstein to Research*. New York: Peter Lang, 153–182.

Morais, A. (2002) Basil Bernstein at the micro level of the classroom. *British Journal of Sociology of Education*, 23(4), 559–569.

Morais, A. & Neves, I. (2018) The quest for high-level knowledge in schools: revisiting the concepts of classification and framing. *British Journal of Sociology of Education*, 39(3), 261–282.

Morgan, S. (2012) Models of college entry in the United States and the challenges of estimating primary and secondary effects. *Sociological Methods & Research*, 41(1), 17–56.

Mountford-Zimdars, A. & Harrison, N. (Eds.) (2016) *Access to Higher Education: Theoretical Perspectives and Contemporary Challenges*. London: Routledge.

Müller, W. & Karle, W. (1993) Social selection in educational systems in Europe. *European Sociological Review*, 9(1), 1–23.

Murphy, J. (1990) A most respectable prejudice: inequality in educational research and policy. *British Journal of Sociology*, 41(1), 29–54.

Murray, K. & Liston, D. (2015) Schooling in capitalism: navigating the bleak pathways of structural fate. *Educational Theory*, 65(3), 245–264.

Nash, R. (1990) Bourdieu on education and cultural reproduction. *British Journal of Sociology of Education*, 11(4), 431–447.

Nash, R. (2005) Boudon, realism and the cognitive habitus: why an explanation of inequality/difference cannot be limited to a model of secondary effects. *Interchange*, 36(3), 275–293.

Nash, R. (2006a) Bernstein and the explanation of social disparities in education: a realist critique of the socio-linguistic thesis. *British Journal of Sociology of Education*, 27(5), 539–553.

Nash, R. (2006b) Controlling for 'ability': a conceptual and empirical study of primary and secondary effects. *British Journal of Sociology of Education*, 27(2), 157–172.

National Audit Office (2008) *Widening Participation in Higher Education*. HC 725 Session 2007–2008. Norwich: The Stationery Office.

NCIHE (National Committee of Inquiry into Higher Education) (1963) *Higher Education*. The Robbins Report. Cmnd 2154. London: Her Majesty's Stationery Office.

NCIHE (National Committee of Inquiry into Higher Education) (1997) *Higher Education in the Learning Society*. The Dearing Report. London: Her Majesty's Stationery Office.

Neugebauer, M. & Schindler, S. (2012) Early transitions and tertiary enrolment: the cumulative impact of primary and secondary effects on entering university in Germany. *Acta Sociologica*, 55(1), 19–36.

Nielsen, F. & Roos, J. (2015) Genetics of educational attainment and the persistence of privilege at the turn of the 21st century. *Social Forces*, 94(2), 535–561.

Niemi, A-M. & Rosvall, P-A. (2013) Framing and classifying the theoretical and practical divide: how young men's positions in vocational education are produced and reproduced. *Journal of Vocational Education and Training*, 65(4), 445–460.

Nixon, D. (2009) 'I can't put a smiley face on': working-class masculinity, emotional labour and service work in the 'New Economy'. *Gender, Work and Organization*, 16(3), 300–322.

Nolan, K. (2011) Oppositional behaviour in urban schooling: toward a theory of resistance for new times. *International Journal of Qualitative Studies in Education*, 24(5), 559–572.

Obermeier, V. & Schneider, T. (2015) Educational choice and risk preferences: how important is relative vs. individual risk preference? *Journal for Educational Research Online*, 7(2), 99–128.

OECD (2010) A family affair: intergenerational social mobility across OECD countries. In *Economic Policy Reforms: Going for Growth*. Paris: OECD Publishing Division.

OECD (2012) *Education at a Glance 2012: OECD Indicators*. Paris: OECD Publishing.

OECD (2014a) *Education at a Glance 2014: OECD Indicators*. Paris: OECD Publishing.

OECD (2014b) *Skills Beyond School: Synthesis Report*. OECD Reviews of Vocational Education and Training. Paris: OECD Publishing.

OECD (2017a) *OECD Employment Outlook 2017*. Paris: OECD Publishing.

OECD (2017b) *Education at a Glance 2017: OECD Indicators*. Paris: OECD Publishing.

ONS (2017a) EMP08: All in employment by occupation. Dataset. Available online at www.ons.gov.uk (Accessed 26 September 2017).

ONS (2017b) JOBS02: Workforce jobs by industry. Dataset. Available online at www.ons.gov.uk (Accessed 26 September 2017).

ONS (2018) Analysis of real earnings and contributions to nominal earnings growth, Great Britain: August 2018. Available online at www.ons.gov.uk (Accessed 7 September 2018).

Pakulski, J. & Waters, M. (1996) *The Death of Class*. London: Sage.

Paterson, L. & Iannelli, C. (2007a) Social class and educational attainment: a comparative study of England, Wales, and Scotland. *Sociology of Education*, 80(4), 330–358.

Paterson, L. & Iannelli, C. (2007b) Patterns of absolute and relative social mobility: a comparative study of England, Wales and Scotland. *Sociological Research Online*, 12(6), 15.

Peters, M. (2018) Affective capitalism, higher education and the constitution of the social body Althusser, Deleuze, and Negri on Spinoza and Marxism. *Educational Philosophy and Theory*, doi:10.1080/00131857.2018.1439720.

Pfeffer, F. (2008) Persistent inequality in educational attainment and its institutional context. *European Sociological Review*, 24(5), 543–565.

Pfeffer, F. (2015) Equality and quality in education: a comparative study of 19 countries. *Social Science Research*, 51, 35–368.

Pfeffer, F. & Hällsten, M. (2012) *Mobility Regimes and Parental Wealth: The United States, Germany and Sweden in Comparison*. Report RR-766. Ann Arbor: Population Studies Centre, University of Michigan.

Pfeffer, F. & Hertel, F. (2015) How has educational expansion shaped social mobility trends in the United States? *Social Forces*, 94(1), 143–180.

Piketty, T. (2014) *Capital in the Twenty-First Century*. Cambridge, MA: Harvard University Press.

Poulantzas, N. (1973) On social classes. *New Left Review*, 78, 27–54.

Power, S. & Whitty, G. (2002) Bernstein and the middle class. *British Journal of Sociology of Education*, 23(4), 595–606.

Power, S., Edwards, T., Whitty, G. & Wigfall, V. (2003) *Education and the Middle Class*. Buckingham: Open University Press.

Prandy, K. (1990) The revised Cambridge scale of occupations. *Sociology*, 24(4), 629–655.

Prandy, K. (1998) Deconstructing classes: critical comments on the revised social classification. *Work, Employment and Society*, 12(4), 743–753.

Raftery, A. & Hout, M. (1993) Maximally maintained inequality: expansion, reform and opportunity in Irish education, 1921–75. *Sociology of Education*, 66, 41–62.

Rawls, J. (1999) *A Theory of Justice*. Revised Edition. Cambridge, MA: Harvard University Press.

Reay, D. (2004) 'It's all becoming a habitus': beyond the habitual use of habitus in educational research. *British Journal of Sociology of Education*, 25(4), 431–444.

Reay, D. (2005) Beyond consciousness? The psychic landscape of class. *Sociology*, 39(5), 911–928.

Reay, D. (2006) The zombie stalking English schools: social class and educational inequality. *British Journal of Educational Studies*, 54(3), 288–307.

Reay, D. (2017) *Miseducation: Inequality, Education and the Working Classes*. Bristol: Policy Press.

Reay, D. & Lucey, H. (2004) Stigmatised choices: social class, social exclusion and secondary school markets in the inner city. *Pedagogy, Culture and Society*, 12(1), 35–51.

Reay, D. & Lucey, H. (2007) 'Unruly places': inner-city comprehensives, middle-class imaginaries and working-class children. *Urban Studies*, 44(7), 1191–1201.

Reay, D., Crozier, G. & Clayton, J. (2009) 'Strangers in paradise?' Working-class students in elite universities. *Sociology*, 43(6), 1103–1121.

Reay, D., Crozier, G. & Clayton, J. (2010) 'Fitting in' or 'standing out': working-class students in UK higher education. *British Educational Research Journal*, 36(1), 107–124.

Reay, D., Crozier, G. & James, D. (2011) *White Middle-Class Identities and Urban Schooling*. Basingstoke: Palgrave Macmillan.

Reay, D., David, M. & Ball, S. (2005) *Degrees of Choice: Social Class, Race and Gender in Higher Education*. Stoke-on-Trent: Trentham Books.

Richardson, W. (2007) In search of the further education of young people in post-war England. *Journal of Vocational Education and Training*, 59(3), 385–418.

Rikowski, G. (1996) Left alone: end time for Marxist educational theory? *British Journal of Sociology of Education*, 17(4), 415–451.

Rikowski, G. (1997) Scorched earth: prelude to rebuilding Marxist educational theory. *British Journal of Sociology of Education*, 18(4), 551–574.

Rikowski, G. (2004) Marx and the education of the future. *Policy Futures in Education*, 2(3–4), 565–577.

Rose, D. (1998) Once more unto the breach: in defence of class analysis yet again. *Work, Employment and Society*, 12(4), 755–767.

Rose, D., Pevalin, D. & O'Reilly, K. (2005) *The National Statistics Socio-economic Classification: Origins, Development and Use*. Basingstoke: Palgrave Macmillan.

Ruggera, I. & Barone, C. (2017) Social closure, micro-class immobility and the intergenerational reproduction of the upper class: a comparative study. *British Journal of Sociology*, 68(2), 194–214.

Russell, L. (2011) *Understanding Pupil Resistance: Integrating Gender, Ethnicity and Class*. Stroud: E&E Publishing.

Salvatori, A. (2015) *The Anatomy of Job Polarisation in the UK*. IZA Discussion Paper No. 9193. Bonn: Forschungsinstitut zur Zukunft der Arbeit.

Sarup, M. (1978) *Marxism and Education*. London: Routledge and Kegan Paul.

Savage, M. (2000) *Class Analysis and Social Transformation*. Buckingham: Open University Press.

Savage, M. (2003) A new class paradigm? *British Journal of Sociology of Education*, 24(4), 535–541.

Savage, M., Cunningham, N., Devine, F., Friedman, S., Laurison, D., McKenzie, L., Miles, A., Snee, H. & Wakeling, P. (2015) *Social Class in the 21st Century*. London: Pelican Books.

Schindler, S. (2017) School tracking, educational mobility and inequality in German secondary education: developments across cohorts. *European Societies*, 19(1), 28–48.

Schindler, S. & Lörz, M. (2012) Mechanisms of social inequality development: primary and secondary effects in the transition to tertiary education between 1976 and 2005. *European Sociological Review*, 28(5), 647–660.

Schmitz, A., Witte, D. & Gengnagel, V. (2017) Pluralizing field analysis: toward a relational understanding of the field of power. *Social Science Information*, 56(1), 49–73.

Schofer, E. & Meyer, J. (2005) The worldwide expansion of higher education in the twentieth century. *American Sociological Review*, 70(6), 898–920.

Sennett, R. & Cobb, J. (1972) *The Hidden Injuries of Class*. Cambridge: Cambridge University Press.

Shavit, Y. & Blossfeld, H.P. (1993) *Persistent Inequality: Changing Educational Attainment in Thirteen Countries*. Boulder, CO: Westview Press.

Shavit, Y. & Müller, W. (2000) Vocational secondary education: where diversion and where safety net? *European Societies*, 2(1), 29–50.

Shavit, Y., Arum, R. & Gamoran, A. (2007) *Stratification in Higher Education: A Comparative Study*. Stanford, CA: Stanford University Press.

Shildrick, T., MacDonald, R., Webster, C. & Garthwaite, K. (2012) *Poverty and Insecurity: Life in Low-Pay, No-Pay Britain*. Bristol: Policy Press.

Shilling, C. (1992) Reconceptualising structure and agency in the sociology of education: structuration theory and schooling. *British Journal of Sociology of Education*, 13(1), 69–87.

Shuttleworth, I. (1995) The relationship between social deprivation, as measured by individual free school meal eligibility, and educational attainment at GCSE in

Northern Ireland: a preliminary investigation. *British Educational Research Journal,* 21(4), 487–504.

Simmons, R. & Smyth, J. (2018) *Education and Working-Class Youth: Reshaping the Politics of Inclusion.* Basingstoke: Palgrave Macmillan.

Simon, B. (1991) *Education and the Social Order 1940–1990.* London: Lawrence and Wishart.

Singh, P. (2017) Pedagogic governance: theorising with/after Bernstein. *British Journal of Sociology of Education,* 38(2), 144–163.

Skeggs, B. (1997) *Formations of Class and Gender: Becoming Respectable.* London: Sage.

Skeggs, B. (2005) *Class, Self, Culture.* London: Routledge.

Skeggs, B. (2015) Stratification or exploitation, domination, dispossession and devaluation? *The Sociological Review,* 63, 205–222.

Small, R. (2005) *Marx and Education.* London: Ashgate.

Smyth, J. (2004) Social capital and the 'socially just school'. *British Journal of Sociology of Education,* 25(1), 19–34.

Snee, H. & Devine, F. (2018) Fair chances and hard work? Families making sense of inequality and opportunity in 21st century Britain. *British Journal of Sociology.* doi:10.1111/1468-4446.12358

Solga, H. (2014) Education, economic inequality and the promises of the social investment state. *Socio-Economic Review,* 12, 269–297.

Solga, H., Protsch, P., Ebner, C. & Brzinsky-Fay, C. (2014) *The German Vocational Education and Training System: Its Institutional Configuration, Strengths, and Challenges.* Discussion Paper SP I 2014–502. Berlin: Wissenschaftszentrum Berlin für Sozialforschung.

Sorokin, P.A. (1927) *Social Mobility.* New York: Harper & Row.

Souto-Otero, M. & Whitworth, A. (2017) Adult participation in higher education and the 'knowledge economy': a cross-national analysis of patterns of delayed participation in higher education across 15 European countries. *British Journal of Sociology of Education,* 38(6), 763–781.

Stahl, G. (2016) Doing Bourdieu justice: thinking with and beyond Bourdieu. *British Journal of Sociology of Education,* 37(7), 1091–1103.

Stahl, G. (2018) Counternarratives to neoliberal aspirations: White working-class boys' practices of value-constitution in formal education. In R. Simmons & J. Smyth (Eds.) *Education and Working-Class Youth: Reshaping the Politics of Inclusion.* Basingstoke: Palgrave Macmillan, 55–78.

Standing, G. (2011) *The Precariat: The New Dangerous Class.* London: Bloomsbury.

Stevenson, T. (1913) Review of the vital statistics of the year 1911. In *The Seventy-Fourth Annual Report of the Registrar-General of Births, Deaths and Marriages in England and Wales (1911),* xii-ci. Cd 6578. London: Wyman and Sons.

Stocké, V. (2007) Explaining educational decision and effects of families' social class position: an empirical test of the Breen–Goldthorpe model of educational attainment. *European Sociological Review,* 23(4), 505–519.

Straehler-Pohl, H. & Gellert, U. (2013) Towards a Bernsteinian language of description for mathematics classroom discourse. *British Journal of Sociology of Education,* 34(3), 313–332.

Strand, S. (2011) The limits of social class in explaining ethnic gaps in educational attainment. *British Educational Research Journal,* 37(2), 197–229.

Strand, S. (2014a) Ethnicity, gender, social class and achievement gaps at age 16: intersectionality and 'getting it' for the white working class. *Research Papers in Education,* 29(2), 131–171.

Strand, S. (2014b) School effects and ethic, gender and socio-economic gaps in educational achievement at age 11. *Oxford Review of Education*, 40(2), 223–245.

Strand, S. (2016) Do some schools narrow the gap? Differential school effectiveness revisited. *Review of Education*, 4(2), 107–144.

Sturgis, P. & Buscha, F. (2015) Increasing intergenerational social mobility: is educational expansion the answer? *British Journal of Sociology*, 66(3), 512–533.

Sullivan, A., Heath, A. & Rothon, C. (2011) Equalisation or inflation? Social class and gender differentials in England and Wales. *Oxford Review of Education*, 37(2), 215–240.

Swann Report (1985) *Education for All: Report of the Committee of Enquiry into the Education of Children from Ethnic Minority Groups*. Cmnd 9453. London: HMSO.

Swartz, D. (2003) From correspondence to contradiction and change: Schooling in Capitalist America revisited. *Sociological Forum*, 18(1), 167–186.

Swedberg, R. (2016) Before theory comes theorizing or how to make theory more interesting. *British Journal of Sociology*, 67(1), 5–22.

Szreter, S. (1984) The genesis of the Registrar General's social classification of occupations. *British Journal of Sociology*, 35(4), 522–546.

Tawney, R.H. (1931) *Equality*. London: George Allen & Unwin.

Taylor, C. (2004) *Modern Social Imaginaries*. Durham, NC: Duke University Press.

Taylor, C. (2018) The reliability of free school meal eligibility as a measure of socio-economic disadvantage: evidence from the Millennium Cohort Study in Wales. *British Journal of Educational Studies*, 66(1), 29–51.

Thijssen, P. (2012) From mechanical to organic solidarity and back: with Honneth beyond Durkheim. *European Journal of Social Theory*, 15(4), 454–470.

Tholen, G. (2017) Symbolic closure: towards a renewed sociological perspective on the relationship between higher education, credentials and the graduate labour market. *Sociology*, 51(5), 1067–1083.

Thomas, V., Wang, Y. & Fan, X. (2001) *Measuring Education Inequality: Gini Coefficients in Education*. Policy Research Working Paper No. 2525. Washington, DC: World Bank.

Thompson, E.P. (1978) *The Poverty of Theory*. London: Merlin Press.

Thompson, R. (2009a) Social class and participation in further education: evidence from the Youth Cohort Study of England and Wales. *British Journal of Sociology of Education*, 30(1), 29–42.

Thompson, R. (2009b) Creativity, knowledge and curriculum in further education: a Bernsteinian perspective. *British Journal of Educational Studies*, 57(1), 37–54.

Thompson, R. (2018) Performance, choice and social class: theorising inequalities in educational opportunity. In R. Simmons & J. Smyth (Eds.) *Education and Working-Class Youth: Reshaping the Politics of Inclusion*. Basingstoke: Palgrave Macmillan, 79–104.

Thompson, R. & Simmons, R. (2013) Social mobility and post-compulsory education: revisiting Boudon's model of social opportunity. *British Journal of Sociology of Education*, 34(5–6), 744–765.

Thomsen, J., Bertilsson, E., Dalberg, T., Hedman, J. & Helland, H. (2017) Higher Education participation in the Nordic countries 1985–2010: a comparative perspective. *European Sociological Review*, 33(1), 98–111.

Tilly, C. (1998) *Durable Inequality*. Berkeley: University of California Press.

Tomlinson, S. (1980) The educational performance of ethnic minority children. *New Community*, 8(3), 213–234.

Torche, F. (2011) Is a college degree still the great equalizer? Intergenerational mobility across levels of schooling in the United States. *American Journal of Sociology*, 117(3), 763–807.

Tutic, A. (2017) Revisiting the Breen-Goldthorpe model of educational stratification. *Rationality and Society*, 29(4), 389–407.

Tyler, I. (2015) Classificatory struggles: class, culture and inequality in neoliberal times. *The Sociological Review*, 63, 493–511.

UNESCO (2012) *International Standard Classification of Education 2011.* Montreal, QC: UNESCO Institute for Statistics.

Van de Werfhorst, H. (2009) Credential inflation and educational strategies: a comparison of the United States and the Netherlands. *Research in Social Stratification and Mobility*, 27(4), 269–284.

Van de Werfhorst, H. & Hofstede, S. (2007) Cultural capital or relative risk aversion? Two mechanisms for educational inequality compared. *British Journal of Sociology*, 58(3), 391–415.

Van de Werfhorst, H. & Mijs, J. (2010) Achievement inequality and the institutional structure of educational systems: a comparative perspective. *Annual Reviews of Sociology*, 36, 407–428.

van Doorn, M., Pop, I. & Wolbers, M. (2011) Intergenerational transmission of education across European countries and cohorts. *European Societies*, 13(1), 93–117.

Wacquant, L. (1989) Towards a reflexive sociology: a workshop with Pierre Bourdieu. *Sociological Theory*, 7(1), 26–63.

Walker, J. (1985) Rebels with our applause? A critique of resistance theory in Paul Willis's ethnography of schooling. *Journal of Education*, 167(2), 63–83.

Warmington, P. (2015) Dystopian social theory and education. *Educational Theory*, 65(3), 265–281.

Waters, J. (2018) Elites. *British Journal of Sociology of Education*, 39(3), 412–419.

Watkins, M. (2018) Little room for capacitation: rethinking Bourdieu on pedagogy as symbolic violence. *British Journal of Sociology of Education*, 39(1), 47–60.

Weber, M. (1978) *Economy and Society: An Outline of Interpretive Sociology.* Berkeley: University of California Press.

Weber, M. (2001) *The Protestant Ethic and the Spirit of Capitalism.* London: Routledge.

Weininger, E. (2005) Foundations of Pierre Bourdieu's class analysis. In E.O. Wright (Ed.) *Approaches to Class Analysis.* Cambridge: Cambridge University Press, 82–118.

Wheelahan, L. & Moodie, G. (2017) Vocational education qualifications' roles in pathways to work in liberal market economies. *Journal of Vocational Education and Training*, 69(1), 10–27.

Whitty, G., Hayton, A. & Tang, S. (2015) Who you know, what you know and knowing the ropes: a review of evidence about access to higher education institutions in England. *Review of Education*, 3(1), 27–67.

WIL (2018) *World Inequality Report.* Available online at https://wir2018.wid.world/ (Accessed 10 September 2018).

Wilkin, A., Derrington, C. & Foster, B. (2009) *Improving the Outcomes for Gypsy, Roma and Traveller Pupils: Literature Review.* Research Report DCSF-RR077. London: Department for Children, Schools and Families.

Willis, P. (1977) *Learning to Labour: How Working-class Kids get Working-class Jobs.* Farnborough: Saxon House.

Willmott, R. (1999) Structure, agency and the sociology of education: rescuing analytical dualism. *British Journal of Sociology of Education*, 20(1), 5–21.

Willmott, R. (2001) The 'mini-renaissance' in Marxist educational sociology: a critique. *British Journal of Sociology of Education*, 22(2), 203–215.

Winter, L. (2018) Relational equality in education: what, how, and why? *Oxford Review of Education*, 44(3), 338–352.

Wright, E.O. (1997) *Class Counts: Comparative Studies in Class Analysis*. Cambridge: Cambridge University Press.

Wright, E.O. (2005) *Approaches to Class Analysis*. Cambridge: Cambridge University Press.

Yaish, M. & Andersen, R. (2012) Social mobility in 20 modern societies: the role of economic and political context. *Social Science Research*, 41, 527–538.

YouGov (2017) How Britain voted at the 2017 general election. Available online at www.yougov.co.uk (Accessed 3 October 2017).Young, M. (1958) *The Rise of the Meritocracy*. London: Thames and Hudson.

Young, M.F.D. (2008) *Bringing Knowledge Back In: From Social Constructivism to Social Realism in the Sociology of Education*. Routledge: London.

Young, M.F.D. & Muller, J. (2013) On the powers of powerful knowledge. *Review of Education*, 1(3), 229–250.

Yuval-Davies, N. (2006) Intersectionality and feminist politics. *European Journal of Women's Studies*, 13(3), 193–209.

INDEX

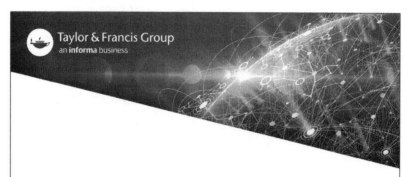